Microsoft®

G000146425

MICROSOFT OFFICE
Microsoft®
OFFICE
USER SPECIALIST

APPROVED COURSEWARE

Step by Step Courseware

Microsoft®
Project 2000
Microsoft Office Application

Core Skills Student Guide

Carl Chatfield, PMP, Timothy Johnson, MCP, and Rebecca Chatfield, Ph.D.

PUBLISHED BY
Microsoft Press
A Division of Microsoft Corporation
One Microsoft Way
Redmond, Washington 98052-6399

Library of Congress Cataloging-in-Publication Data
Microsoft Project 2000 Step by Step Courseware Core Skills / Student Guide
    p. cm.
   ISBN 0-7356-1119-X / (1 color) -- 0-7356-1120-3 / (4 color)
   Data pending.

Printed and bound in the United States of America.

1 2 3 4 5 6 7 8 9   QWT   6 5 4 3 2 1

Distributed in Canada by Penguin Books Canada Limited.

A CIP catalogue record for this book is available from the British Library.

Microsoft Press books are available through booksellers and distributors worldwide. For further information about international editions, contact your local Microsoft Corporation office or contact Microsoft Press International directly at fax (425) 936-7329. Visit our Web site at mspress.microsoft.com. Send comments to *mspinput@microsoft.com*.

Acquisitions Editor: Kong Cheung
Project Editor: Kim Fryer
Technical Editor: Brian Johnson
Copy Editor: Roger LeBlanc
Production/Layout: Barb Runyan
Electronic Artist: Michael Kloepfer

Contents

Course Overview

Welcome to the *Step by Step Courseware* series for Microsoft Office 2000 and Microsoft Windows 2000 Professional. This series facilitates classroom learning, letting you develop competence and confidence in using an Office application or operating system software. In completing courses taught with *Step by Step Courseware*, you learn to use the software productively and discover how to make the software work for you. This series addresses core-level and expert-level skills in Microsoft Word 2000, Microsoft Excel 2000, Microsoft Access 2000, Microsoft Outlook 2000, Microsoft FrontPage 2000, Microsoft Project 2000, and Microsoft Windows 2000 Professional, and core-level skills in Microsoft Power-Point 2000.

The *Step by Step Courseware* series provides:

- A time-tested, integrated approach to learning.
- Task-based, results-oriented learning strategies.
- Exercises based on business scenarios.
- Complete preparation for Microsoft Office User Specialist (MOUS) certification.
- Attractive student guides with full-featured lessons.
- Lessons with accurate, logical, and sequential instructions.
- Comprehensive coverage of skills from the basic to the expert level.
- Review of core-level skills provided in expert-level guides.
- A CD-ROM with practice files.

A Task-Based Approach Using Business Scenarios

The *Step by Step Courseware* series builds on the strengths of the time-tested approach that Microsoft developed and refined for its Step by Step series. Even though the Step by Step series was created for self-paced training, instructors have long used it in the classroom. For the first time, this popular series has been adapted specifically for the classroom environment. By studying with a task-based approach, you learn more than just the features of the software. You learn how to accomplish real-world tasks so that you can immediately increase your productivity using the software application.

The lessons are based on tasks that you might encounter in the everyday work world. This approach allows you to quickly see the relevance of the training. The task-based focus is woven throughout the series, including lesson organization within each unit, lesson titles, and scenarios chosen for practice files.

An Integrated Approach to Training

The *Step by Step Courseware* series distinguishes itself from other series on the market with its consistent delivery and completely integrated approach to learning across a variety of print and online training media. With the addition of the *Step by Step Courseware* series, which supports classroom instruction, the *Step by Step* training suite now provides a flexible and unified training solution.

Print-Based Self-Training in the Step by Step Training Suite

The proven print-based series of stand-alone *Step by Step* books has consistently been the resource that customers choose for developing software skills on their own.

Online Training in the Step by Step Training Suite

For those who prefer online training, the *Step by Step Interactive* products offer highly interactive online training in a simulated work environment, complete with graphics, sound, video, and animation delivered to a single station (self-contained installation), local area network (LAN), or intranet. *Step by Step Interactive* has a network administration module that allows a training manager to track the progress and quiz results for students using the training. For more information, see *mspress.microsoft.com*.

Preparation for Microsoft Office User Specialist (MOUS) Certification

This series has been certified as approved courseware for the Microsoft Office User Specialist certification program. Students who have completed this training are prepared to take the related MOUS exam. By passing the exam for a particular Office application, students demonstrate proficiency in that application to their employers or prospective employers. Exams are offered at participating test centers. For more information, see *www.mous.net*.

A Sound Instructional Foundation

All products in the *Step by Step Courseware* series apply the same instructional strategies, closely adhering to adult instructional techniques and reliable adult learning principles. Lessons in the *Step by Step Courseware* series are presented in a logical, easy-to-follow format, helping you find information quickly and learn as efficiently as possible. To facilitate the learning process, each lesson follows a consistent structure.

Designed for Optimal Learning

The following "Lesson Features" section shows how the colorful and highly visual series design makes it easy for you to see what to read and what to do when practicing new skills.

Lessons break training into easily assimilated sessions. Each lesson is self-contained, and lessons can be completed in sequences other than the one presented in the table of contents. Sample files for the lessons don't depend on completion of other lessons. Sample files within a lesson assume only that you are working sequentially through a complete lesson.

The *Step by Step Courseware* series features:

- **Lesson objectives.** Objectives clearly state the instructional goals for each lesson so that you understand what skills you will master. Each lesson objective is covered in its own section, and each section or topic in the lesson is covered in a consistent way. Lesson objectives preview the lesson structure, helping you grasp key information and prepare for learning skills.

- **Informational text for each topic.** For each objective, the lesson provides easy-to-read, technique-focused information.

- **Hands-on practice.** Numbered steps give detailed, step-by-step instructions to help you learn skills. The steps also show results and screen images to match what you should see on your computer screen. The accompanying CD contains sample files used for each lesson.

- **Full-color illustrations in color student guides.** Illustrated screen images give visual feedback as you work through exercises. The images reinforce key concepts, provide visual clues about the steps, and give you something to check your progress against.

- **MOUS icon.** Each section or sidebar that covers a MOUS certification objective has a MOUS icon in the margin at the beginning of the section. The number of the certification objective is also listed.

- **Tips.** Helpful hints and alternate ways to accomplish tasks are located throughout the lesson text.

- **Important.** If there is something to watch out for or something to avoid, this information is added to the lesson and indicated with this heading.

- **Sidebars.** Sidebars contain parenthetical topics or additional information that you might find interesting.

- **Margin notes.** Margin notes provide additional related or background information that adds value to the lesson.

- **Button images in the margin.** When the text instructs you to click a particular button, an image of the button and its label appear in the margin.

- **Lesson Glossary.** Terms with which you might not be familiar are defined in the glossary. Terms in the glossary appear in boldface type within the lesson and are defined upon their first use within lessons.

- **Quick Quiz.** You can use the short-answer Quick Quiz questions to test or reinforce your understanding of key topics within the lesson.

Lesson Features

Lesson objectives clearly state the instructional goals for each lesson so that you understand what skills you will master.

Lesson introductions list the practice files for the lesson and explain any necessary file preparation.

Each topic begins with explanatory information that teaches concepts and techniques.

Important notes state warnings or cautions.

The Microsoft Office User Specialist (MOUS) logo indicates that the section covers a task that will be tested on the certification exam.

Tips provide helpful hints and alternative ways to complete tasks.

Numbered steps provide detailed instructions to guide you through practicing new skills.

Illustrations give you visual feedback as you work through the lesson.

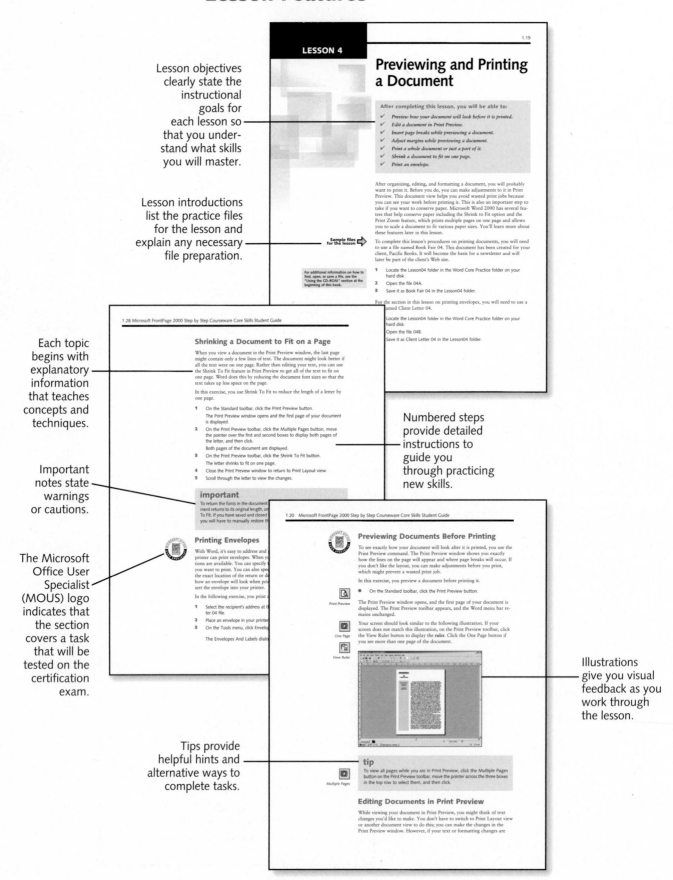

Margin notes provide additional information.

Lesson Glossary defines key terms shown in boldface within the lesson.

Lesson Wrap-Up covers remaining file administration details to end the lesson.

Quick Quiz short-answer questions quiz you on the lesson concepts.

Putting It All Together exercises challenge you to apply what you've learned and require you to apply skills in a new way.

Quick Reference summarizes skills learned in the lesson.

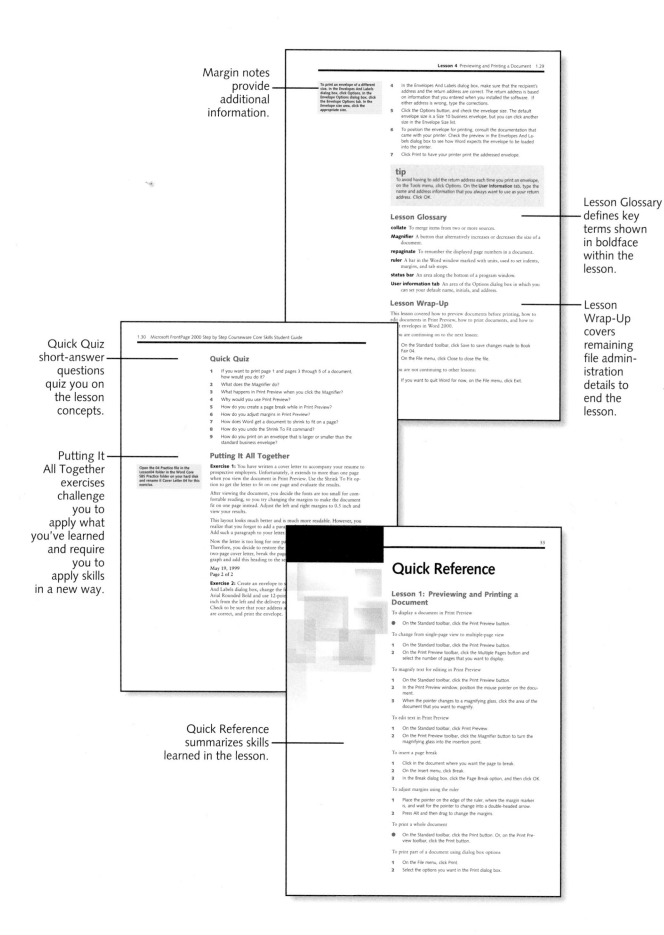

Lesson 4 Previewing and Printing a Document   1.29

To print an envelope of a different size, in the Envelopes And Labels dialog box, click Options. In the Envelope Options dialog box, click the Envelope Options tab. In the Envelope size area, click the appropriate size.

4   In the Envelopes And Labels dialog box, make sure that the recipient's address and the return address are correct. The return address is based on information that you entered when you installed the software.   If either address is wrong, type the corrections.

5   Click the Options button, and check the envelope size. The default envelope size is a Size 10 business envelope, but you can click another size in the Envelope Size list.

6   To position the envelope for printing, consult the documentation that came with your printer. Check the preview in the Envelopes And Labels dialog box to see how Word expects the envelope to be loaded into the printer.

7   Click Print to have your printer print the addressed envelope.

tip
To avoid having to add the return address each time you print an envelope, on the Tools menu, click Options. On the **User Information** tab, type the name and address information that you always want to use as your return address. Click OK.

Lesson Glossary

collate   To merge items from two or more sources.

Magnifier   A button that alternatively increases or decreases the size of a document.

repaginate   To renumber the displayed page numbers in a document.

ruler   A bar in the Word window marked with units, used to set indents, margins, and tab stops.

status bar   An area along the bottom of a program window.

User information tab   An area of the Options dialog box in which you can set your default name, initials, and address.

Lesson Wrap-Up

This lesson covered how to preview documents before printing, how to edit documents in Print Preview, how to print documents, and how to print envelopes in Word 2000.

u are continuing on to the next lesson:

On the Standard toolbar, click Save to save changes made to Book Fair 04.
On the File menu, click Close to close the file.

u are not continuing to other lessons:

If you want to quit Word for now, on the File menu, click Exit.

1.30   Microsoft FrontPage 2000 Step by Step Courseware Core Skills Student Guide

Quick Quiz

1   If you want to print page 1 and pages 3 through 5 of a document, how would you do it?
2   What does the Magnifier do?
3   What happens in Print Preview when you click the Magnifier?
4   Why would you use Print Preview?
5   How do you create a page break while in Print Preview?
6   How do you adjust margins in Print Preview?
7   How does Word get a document to shrink to fit on a page?
8   How do you undo the Shrink To Fit command?
9   How do you print on an envelope that is larger or smaller than the standard business envelope?

Putting It All Together

Open the 04 Practice file in the Lesson04 folder in the Word Core SBS Practice folder on your hard disk and rename it Cover Letter 04 for this exercise.

Exercise 1: You have written a cover letter to accompany your resume to prospective employers. Unfortunately, it extends to more than one page when you view the document in Print Preview. Use the Shrink To Fit option to get the letter to fit on one page and evaluate the results.

After viewing the document, you decide the fonts are too small for comfortable reading, so you try changing the margins to make the document fit on one page instead. Adjust the left and right margins to 0.5 inch and view your results.

This layout looks much better and is much more readable. However, you realize that you forgot to add a para
Add such a paragraph to your letter.

Now the letter is too long for one p
Therefore, you decide to restore the
two-page cover letter, break the page
graph and add this heading to the se
May 19, 1999
Page 2 of 2

Exercise 2: Create an envelope to s
And Labels dialog box, change the f
Arial Rounded Bold and use 12-poin
inch from the left and the delivery a
Check to be sure that your address a
are correct, and print the envelope.

33

Quick Reference

Lesson 1: Previewing and Printing a Document

To display a document in Print Preview

● On the Standard toolbar, click the Print Preview button.

To change from single-page view to multiple-page view

1   On the Standard toolbar, click the Print Preview button.
2   On the Print Preview toolbar, click the Multiple Pages button and select the number of pages that you want to display.

To magnify text for editing in Print Preview

1   On the Standard toolbar, click the Print Preview button.
2   In the Print Preview window, position the mouse pointer on the document.
3   When the pointer changes to a magnifying glass, click the area of the document that you want to magnify.

To edit text in Print Preview

1   On the Standard toolbar, click Print Preview.
2   On the Print Preview toolbar, click the Magnifier button to turn the magnifying glass into the insertion point.

To insert a page break

1   Click in the document where you want the page to break.
2   On the Insert menu, click Break.
3   In the Break dialog box, click the Page Break option, and then click OK.

To adjust margins using the ruler

1   Place the pointer on the edge of the ruler, where the margin marker is, and wait for the pointer to change into a double-headed arrow.
2   Press Alt and then drag to change the margins.

To print a whole document

● On the Standard toolbar, click the Print button. Or, on the Print Preview toolbar, click the Print button.

To print part of a document using dialog box options

1   On the File menu, click Print.
2   Select the options you want in the Print dialog box.

■ **Putting It All Together exercises.** These exercises give you another opportunity to practice skills that you learned in the lesson. Completing these exercises helps you to verify whether you understand the lesson, to reinforce your learning, and to retain what you have learned by applying what you have learned in a different way.

■ **Quick Reference.** A complete summary of steps for tasks taught in each lesson is available in the back of the guide. This is often the feature that people find most useful when they return to their workplaces. The expert-level guides include the references from the core-level guides so that you can review or refresh basic and advanced skills on your own whenever necessary.

■ **Index.** Student guides are completely indexed. All glossary terms and application features appear in the index.

Suggestions for Improvements

Microsoft welcomes your feedback on the *Step by Step Courseware* series. Your comments and suggestions will help us to improve future versions of this product. Please send your feedback to SBSCfdbk@microsoft.com.

Support requests for Microsoft products should not be directed to this alias. Please see "Using the CD-ROM" for information on support contacts.

Conventions and Features Used in This Book

This book uses special fonts, symbols, and heading conventions to high-light important information or to call your attention to special steps. For more information about the features available in each lesson, refer to the "Course Overview" section on page vii.

Convention	Meaning
Practice files for the lesson	This icon identifies the section that lists the files that the lesson will use and explains any file preparation that you need to take care of before starting the lesson.
Most items you see in Microsoft Project support ToolTips. Point to the dates on the timescale or task bars in the Gantt Chart or to buttons on the toolbars to see some of the available ToolTips.	Notes in the margin area are pointers to information provided elsewhere in the workbook or provide brief notes related to the text or procedures.
New!	This icon indicates a new or greatly improved feature in this version of the software product and includes a short description of what is new.
Proj2000-1-17	This icon indicates that the section where this icon appears covers a Microsoft Office User Specialist (MOUS) exam objective. The number below the icon is the MOUS objective number. For a complete list of the MOUS objectives, see the "MOUS Objectives" section on page xxi.
tip	Tips provide helpful hints or alternative procedures related to particular tasks.
important	Importants provide warnings or cautions that are critical to exercises.
🖫	When a toolbar button is referenced in the lesson, the button's picture is shown in the margin.
Alt+Tab	A plus sign (+) between two key names means that you must press those keys at the same time. For example, "Press Alt+Tab" means that you hold down the Alt key while you press Tab.
Boldface type	This formatting indicates text that you need to type Or It indicates a glossary entry that is defined at the end of the lesson.

Using the CD-ROM

The CD-ROM included with this student guide contains the practice files that you will use as you perform the exercises in the books. By using the practice files, you won't waste time creating the samples used in the lessons, and you can concentrate on learning how to use Microsoft Project 2000. With the files and the step-by-step instructions in the lessons, you will also learn by doing, which is an easy and effective way to acquire and remember new skills.

System Requirements

Your computer system must meet the following minimum requirements in order for you to install the practice files from the CD-ROM and to run Microsoft Project 2000.

important

The Microsoft Project 2000 software is not provided on the companion CD-ROM. This course assumes that you have already purchased and installed Microsoft Project 2000.

- A personal computer running Microsoft Project 2000 on a Pentium 75-megahertz (MHz) or higher processor with the Microsoft Windows 95 or later operating system with 20 MB of RAM or with the Microsoft Windows NT Workstation version 4.0 operating system with Service Pack 3 or with the Microsoft Windows 2000 Professional operating system and 36 MB of RAM.
- Internet Explorer 4 or later (Lesson 9 of the Core Skills course).
- Microsoft Word (to read the Test Bank)
- At least 110 MB of available disk space.
- A CD-ROM drive.
- A monitor with VGA or higher resolution (Super VGA recommended; 15-inch monitor or larger recommended).
- A Microsoft mouse, a Microsoft IntelliMouse, or other compatible pointing device.
- A 9600 baud modem, although 14,400 or higher baud is recommended.
- Multimedia computer required to access sound and other multimedia effects.
- Some Internet functionality might require Internet access and payment of a separate fee to a service provider.

Microsoft Project
Central Setup Instructions

To complete Lesson 9 of the Core Skills course, you will need access to the Microsoft Project Central client and server components. Project Central has setup requirements beyond those of Microsoft Project.

Web Server Installation Requirements

Hardware and system requirements for the Project Central server installations are as follows:

- Windows NT Server version 4.0 with Service Pack 4 or later, or Microsoft Windows 2000 (Server or Professional)

- If you use Windows NT 4.0, then you also need Windows NT 4.0 Option Pack so that you can install Microsoft Internet Information Server version 4.0. If you use Windows 2000, you must install Microsoft Internet Information Server 5.0, which is shipped with Windows 2000.

- If you use Windows NT 4.0, you must install Microsoft Internet Service Manager as an option with Microsoft Internet Information Server 4.0. If you do not have Windows NT Server, you can also use Windows NT 4.0 Option Pack with Windows NT Workstation; however, you will be limited to 10 connections.

- Microsoft SQL Server 7.0 or later, Oracle Server 8.0 or later, or Microsoft Data Engine (MSDE). MSDE is included and installed with the Microsoft Project Central server setup. MSDE is installed if it's not already on the system and SQL Server is not installed. Microsoft Data Access Components (MDAC) version 2.5 is also installed with the Project Central server setup if you do not have Windows 2000.

- Available hard-disk space: 100–150 MB recommended

- Processor: Intel Pentium 200 MHz or higher, or similar processor

- Memory requirements: 128 MB RAM or more

The hard disk and memory requirements are for a default installation. Your hard disk and memory requirements may vary depending on your configuration and the options you choose to install.

Project Central server and Microsoft Project can be installed on the same computer if necessary. Shared components of Project Central server and Microsoft Project 2000 will be installed in the folder, \Program Files\Microsoft Office\Office\1033 (or the appropriate folder for the language version you use).

Once installed, clients can connect to the Microsoft Project Central server using either Internet Explorer or the Browser Module for Microsoft Project Central. Clients accessing the Microsoft Project Central server must have a Microsoft Project Central client access license.

If You Need to Install and Uninstall the Practice Files

Your instructor might already have installed the practice files before you arrive in class. However, your instructor might ask you to install the practice files on your own at the start of class. Also, you will need to first install the practice files if you want to work through any of the exercises in this book on your own at home or at your place of business after class.

To install the practice files on a classroom computer:

1   Insert the CD-ROM in the CD-ROM drive.

A menu screen appears.

important

If the menu screen does not appear, start Windows Explorer. In the left pane, locate the icon for your CD-ROM, and click this icon. In the right pane, double-click the file StartCD.

2   Click Install Practice Files, and follow the directions on the screen.

The recommended options are pre-selected for you.

3   After the practice files have been installed, click Exit.

4   A folder called MS Project Core Practice has been created on the hard disk, the practice files have been placed in that folder, and a shortcut to the Microsoft Press Web site has been added to your desktop. Remove the CD-ROM from the CD-ROM drive.

Use the following steps when you want to delete (uninstall) the lesson practice files from your hard disk. Your instructor might ask you to perform these steps at the end of class. Also, you should perform these steps if you have worked through the exercises at home or at your place of business and want to work through the exercises again. Deleting the practice files and then reinstalling them ensures that all files and folders are in their original condition if you decide to work through the exercises again.

To uninstall the exercise files:

1   On the Windows taskbar, click the Start button, point to Settings, and then click Control Panel.

2   Double-click the Add/Remove Programs icon.

3   Click MS Project Core Practice in the list, and click Add/Remove. (If your computer has Windows 2000 Professional installed, click the Remove or Change/Remove button.)

4   Click Yes when the confirmation dialog box appears.

Using the Practice Files

Each lesson in this book explains when and how to use any practice files for that lesson. The lessons are built around scenarios that simulate a real project life cycle so that students can easily apply the skills they learn to their own work. The scenarios in the lessons are in the context of a fictitious project: a toy commercial project. You play the role of a project manager for a film and video production company, Industrial Smoke and Mirrors.

The following is a list of all files and folders used in the lessons.

File Name	Description
Lesson 1 - folder	Students create their own files in the Lesson 1 folder
Lesson 2 - folder	
2A	File used in Lesson 2
Putting It All Together 2	File used in Putting It All Together
Lesson 3 - folder	
3A	File used in Lesson 3
Putting It All Together 3	File used in Putting It All Together
Lesson 4 - folder	
4A	File used in Lesson 4
Putting It All Together 4	File used in Putting It All Together
Lesson 5 - folder	
5A	File used in Lesson 5
Putting It All Together 5	File used in Putting It All Together
Lesson 6 - folder	
6A	File used in Lesson 6
Putting It All Together 6	File used in Putting It All Together
Lesson 7 - folder	
7A	File used in Lesson 7
Putting It All Together 7	File used in Putting It All Together
Lesson 8 - folder	
8A	File used in Lesson 8
8B	File used in Lesson 8
8C	File used in Lesson 8
Putting It All Together 8	File used in Putting It All Together
Lesson 9 - folder	
9A	File used in Lesson 9
Lesson 10 - folder	
10A	File used in Lesson 8
10B	File used in Lesson 8
Putting It All Together 10A	File used in Putting It All Together
Putting It All Together 10B	File used in Putting It All Together

File Name	Description
Lesson 11 - folder	
11A	File used in Lesson 11
11B	File used in Lesson 11
Putting It All Together 11	File used in Putting It All Together
Lesson 12 - folder	
12A	File used in Lesson 8
Letter To Client	File used in Lesson 8
Sample Task List	File used in Lesson 8
Putting It All Together 12	File used in Putting It All Together

Replying to Install Messages

When you work through some lessons, you might see a message indicating that the feature that they are trying to use is not installed. If you see this message, insert the Microsoft Project 2000 CD-ROM in your CD-ROM drive and click Yes to install the feature.

Locating the Practice Files

After you (or your instructor) have installed the practice files, all files that you need for these courses will be stored in a folder named MS Project Core Practice that is located on your hard disk. To navigate to this folder from within Microsoft Project:

1   On the Standard toolbar, click the Open button.

2   Click the Look In down arrow, and click the icon for your hard disk.

3   Double-click the folder named MS Project Core Practice.

4   Double-click the specific folder name that corresponds to the lesson you want.

Practice files for the lesson

All the files for the lessons appear within the MS Project Core Practice folder.

On the first page of each lesson, look for the margin icon *Pracitce files for this lesson*. This icon points to the paragraph that explains which file(s) you will need to work through the lesson exercises.

If You Need Additional Help

If you have any problems regarding the use of the CD-ROM for this book or if you need additional help with the practice files, you should first consult your instructor. If you are using the CD-ROM at home or at your place of business and need additional help with the practice files, see the Microsoft Press Web site at *http://mspress.microsoft.com/support*.

important

Please note that support for the Microsoft Project 2000 software product itself is not offered through the above Web site. For help using Microsoft Project 2000 rather than this Microsoft Press book, you can visit *www.microsoft.com/support* or call Microsoft Project 2000 Technical Support at (425) 454-2030 Monday through Friday between 5 A.M. and 9 P.M. Pacific Standard Time and 9 A.M. to 3 P.M. Pacific Standard Time Saturdays, excluding holidays. Microsoft Product Support does not provide support for this course.

MOUS Objectives

Core Skills

(continued)

Objective	Activity	Page(s)
Proj2000-3-3	Identify lost elements when saving a project to Project 98	12.8
Proj2000-3-4	Copy picture and save as a web page	12.1, 12.3
Proj2000-3-5	Share formatting elements with other projects	11.3
Proj2000-3-6	Modify a standard report	7.5
Proj2000-3-7	Copy Gantt chart and paste to Word or Excel	12.5
Proj2000-3-8	Copy and paste to Excel	12.5
Proj2000-3-9	Publish project information using Project Central	9.1
Proj2000-3-10	Set page setup options	7.2
Proj2000-3-11	Create a standard report	7.5
Proj2000-4-1	Display the critical path	4.13
Proj2000-4-2	Differentiate work from duration	3.3
Proj2000-5-1	Reset table defaults	11.3
Proj2000-5-2	Create and apply custom outline codes and predefined filters	5.7
Proj2000-5-3	Create outline codes	5.4
Proj2000-5-4	Create a custom grouping	5.4
Proj2000-5-5	Format bar styles	6.1
Proj2000-5-6	Sort a view	5.1
Proj2000-5-7	Create and apply a custom filter	5.7
Proj2000-5-8	Create a custom table	6.6
Proj2000-5-9	Create a custom view	6.9
Proj2000-5-10	Format a time scale	4.15
Proj2000-5-11	Utilize grouping functions	5.4
Proj2000-5-12	Apply a filter using AutoFilter	5.7
Proj2000-5-13	Insert a column in a table	6.5
Proj2000-6-1	Set baselines for a master project	10.1
Proj2000-6-2	Add a task to a master project	10.1
Proj2000-6-3	Add cross-project links	10.4
Proj2000-6-4	Insert multiple projects to a master project (one at a time)	10.1

Taking a Microsoft Office User Specialist Certification Test

The Microsoft Office User Specialist (MOUS) program is the only Microsoft-approved certification program designed to measure and validate your skills with the Microsoft Office family of desktop productivity applications: Microsoft Word, Microsoft Excel, Microsoft PowerPoint, Microsoft Access, Microsoft Outlook, and Microsoft Project.

By becoming certified, you demonstrate to employers that you have achieved a predictable level of skills in the use of a particular Office application. Certification is often required by employers either as a condition of employment or as a condition of advancement within the company or other organization. The certification examinations are sponsored by Microsoft but administered through Nivo International.

For each Microsoft Office 2000 application, two levels of MOUS tests are currently or will soon be available: core and expert. For a core-level test, you demonstrate your ability to use an application knowledgeably and without assistance in a day-to-day work environment. For an expert-level test, you demonstrate that you have a thorough knowledge of the application and can effectively apply all or most of the features of the application to solve problems and complete tasks found in business.

Preparing to Take an Exam

Unless you're a very experienced user, you'll need to use a test preparation course to prepare to complete the test correctly and within the time allowed. The *Step by Step Courseware* training program is designed to prepare you for either core-level or expert-level knowledge of a particular Microsoft Office application. By the end of this course, you should have a strong knowledge of all exam topics, and with some additional review and practice on your own, you should feel confident in your ability to pass the appropriate exam.

After you decide which exam to take, review the list of objectives for the exam. This list can be found in the "MOUS Objectives" section at the front of the appropriate *Step by Step Courseware* student guide; the list of MOUS objectives for this book begins on page xxi. You can also easily identify tasks that are included in the objective list by locating the MOUS logo in the margin of the lessons in this book.

For an expert-level test, you'll need to be able to demonstrate any of the skills from the core-level objective list, too. Expect some of these core-level tasks to appear on the expert-level test. In the *Step by Step Courseware Expert Skills Student Guide*, you'll find the core skills included in the "Quick Reference" section at the back of the book.

You can also familiarize yourself with a live MOUS certification test by downloading and installing a practice MOUS certification test from *www.mous.net*.

To take the MOUS test, first see *www.mous.net* to locate your nearest testing center. Then call the testing center directly to schedule your test. The amount of advance notice you should provide will vary for different testing centers, and it typically depends on the number of computers available at the testing center, the number of other testers who have already been scheduled for the day on which you want to take the test, and the number of times per week that the testing center offers MOUS testing. In general, you should call to schedule your test at least two weeks prior to the date on which you want to take the test.

When you arrive at the testing center, you might be asked for proof of identity. A driver's license or passport is an acceptable form of identification. If you do not have either of these items of documentation, call your testing center and ask what alternative forms of identification will be accepted. If you are retaking a test, bring your MOUS identification number, which will have been given to you when you previously took the test. If you have not prepaid or if your organization has not already arranged to make payment for you, you will need to pay the test-taking fee when you arrive. The current test-taking fee is $50 (U.S.).

Test Format

All MOUS certification tests are live, performance-based tests. There are no multiple-choice, true/false, or short answer questions. Instructions are general: you are told the basic tasks to perform on the computer, but you aren't given any help in figuring out how to perform them. You are not permitted to use reference material other than the application's Help system.

As you complete the tasks stated in a particular test question, the testing software monitors your actions. An example question might be:

> Change the Calendar view to Work Week, and schedule an appointment next Tuesday at 9:00 A.M. with the subject *Department Meeting*. Set the recurrence to weekly, and set a reminder for the appointmetnt five minutes in advance of the appointment time.

The sample tests available from *www.mous.net* give you a clear idea of the type of questions that you will be asked on the actual test.

When the test administrator seats you at a computer, you'll see an online form that you use to enter information about yourself (name, address, and other information required to process your exam results). While you complete the form, the software will generate the test from a master test bank and then prompt you to continue. The first test question will appear in a window. Read the question carefully, and then perform all the tasks stated in the test question. When you have finished completing all tasks for a question, click the Next Question button.

You have 45 to 60 minutes to complete all questions, depending on the test that you are taking. The testing software assesses your results as soon as you complete the test, and the results of the test can be printed by the test administrator so that you will have a record of any tasks that you performed incorrectly. A passing grade is 75 percent or higher. If you pass, you will receive a certificate in the mail within two to four weeks. If you do not pass, you can study and practice the skills that you missed and then schedule to retake the test at a later date.

Tips for Successfully Completing the Test

The following tips and suggestions are the result of feedback received by many individuals who have taken one or more MOUS tests:

- Make sure that you are thoroughly prepared. If you have extensively used the application for which you are being tested, you might feel confident that you are prepared for the test. However, the test might include questions that involve tasks that you rarely or never perform when you use the application at your place of business, at school, or at home. You must be knowledgeable in *all* the MOUS objectives for the test that you will take.

- Read each exam question carefully. An exam question might include several tasks that you are to perform. A partially correct response to a test question is counted as an incorrect response. In the example question on the previous page, you might change the calendar view, create the appointment, and set the recurrence, but forget to set the reminder. This would count as an incorrect response and would result in a lower test score.

- You are allowed to use the application's Help system, but relying on the Help system too much will slow you down and possibly prevent you from completing the test within the allotted time. Use the Help system only when necessary.

- Keep track of your time. The test does not display the amount of time that you have left, so you need to keep track of the time yourself by monitoring your start time and the required end time on your watch or a clock in the testing center (if there is one). The test program displays the number of items that you have completed along with the total number of test items (for example, "35 of 40 items have been completed"). Use this information to gauge your pace.

- If you skip a question, you cannot return to it later. You should skip a question only if you are certain that you cannot complete the tasks correctly.

- Don't worry if the testing software crashes while you are taking the exam. The test software is set up to handle this situation. Find your test administrator and tell him or her what happened. The administrator will work through the steps required to restart the test. When the test restarts, it will allow you to continue where you left off. You will have the same amount of time remaining to complete the test as you did when the software crashed.

■   As soon as you are finished reading a question and you click in the
     application window, a condensed version of the instruction is dis-
     played in a corner of the screen. If you are unsure whether you
     have completed all tasks stated in the test question, click the
     Instructions button on the test information bar at the bottom of
     the screen and then reread the question. Close the instruction win-
     dow when you are finished. Do this as often as necessary to
     ensure you have read the question correctly and that you have
     completed all the tasks stated in the question.

If You Do Not Pass the Test

If you do not pass, you can use the assessment printout as a guide to practice the items that you missed. There is no limit to the number of times
that you can retake a test; however, you must pay the fee each time that
you take the test. When you retake the test, expect to see some of the same
test items on the subsequent test; the test software randomly generates the
test items from a master test bank before you begin the test. Also expect to
see several questions that did not appear on the previous test.

LESSON 1

Entering and Organizing Tasks

After completing this lesson, you will be able to:

✔ *Create a new Microsoft Project file based on a template.*

✔ *Customize the menus and toolbars in Microsoft Project.*

✔ *Create a new Microsoft Project file, and set the project start date.*

✔ *Enter a task list that describes work to be done in the project.*

✔ *Estimate durations for the task list you have created.*

✔ *Enter a milestone to signify an important event in the project.*

✔ *Create summary tasks to represent broad phases of project work.*

✔ *Link tasks to indicate the order in which work should be done.*

✔ *Adjust task links to more finely control when tasks should start.*

✔ *Create notes and hyperlinks for tasks.*

Practice files for the lesson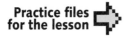

For additional information about how to find and open files used in this book, see the "Using the CD-ROM" section at the beginning of this book.

In this lesson, you will be introduced to some parts of the Microsoft Project interface, and you will create the project file that you will work with throughout the lessons in this book.

Microsoft Project is a member of the Microsoft Office family of desktop programs, so much of what you see in Microsoft Project is similar to what you see in Microsoft Word, Microsoft Excel, and Microsoft Access. The organization of the menu bar and toolbar, for example, is very similar. You have access to the same online Help tools, such as the Office Assistant and **ToolTips**, throughout Microsoft Project. Much of what you do with Microsoft Project is distinct from what you do with other Office programs, however.

For the scenario in this book, imagine that you are the project manager for Industrial Smoke and Mirrors, a small film and video production company. Your company recently installed Microsoft Project 2000, and you are eager to use it to manage a toy commercial project that is getting under way.

To complete the procedures in this lesson, you will create a new Microsoft Project file.

Getting Started with Microsoft Project

In this exercise, you start Microsoft Project, create a file based on a template, and see some of the major areas of the default Microsoft Project interface.

1   On the Windows taskbar, click the Start button.

The Start menu appears.

2   On the Start menu, point to Programs, and then click Microsoft Project.

Microsoft Project appears. Your screen should look similar to the following illustration.

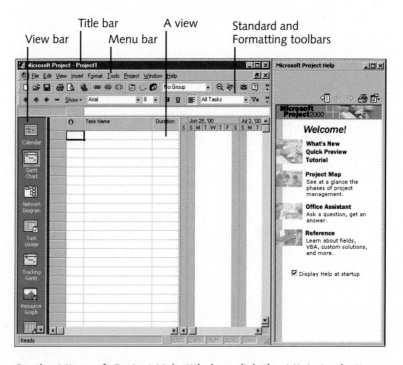

3   On the Microsoft Project Help title bar, click the Minimize button.

The Help window minimizes, and the Microsoft Project window expands to fill the screen. Next you will view the templates included with Microsoft Project and create a project file based on one of them.

4   On the File menu, click New.

The New dialog box appears.

5   Click the Project Templates tab.

Your screen should look similar to the following illustration.

When you start Microsoft Project, the tiled Help window appears. To stop Help from appearing when you start Microsoft Project, clear the Display Help At Startup box in the Help window. If you later change your mind about Help displaying on startup, on the Tools menu, click Options, and then on the General tab click the Display Help On Startup box.

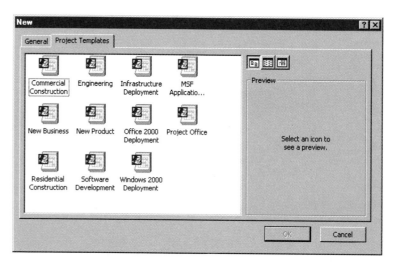

All of the templates you see here have been developed by project management professionals just for Microsoft Project 2000.

6 Select Residential Construction, and then click OK.

Microsoft Project creates a file based on the Residential Construction template, and the Project Information dialog box appears.

Every project is scheduled from either a start date or a finish date.

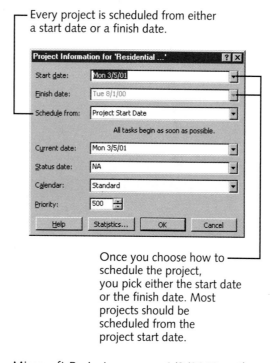

Once you choose how to schedule the project, you pick either the start date or the finish date. Most projects should be scheduled from the project start date.

Microsoft Project proposes 1/3/2000 as the project start date.

7 In the Start Date field, enter the current date, and then click OK.

Your screen should look similar to the following illustration, although the exact dates you see in the Gantt Chart probably differ.

Most items you see in Microsoft
Project support ToolTips. Point to the
dates on the timescale or task bars in
the Gantt Chart or to buttons on the
toolbars to see some of the available
ToolTips.

Microsoft Project adjusts the initial tasks in the project
to begin at the project start date you specify.

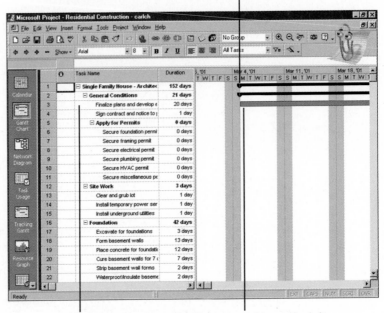

The Gantt Chart view is divided into a table on the left
and a graphical chart with a timescale on the right.
The bars on the right correspond to tasks on the left.

Try Out the Office Assistant

If you use Office programs such as Excel and Word, you are probably
familiar with the **Office Assistant**, an animated character that appears
in the program's window. The primary purpose of the Office Assistant
in Microsoft Project is to locate Help topics based on questions you ask.
To try it, click the Office Assistant and in the What Would You Like To
Do box, type **Tell me about Templates in Project** and then click Search.
The Office Assistant locates and displays the topics that are most closely
related to the keywords or concepts in your question. Click the first topic
listed, "Templates included with Microsoft Project." If you would like
to learn more about these templates, read the topic that appears in the
Microsoft Project Help window. To close the list of found topics, click
the Office Assistant.

If you prefer not to use the Office Assistant, you can still use the same
underlying tools to get access to Help topics. In the Microsoft Project
Help window, click the Show button to see the navigation tabs available
with Help. Click the Answer Wizard tab. Type the same question again,
and then click Search. You will see similar results. The Answer Wizard
tab is available whether or not the Office Assistant is displayed. To display Help without using the Office Assistant, open the Help menu, and
click Contents And Index.

Working with Menus and Toolbars

Most of the instructions you give to Microsoft Project are given through the Menu bar and toolbars. Initially, Microsoft Project displays the Menu bar and 2 of its 13 toolbars: Standard and Formatting.

Like other Microsoft Office 2000 applications, Microsoft Project customizes the menus and toolbars for you, based on how frequently you use specific commands or toolbar buttons. The most frequently used commands and buttons will remain visible on the menus and toolbars, while the commands and buttons you do not use will be temporarily hidden.

> **tip**
>
> Most items and screen regions you see in Microsoft Project support **short-cut menus**. To see some of the available shortcut menus, right-click items such as task bars in the Gantt Chart or buttons on the toolbars.

In this exercise, you learn to customize the behavior of the menus and toolbars in Microsoft Project.

1 Click the Tools menu.

Microsoft Project initially displays only a portion of all commands on the Tools menu.

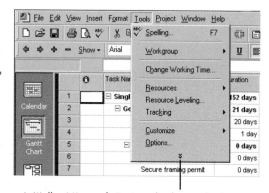

Initially, Microsoft Project displays only the most commonly used commands on a menu. Click the chevron shown here to see all commands.

2 Click the chevron at the bottom of the menu.

Microsoft Project expands the Tools menu to show all commands. The commands that initially were hidden now appear with a lighter gray background.

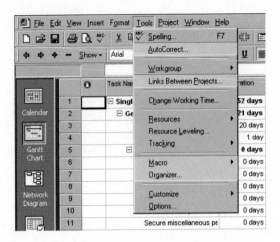

tip

To quickly expand a menu, you can double-click the menu name.

3   Point to Customize, and in the submenu that appears, click Toolbars.

Microsoft Project displays the Customize dialog box.

4   Click the Options tab.

To disable the personalized
menu behavior, clear this box.

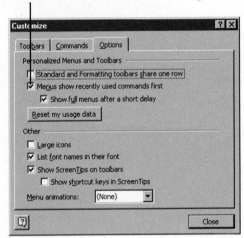

Here you can control the behavior of menus and toolbars in Microsoft Project.

5   Select the Standard And Formatting Toolbars Share One Row check box, and then click Close.

Microsoft Project rearranges the Standard and Formatting toolbars so that they appear side by side rather than stacked. Your screen should look similar to the following illustration.

When the toolbars are arranged side by side, there is more vertical space for the Microsoft Project data.

6 Click More Buttons on the Standard or Formatting toolbar.

Microsoft Project displays the buttons that do not fit on the single row. As you use Microsoft Project, the program will show the buttons you use most often on the toolbar, but will hide those you do not use and place them in this secondary list.

7 On the Tools menu, point to Customize, and then click Toolbars.

8 Click the Options tab, clear the Standard And Formatting Toolbars Share One Row check box, and then click Close.

Microsoft Project rearranges the Standard and Formatting toolbars so that they once again appear stacked.

9 On the File menu, click Close.

10 When prompted to save changes to the Residential Construction file, click No.

Proj2000-1-17

Creating a Project File

The first step in starting a new project is to establish the start or finish date of the project. Every project starts on one date and finishes on a later date. Sometimes you know the planned project start date, the planned project finish date, or both. However, when working with Microsoft Project you specify one date, not both: the project start date or the project finish date. Why? Because after you enter the project start or finish date and the **durations** of the tasks, Microsoft Project calculates the other date for you. Remember that Microsoft Project is not just a static repository of your project information; it is an active scheduling tool.

Most projects should be scheduled from a start date, even if you know that the project must end by a certain date. Scheduling from a start date causes all tasks to start as soon as possible, and it gives you the greatest scheduling flexibility. In later lessons, you will see this flexibility in action as we work with a project that is scheduled from a start date.

Now you are ready to create the project plan you will use throughout this training program. In this exercise, you create a file and specify the project's start date.

1 On the Standard toolbar, click New.

Microsoft Project creates a file, and the Project Information dialog box appears.

2 In the Start Date box, click the down arrow button.

A small monthly calendar appears. By default, Microsoft Project uses the current date as the project start date. However, in this exercise, you change the project start date to June 4, 2001.

3 Click the left or right arrow button until June 2001 is displayed.

4 Click June 4.

tip

You use this type of calendar in several places in Microsoft Project. Here is a handy shortcut for quickly picking a date with the calendar: click the name of the month to display a pop-up menu of all months, and then select the month you want. Next click the year to display up and down arrows, and then type or select the year you want.

The monthly calendar closes, and the Start Date box contains the date 6/4/2001.

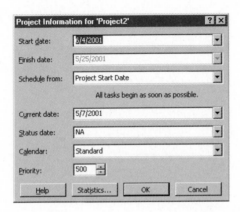

5   Click OK to close the Project Information dialog box.

To conclude this exercise, you will save the Microsoft Project file.

6   On the Standard Toolbar, click the Save button.

Because this project file has not previously been saved, the Save As dialog box appears.

7   Locate the Lesson 1 folder in the MS Project Core Practice folder located on your hard disk.

8   In the File Name box, type **Wingtip Toys Commercial 1**

9   Click Save to close the Save As dialog box.

Microsoft Project saves the file as Wingtip Toys Commercial 1.

Entering Tasks

In Microsoft Project, one place you enter tasks is in the Gantt Chart view. In the default Gantt Chart view, the bar chart appears in the right side, and a table appears in the left side of the view. (The **Entry table** appears by default, but you can display other tables as well.) Although the table might look similar to an Excel spreadsheet grid, it behaves more like a database table. Each row of the table describes a single task, which is assigned a **Task ID**. Task IDs appear on the left side of the task's row, and the column headings, such as Task Name and Duration, are field labels. The intersection of a row (or task) and a column is called a cell or **field**. In fact, the internal architecture of a file from Microsoft Project has much more in common with that of a file from a database program such as Access than it does with that of a file from a spreadsheet program such as Excel.

In this exercise, you enter the first tasks required in the film project.

1   In the Gantt Chart view, click the cell directly below the Task Name column heading.

2   Type **Review script**, and then press Enter.

Your screen should look similar to the following illustration.

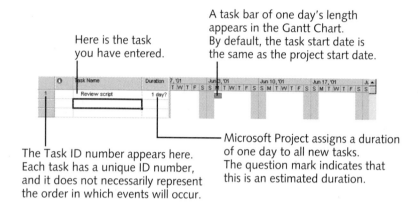

Here is the task you have entered.

A task bar of one day's length appears in the Gantt Chart. By default, the task start date is the same as the project start date.

The Task ID number appears here. Each task has a unique ID number, and it does not necessarily represent the order in which events will occur.

Microsoft Project assigns a duration of one day to all new tasks. The question mark indicates that this is an estimated duration.

3   Enter the following task names below Review script, pressing Enter after each task name.

```
Develop script breakdown and schedule
Develop production boards
Pick locations
Hold auditions
Reserve camera equipment
Reserve sound equipment
```

Your screen should look similar to the following illustration.

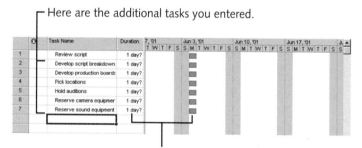

Here are the additional tasks you entered.

New tasks have a default estimated duration of one day and are not linked.

Proj2000-1-5

Estimating Durations

A task's duration is the amount of time you expect it will take to complete the task. Microsoft Project determines the overall duration of a project by calculating the difference between the earliest start date and the latest finish date of the tasks that compose the project. The project's duration is affected by other factors, such as task relationships, to be discussed in later lessons. Because Microsoft Project distinguishes between working and nonworking time, a task's duration does not necessarily correlate to elapsed time.

For example, a project might have a project calendar with working time defined as 9:00 A.M.–5:00 P.M. Monday through Friday, leaving non-working time defined as evenings and weekends. If you estimate that a task will take 16 hours of working time, you could enter its duration as **2d** to schedule work over two 8-hour workdays. You should then expect that starting the task at 9:00 A.M. on a Friday means that it would not be completed until 5:00 P.M. on the following Monday. No work would be scheduled over the weekend, because Saturday and Sunday have been defined as nonworking time.

You can schedule tasks to occur over working and nonworking time, however. To do this, assign an **elapsed duration** to a task. For example, you might have the tasks "Pour foundation concrete" and "Remove foundation forms" in a construction project. If so, you might also want a task called "Wait for concrete to cure" because you do not want to remove the forms until the concrete has cured. The task "Wait for concrete to cure" should have an elapsed duration because the concrete will cure over a contiguous range of days, whether they are working or nonworking days. If the concrete takes 48 hours to cure, you can enter the duration for that task as **2ed**, schedule the task to start on Friday at 9 A.M., and expect it to be complete by Sunday at 9 A.M. In most cases, however, you will work with nonelapsed durations in Microsoft Project.

Microsoft Project can work with task durations that range from minutes to months. Depending on the scope of your project, you will probably want to work with task durations on the scale of hours, days, and weeks. You should consider two general rules when estimating task durations:

■   Project duration often correlates to task duration; long projects tend to have tasks with longer durations than short projects.

> Although it is beyond the scope of this courseware, Program Evaluation and Review Technique (PERT) analysis can be a useful tool for estimating task durations. For more information, ask the Office Assistant in Microsoft Project how to "Estimate task durations by using PERT analysis."

Defining the Right Tasks for the Right Deliverable

Every project has an ultimate goal or intent: the reason why the project was started to begin with. This is referred to as the project **deliverable**. This deliverable is usually a product, such as a short film, or a service or event, such as a software training session. Defining the right tasks to create the right deliverable is an essential skill for a project manager. The task lists you create in Microsoft Project should describe all the work required, and only the work required, to complete the project successfully.

In developing your task lists, it is helpful to distinguish product scope from project scope. **Product scope** describes the quality, features, and functions of the deliverable of the project. In the scenario used in this book, for example, the product deliverable is a short film. **Project scope**, on the other hand, describes the work required to deliver such a product or service. In our scenario, the project scope includes detailed pre-production, production, and post-production tasks relating to the creation of a documentary film.

■   If you track progress against your project plan (described in Lesson 8), you need to think about the level of detail you want to apply to your project's tasks. If you have a multiyear project, for example, it might not be practical or even possible to track tasks that are measured in minutes or hours. In general, you should measure task durations at the lowest level of detail or control you care about, but no lower.

When working in Microsoft Project, you can use abbreviations for durations.

If You Enter This Abbreviation	It Appears Like This	And Means
m	min	minute
h	hr	hour
d	day	day
w	wk	week
mo	mon	month
em	emin	elapsed minute
eh	ehr	elapsed hour
ed	eday	elapsed day
ew	ewk	elapsed week
emo	emon	elapsed month

Microsoft Project 2000 supports entering month durations.

Microsoft Project uses standard values of minutes and hours for durations: one minute equals 60 seconds, and one hour equals 60 minutes. However, you can define the duration of days, weeks, and months for your project. To do this, you must first open the Tools menu, choose the Options command, and display the Calendar tab, illustrated on the following page.

How Do You Come Up with Accurate Task Durations?

For the project you work on in this book, the durations are supplied for you. For your real-world projects, you will often have to estimate task durations. Some good sources of task duration estimates include:

■   Historical information from previous, similar projects.

■   Estimates from the people who will complete the tasks.

■   The expert judgment of people who have managed similar projects.

■   Professional or industry organizations dedicated to whatever subject the project is about.

For complex projects, you probably would employ a combination of these and other methods to estimate task durations. Inaccurate task duration estimates are a major source of **risk** in any project, so making good estimates is well worth the effort.

With a setting of 8 working hours per day,
a 2-day task duration is equal to 16 hours.

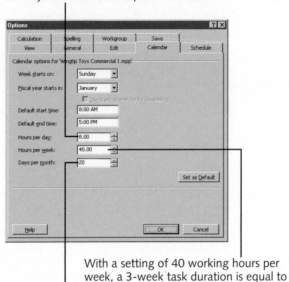

With a setting of 40 working hours per
week, a 3-week task duration is equal to
120 hours.

With a setting of 20 working days per month,
a one-month task duration is equal to 160 hours
(or 8 hours per day x 20 days per month).

The exercises in this book require the default values: 8 hours per day, 40 hours per week, and 20 days per month.

In this exercise, you enter durations for the tasks you created earlier in the lesson. When you created those tasks, Microsoft Project entered an estimated duration of 1 day for each. (The question mark in the Duration field indicates that the duration is an explicit estimate, although really you should consider all task durations to be estimates until the task is completed.)

1 In the Gantt Chart view, click the cell directly below the Duration column heading.

The Duration field for Task 1, "Review script," is selected.

2 Type **2w** and then press Enter.

The value 2 wks (short for 2 weeks) appears in the Duration field.

3 Enter the following durations for the remaining tasks.

Task ID	Task Name	Duration
2	Develop script breakdown and schedule	1w
3	Develop production boards	1mo
4	Pick locations	6w?
5	Hold auditions	2w
6	Reserve camera equipment	1w
7	Reserve sound equipment	5d

Typing a question mark after a duration (for example, 6w?) is a good way to mark estimated durations that you might want to update after you know more about the scope of the task. You can later filter for tasks with estimated durations. On the Project menu, click Filtered For, and then click Tasks With Estimated Durations. For more information about filtering, see Lesson 9.

Your screen should look similar to the following illustration.

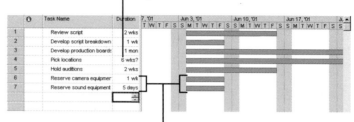

The question mark indicates an explicit estimated duration.

Although the durations of these two tasks were entered differently (1 week and 5 days), the durations are equal.

You might recall from the discussion above that, by default, 1 week equals 40 hours, as does 5 days. You can see that the bar lengths of Task 6 (with a duration of one week) and Task 7 (with a duration of five days) are equal in the Gantt Chart.

Proj2000-1-16

Entering a Milestone

You might want to track an important event for your project, such as when the Pre-Production phase of the project will end. To do this, you will create a **milestone**.

Milestones are significant events that are either reached within the project (completion of a phase of work, for example) or imposed upon the project (a deadline by which to apply for funding, for example). Because the milestone itself does not normally include any work, milestones are represented as tasks with zero duration.

In this exercise, you create a milestone.

A milestone usually identifies a significant event or the completion of a phase of work. But the milestone itself requires no work, and it, therefore, has a duration of zero days. However, you can mark a task of any duration as a milestone if you want. Double-click the task name to display the Task Information dialog box, and then click the Advanced tab. Click Mark Task As Milestone.

1 In the Task column of the Gantt Chart view, click the next empty cell below the name of Task 7, "Reserve sound equipment."

2 Type **Pre-Production complete!** and then press Tab.

3 In the Duration field, type **0d** and then press Enter.

The milestone is added to your file. Your screen should look similar to the following illustration.

On the Gantt Chart, the milestone appears as a black diamond.

Proj2000-1-14

Organizing Tasks into Phases

If you have a complex set of tasks, you should consider organizing them into phases, or groups of closely related tasks. In Microsoft Project, phases are represented by **summary tasks**.

A summary task behaves differently from other tasks. You cannot edit its duration, start date, or other calculated values directly because they are derived from the detail tasks, called subtasks. Summary tasks are useful for getting information about phases of project work.

In this exercise, you create a summary task and insert additional tasks.

1   In the Gantt Chart view, click the name of Task 1, "Review script."

2   On the Insert menu, click New Task.

3   In the Task Name field for the new task, type **Pre-Production** and press Enter.

   You will next add two high-level activities, whose details you will fill in later.

4   Type the following task names below Task 9, "Pre-Production complete!," pressing Enter after each task name.

   Production

   Post-Production

   Finally, you will make Task 1, "Pre-Production," a summary task by indenting the subtasks below it.

Project Management Focus: Top-Down and Bottom-Up Planning

There are two common approaches to developing tasks and phases: **top-down** and **bottom-up** planning.

Top-Down Planning	Bottom-Up Planning
Identifies major phases or products of the project and then fills in the tasks required to complete those phases. Complex projects might have several layers of subordinate phases.	Identifies as many of the bottom level detailed tasks as possible and then organizes them under logical groups of phases or summary tasks.
Works from general to specific.	Works from specific to general.

Project goals often flow from the top down, and project planning details flow from the bottom up. Creating accurate tasks and phases for most complex projects really requires a combination of top-down and bottom-up planning. For some project work, you will already know the low-level tasks, but for others, you might initially know only the broader project goals.

5 Select Tasks 2 through 9.

6 On the Formatting toolbar, click the Indent button.

Task 1 becomes a summary task, and a summary task bar for it appears in the Gantt Chart. Your screen should look similar to the following illustration.

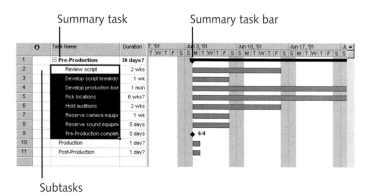

Summary task   Summary task bar

Subtasks

Proj2000-1-19

Linking Tasks

Projects require tasks to be done in a specific order. For example, the task of filming a scene must be completed before the task of editing the filmed scene can occur. These two tasks have a finish-to-start **relationship**, which has two aspects.

- The second task must occur after the first task; this is a **sequence**.

- The second task can occur only if the first task is completed; this is a **dependency**.

In Microsoft Project, the first task ("Film the scene") is called the **predecessor** because it precedes tasks that depend on it. The second task ("Edit the filmed scene") is called the **successor** because it succeeds tasks on which it is dependent. Any task can be a predecessor for one or more successor tasks. Likewise, any task can be a successor to one or more predecessor tasks.

This might sound complicated, but it turns out tasks can have one of only four types of task relationships:

This Task Relationship	Means	Looks Like This in the Gantt Chart	Example
finish-to-start (FS)	The finish date of the predecessor task determines the start date of the successor task.		A film scene must be shot before it can be edited.
start-to-start (SS)	The start date of the predecessor task determines the start date of the successor task.		Reviewing a script and developing the script breakdown and schedule are closely related, and should occur simultaneously.
finish-to-finish (FF)	The finish date of the predecessor task determines the finish date of the successor task.		Tasks that require specific equipment must end when the task that represents the duration of the equipment rental ends.
start-to-finish (SF)	The start date of the predecessor task determines the finish date of the successor task.		Rarely used; has some application when tracking accounting tasks.

Task relationships appear in several ways in Microsoft Project. The most common places to see task relationships are:

■ In the Gantt Chart and Network Diagram views, task relationships appear as the lines connecting tasks.

■ In tables, such as the Entry table, Task ID numbers of predecessor tasks appear in the Predecessor fields of successor tasks.

You create task relationships by creating **links** between tasks. In this exercise, you use different methods to create links between several tasks, creating finish-to-start relationships.

1 In the Gantt Chart view, click the name of Task 2, "Review script," and then drag to the name of Task 3, "Develop script breakdown and schedule."

Tasks 2 and 3 are selected.

2 On the Standard toolbar, click the Link Tasks button.

Tasks 2 and 3 are linked with a finish-to-start relationship. Note that Microsoft Project changed the start date of Task 3 to the next working day following the completion of Task 2.

Clicking the Link Tasks button creates a finish-to-start (FS) task relationship. For instructions on creating other types of task relationships, see "Adjusting Task Relationships" later in this lesson.

Your screen should look similar to the following illustration.

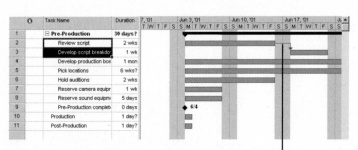

To unlink tasks, select the tasks you want to unlink, and then click the Unlink Tasks button. If you unlink a single task that is part of a chain of linked tasks with finish-to-start relationships, Microsoft Project reestablishes links between the remaining tasks.

This link line indicates a finish-to-start relationship between these two tasks. Note that this link line extends over the weekend, which is nonworking time.

Next you will link two tasks in another way.

3 Select the name of Task 4, "Develop production boards."

4 On the Standard toolbar, click the Task Information button.

The Task Information dialog box appears.

5 Click the Predecessors tab.

6 Click the empty cell below the Task Name column heading, and then click the down arrow button that appears.

7 In the Task Name list, click Develop script breakdown and schedule, and press Enter. Your screen should look similar to the following illustration.

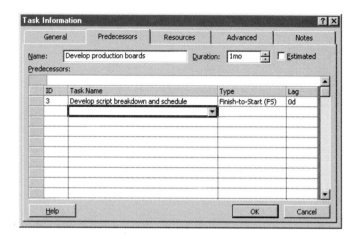

8   Click OK to close the Task Information dialog box.

Tasks 3 and 4 are linked with a finish-to-start relationship. Next you will verify this task relationship by viewing the Predecessors column.

9   At the bottom of the Entry table, drag the scroll box to the right until you can see the Predecessors column.

You can see Task 3 in the Predecessor field for Task 4. Your screen should look similar to the following illustration.

The Task IDs of predecessor tasks appear in the Predecessors column.

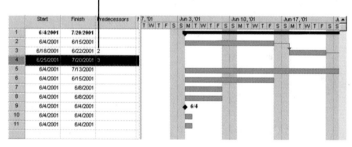

10   At the bottom of the Entry table, drag the scroll box to the left until the leftmost column is visible again.

Next you link the remaining tasks in a single step.

tip

To see the complete name of a task or any other field that does not fit within the width of a column, point to the cell for a moment. The full name will appear in a ToolTip.

11   Select Tasks 4 through 9.

12   On the Standard toolbar, click the Link Tasks button.

The remaining tasks are linked with finish-to-start relationships. Your screen should look similar to the following illustration.

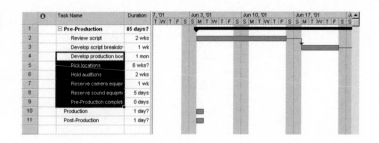

You can also create a finish-to-start relationship between tasks right in the Gantt Chart. Point to the task bar of the predecessor task until the pointer changes to a four-pointed star. Then drag up or down to the task bar of the successor task.

Proj2000-2-11

Adjusting Task Relationships

When you enter tasks in Microsoft Project and link them by clicking the Link Tasks button on the Standard toolbar, the tasks are given a finish-to-start (FS) relationship. This might be fine for most tasks, but you will probably want to change some task relationships. Here are some examples of tasks that require relationships other than finish-to-start.

■ You can start setting up the lighting for a film scene as soon as you start setting up the props (start-to-start relationship). This reduces the overall time required to complete the two tasks, as they are completed in parallel.

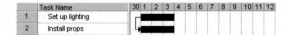

■ Planning the scene filming sequence can begin before the script is complete, but it can not finish until after the script is complete. You want the two tasks to finish at about the same time (finish-to-finish relationship).

Task relationships should reflect the sequence in which work should be done. Once you have established the correct task relationships, you can fine-tune your schedule by entering overlap (called lead time) or delay (called lag time) between the finish or start dates of predecessor and successor tasks.

Assuming two tasks have a finish-to-start relationship:

■ Lead time causes the successor task to begin before its predecessor task concludes.

■ Lag time causes the successor task to begin some time after its predecessor task concludes.

Here is an illustration of how lead and lag time affect task relationships. Let's say you initially planned the following three tasks using finish-to-start relationships:

Initially the tasks are linked with finish-to-start relationships, so the successor tasks begin as soon as the predecessor tasks finish.

Before Task 8 can start, you need to allow an extra day for the paint applied in Task 7 to dry. You do not want to add a day to the duration of Task 7 because no real work will occur on that day. Instead, you enter a one-day lag between Tasks 7 and 8:

This lag time causes a delay in the start of the successor task.

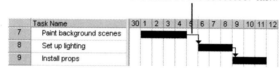

However, Task 9 can start as soon as Task 8 is halfway completed; to make this happen, you enter a 50% lead time between Tasks 8 and 9:

This lead time causes the successor task to start before the predecessor task finishes.

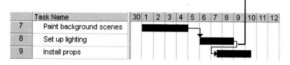

Places you can enter lead or lag time include the Task Information dialog box and the Predecessors column in the Entry table.

You can enter lead and lag time as units of time (for example, 2 days) or as a percentage of the duration of the predecessor task (for example, 50%). Lag time is entered in positive units, lead time in negative units (for example, –2 days or –50%). You can apply lead or lag time to any type of task relationship: finish-to-start, start-to-start, and so on.

In this exercise, you change task relationships and enter lead and lag time between predecessor and successor tasks.

1   In the Entry table, double-click the name of Task 7, "Reserve camera equipment."

   The Task Information dialog box appears.

Double-clicking a task name displays the Task Information dialog box.

2   Click the Predecessors tab.

3   In the Lag field for predecessor Task 6, type **-50%**, and press Enter.

To enter lead time against a predecessor task,
enter it as negative lag time either in units
of time such as days, or as a percentage
of the duration of the predecessor task.

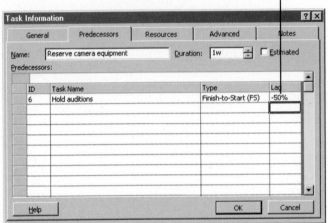

Entering lag time as a negative value produces lead time.

4   Click OK to close the Task Information dialog box.

5   To see how the lag time affects the scheduling of the successor task,
on the Standard toolbar, click the Go To Selected Task button.

Lead time causes the successor task to start before
the predecessor task has finished, although the
two tasks still have a finish-to-start relationship.

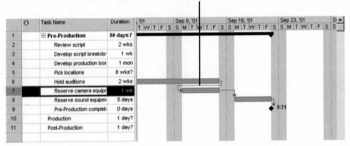

Microsoft Project scrolls the Gantt Chart to display the Gantt bar for
Task 7. Task 7 is now scheduled to start when Task 6 is 50% complete. Should the duration of Task 6 change, Microsoft Project will reschedule the start of Task 7.

Next you will change the task relationship between two tasks.

6   In the Gantt Chart view, double-click the name of Task 8, "Reserve
sound equipment."

The Task Information dialog box appears. The Predecessors tab should
be visible.

7   Click in the Type field for predecessor Task 7. Select Start-to-Start
(SS), and click OK.

Microsoft Project changes the task relationship between Tasks 7 and 8
to start-to-start.

The start-to-start task relationship causes the two tasks to start at the same time. Should the start of the predecessor task change, the start of the successor task would change as well.

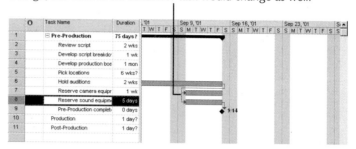

Assigning tasks start-to-start relationships or entering lead times where appropriate are both excellent techniques to shorten overall project duration. Microsoft Project cannot automatically make such schedule adjustments for you, however. As project manager, you must analyze the sequences and relationships of your tasks and make those adjustments where appropriate.

Proj2000-1-20
Proj2000-3-2

Documenting Task Details with Notes and Hyperlinks

You can record any additional information about a task that you want in a **note**. For example, if the duration of a task is based on important information that should be recorded, it is a good idea to record the reason in a note. That way, the information resides in the Microsoft Project file and can be easily viewed or printed.

There are three types of notes: task notes, resource notes, and assignment notes. Task notes appear on the Notes tab in the Task Information dialog box. (You can open the Task Information dialog box by selecting the Task Information command from the Microsoft Project menu.) Notes in Microsoft Project support a wide range of text formatting options; you can even link to or store graphic images and other types of files in Microsoft Project notes.

Hyperlinks allow you to connect a specific task to another file, a specific location in a file, a page on the World Wide Web, or a page on an intranet.

In this exercise, you enter task notes and hyperlinks to document important information about some tasks. You will work with resource notes in Lesson 7 and with assignment notes in Lesson 8.

1   Select the name of Task 7, "Reserve camera equipment."

2   On the Standard toolbar, click the Task Notes button.

Microsoft Project displays the Task Information dialog box with the Notes tab visible.

3   In the Notes box, type **Don't forget to locate a Steadicam.** Then click OK.

A note icon appears in the Indicators column.

4   Point to the note icon.

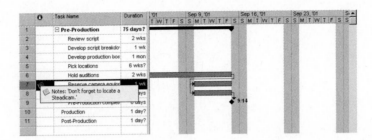

The note appears in a ToolTip. For notes that are too long to appear in a ToolTip, you can click the note icon to display the full text of the note.

To conclude this exercise, you create a hyperlink.

5   Select the name of Task 8, "Reserve sound equipment."

6   On the Standard toolbar, click the Insert Hyperlink button.

The Insert Hyperlink dialog box appears.

7   In the Type The File Or Web Page Name box, type
http://www.widgets-inc-10.com

8   In the Text To Display box, type **Web site of good audio rental company** and then click OK.

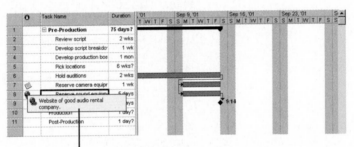

Hover your mouse pointer over a hyperlink indicator, and Microsoft Project displays the text you entered when you created the hyperlink.

A hyperlink icon appears in the Indicators column. Pointing to the icon displays the descriptive text you typed above. Clicking the icon opens the Web page in your browser.

Lesson Wrap-Up

In this lesson, you learned how to create a new Microsoft Project file and enter an initial task list.

If you are continuing on to other lessons:

●   On the File menu, click Close to close the file. When you are prompted to save changes, click Yes, and then save without a **baseline.**

If you are not continuing on to other lessons:

1   On the File menu, click Close to close the file. If you are prompted to save changes, click No.

2   On the File menu, click Exit.

Microsoft Project closes.

Lesson Glossary

baseline The original project plan, saved for later comparison. The baseline includes the planned start and finish dates of tasks and assignments and their planned costs. Each Microsoft Project file can have at most one baseline.

bottom-up planning Developing a project plan by starting with the lowest-level tasks before organizing them into broad phases.

deliverable The final product, service, or event a project is intended to create.

dependency A link between a predecessor task and a successor task. A dependency controls the start or finish of one task relative to the start or finish of the other task. The most common dependency is finish-to-start, in which the finish date of the predecessor task determines the start date of the successor task.

duration The length of working time you expect it will take to complete a task.

elapsed duration The total length of working and nonworking time you expect it will take to complete a task.

Entry table The grid in the left side of the default Gantt Chart view.

field The lowest-level information about a task, resource, or assignment; also called a cell.

Gantt Chart view One of several predefined views in Microsoft Project. The Gantt Chart view consists of a table (the Entry table by default) on the left side and a graphical bar chart on the right side.

link A logical relationship between tasks that controls sequence and dependency. In the Gantt Chart and Network Diagram views, links appear as lines between tasks.

milestone A significant event that might be reached within the project or imposed upon the project. In Microsoft Project, milestones are normally represented as tasks with zero duration.

predecessor A task whose start or end date determines the start or finish of another task or tasks, called successor tasks.

product scope The quality, features, and functions (often called specifications) of the deliverable of the project.

project scope The work required to produce a deliverable with agreed-upon quality, features, and functions.

relationship The type of dependency between two tasks, visually indicated by a link line. The types of relationships include finish-to-start, start-to-start, finish-to-finish, and start-to-finish. Also known as a link, a logical relationship, a task dependency, or a precedence relationship.

risk Any event that decreases the likelihood of completing the project on time, within budget, and to specification.

shortcut menu A menu you display by pointing to an item on the screen and then clicking the right mouse button. Shortcut menus contain only the commands that apply to the item to which you are pointing.

sequence The chronological order in which tasks occur. A sequence is ordered from left to right in most views that include a time scale, for example, the Gantt Chart view.

successor A task whose start or finish is driven by another task or tasks, called predecessor tasks.

summary task A task that is made up of and summarizes the subtasks below it. In Microsoft Project, phases of project work are represented by summary tasks.

Task ID A unique number that Microsoft Project assigns to each task in a project. In the Entry table, the Task ID appears in the far left column.

ToolTip A short description of an item on the screen, such as a toolbar, button, or bar. To see a ToolTip, briefly point to an item.

top-down planning Developing a project plan by identifying the highest-level phases or summary tasks before breaking them into lower-level components or subtasks.

Quick Quiz

1   How do you use the Answer Wizard to search Help without using the Office Assistant?

2   How do you display all the commands on Microsoft Project menus?

3   When creating a new Microsoft Project file, why do you specify the project start date or finish date, but not both?

4   In Microsoft Project, what is a cell?

5   What is the difference between the duration and the elapsed duration of a task?

6   How do you quickly create a milestone task?

7   Why can't you directly edit the duration of a summary task?

8   What are predecessors and successors?

9   What are the four types of task relationships, or links, and what are their abbreviations?

10   A task has a note. What is the easiest way to read the note?

Putting It All Together

Exercise 1: If necessary, start Microsoft Project. Create a new file with a project start date of May 7, 2001. Enter the following tasks and durations into the new file:

```
Pre-Production, (leave at 1d? duration)
Develop script breakdown, 2w
Develop choreography, 3w
Production, (leave at 1d? duration)
Rehearsal, 3d
Shoot, 2d
Post-Production, (leave at 1d? duration)
Fine cut edit, 1w
Add final music, 1w
```

Save the document in the Lesson 1 folder located in the MS Project Core Practice folder on your hard disk with the name Music Video 1.

Exercise 2: Make Tasks 1, 4, and 7 summary tasks. Link all tasks with finish-to-start relationships, and then save and close the document without a baseline.

LESSON 2

Setting Up Resources

After completing this lesson, you will be able to:

✔ *Set up basic resource information for the people who work on your projects.*

✔ *Enter basic resource information for the equipment that will be used in your projects.*

✔ *Update individual resource calendars.*

✔ *Enter basic resource information for the materials that will be consumed as your project progresses.*

✔ *Set up cost information for your resources.*

✔ *Create a resource note.*

Resources are the people, equipment, and material needed to complete the tasks in a project. Microsoft Project focuses on two aspects of resources: their availability and their costs. Availability determines when specific resources can work on tasks and how much work they can do, and costs refer to how much money will be required to pay for those resources.

In this lesson, you will set up some of the resources you need to complete the toy commercial project. Managing resources effectively is one of the most powerful advantages of using Microsoft Project over task-focused planning tools, such as paper-based organizers. You do not need to set up resources and assign them to tasks in Microsoft Project; however, without this information, you might have less control over who does what work, when, and at what cost. Setting up resource information in Microsoft Project takes a little effort, but the time is well spent if your project is primarily driven by time or cost constraints. (And nearly all complex projects are driven by one, if not both, of these factors.)

Practice files for the lesson

To complete the procedures in this lesson, you will need to use a file named Wingtip Toys Commercial 2. Open the Lesson 2 folder in the MS Project Core Practice folder located on your hard disk. Open the file 2A, and save it without a baseline as Wingtip Toys Commercial 2 in the Lesson 2 folder.

Setting Up People Resources

Microsoft Project works with two types of resources: work resources and material resources. **Work resources** are the people and equipment that do the work of the project. You will learn about material resources later in this lesson.

Here are some examples of work resources.

Work Resource	Example
Individual people identified by name	Jon Ganio; Jim Hance
Individual people identified by job title or function	Director; Camera operator
Groups of people who have common skills (when assigning such inter-changeable resources to a task, you do not care who the individual resource is, as long as the resource has the right skills)	Electricians; Carpenters; Extras
Equipment	16-mm camera; 1000-watt light

Equipment resources need not be portable; a fixed location or piece of machinery (for example, a film editing studio) can also be considered equipment.

All projects require some people resources, and some projects require only people resources. Although Microsoft Project is not a complete resource or asset management system, it can help you make smarter decisions about how to manage work resources and at what financial cost.

In this exercise, you set up resource information for several people resources in the Resource Sheet view.

1   On the View Bar, click Resource Sheet.

2   On the Resource Sheet, click the cell directly below the Resource Name column heading.

3   Type **Garrett R. Vargas** and press Tab.

Microsoft Project creates a new resource record with a default type of Work and the Max. Units field set to 100%.

4   In the Type field, make sure that Work is selected, and press Tab.

The two types of resources are work (people and equipment) and material.

If you cannot see the Resource Sheet button on the View Bar, click the down arrow button at the bottom of the View Bar until the Resource Sheet button appears.

5   Press Tab again to get to the Initials field.

In the Initials field, Microsoft Project supplied the first initial from the resource name. But, for this project, you want to use at least two initials per resource. In a later exercise, you'll reformat a Gantt Chart view to display resource initials next to Gantt bars.

Because you are entering a work resource, you can skip the Material Label field.

6   In the Initials field, type **GV** and press Tab.

7   Press Tab again to skip over the Group field.

8   In the Max. Units field, make sure that 100% is selected, and click the next empty cell in the Resource Name column. Your screen should look similar to the following illustration.

Here is the resource information you've entered.

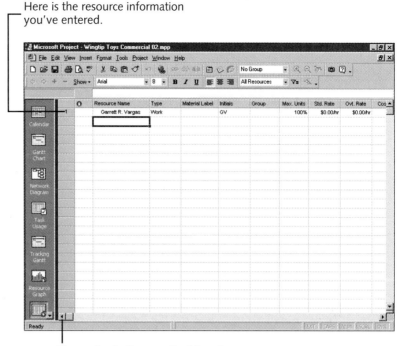

To see the buttons on the View Bar, click this scroll button.

You will work with cost information later in the lesson, but the **Max. Units** field merits some explanation now. This field represents the maximum capacity of a resource to accomplish any task. Specifying that Garrett R. Vargas has 100% maximum units means that 100% of Garrett's time is available to work on the tasks to which you assign him. Microsoft Project will alert you if you assign Garrett to more tasks than he can accomplish at 100% maximum units (or, in other words, if Garrett becomes **overallocated**).

You can also have a resource that represents multiple people. Next you will set up such a resource.

In Lesson 3, you will assign these resources to tasks.

9 In the Resource Name field below the first resource, type **Electrician**, and then press Tab.

10 In the Type field, make sure that Work is selected, and then press Tab twice.

11 In the Initials field, type **EL** and then press Tab twice.

12 In the Max. Units field, type or select 200%, and then press Tab. Your screen should look similar to the following illustration.

If you prefer, you can enter maximum units as partial or whole numbers (for example, .5, 1, 2) rather than as percentages (50%, 100%, or 200%). To use this format, open the Tools menu, click Options, and then click the Schedule tab. In the Assignment Units As A box, click Decimal.

The resource named Electrician does not represent a single person; instead, it represents a category of interchangeable people called electricians. Because the Electrician resource has Max. Units set to 200%, you can plan on two electricians being available to work full-time every workday. At this point in the planning phase, you do not know exactly who these electricians will be, and that's okay. You can still proceed with more general planning.

13   Enter the remaining resource information into the Resource Sheet. For each resource, make sure **Work** is selected in the Type field.

Resource Name	Initials	Max. Units
Jim Hance	JH	100%
Scott Cooper	SC	100%
Jo Brown	JB	100%
Patti Mintz	PM	100%
Peter Kelly	PK	100%
John Rodman	JR	100%
Jonathan Mollerup	JM	50%
Jon Ganio	JG	75%

Your screen should look similar to the following illustration.

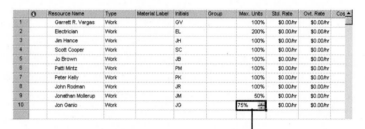

When you create a new resource, Microsoft Project assigns it 100% max. units by default. You change the resource's max. units here.

What Is the Best Way to Enter Resource Names?

In Microsoft Project, resource names can refer to specific people (for example, Jon Ganio or Jim Hance) or to specific job titles (for example, Camera Operator or Actor). Use whatever makes the most sense for your needs and for those who will see the project information you publish. The important questions to ask are, "Who will see these resource names?" and "How will they identify the resources?" This includes both working with resource names in Microsoft Project and viewing them in information published from Microsoft Project. For example, in the default Gantt Chart view, the name of the resource, as you enter it in the Resource Name field, appears next to the bars of the tasks to which that resource is assigned.

A resource might be somebody already on staff or a position to be filled later. If you have not yet filled all of the resource positions required, you will not necessarily have real people's names yet. If this is the case, use placeholder names such as functional titles when setting up resources in Microsoft Project.

Setting Up Equipment Resources

You set up people and equipment resources in exactly the same way in Microsoft Project. However, you should be aware of important differences in how you can schedule these two types of resources. For example, most people resources have a working day of no more than 12 hours, but equipment resources might work around the clock. Moreover, people resources might be more flexible in the tasks they can perform, but equipment resources tend to be more specialized. For example, a director of photography for a film might also act as a camera operator in a pinch, but a movie camera cannot replace an editing studio.

You do not need to track every piece of equipment that will be used in your project, but you might want to set up equipment resources when

■ Multiple teams or people might need a piece of equipment to do different tasks simultaneously, and the equipment might be overbooked.

■ You want to plan and track costs associated with the equipment.

In this exercise, you enter information about equipment resources in the Resource Information dialog box.

1 On the Resource Sheet, click the empty cell in the Resource Name column under Jon Ganio.

2 On the Standard toolbar, click the Resource Information button.

The Resource Information dialog box appears.

You can also double-click a resource name or an empty cell in the Resource Name column to display the Resource Information dialog box.

3 Click the General tab.

In the upper portion of the General tab, you might recognize the fields you saw in the Resource Sheet view. As with many types of information in Microsoft Project, you can usually work in at least two interfaces: a table and a dialog box.

4 In the Resource Name field, type **16-mm Camera** and press Tab.

5 In the Resource Type field, select Work, and press Tab.

6 In the Initials field, type **16mm**. Your screen should look similar to the following illustration.

The Resource Information dialog box contains a button labeled Details. If you have an e-mail program that complies with the Messaging Application Programming Interface (MAPI) and the program is installed on the same computer as Microsoft Project, you can click Details to see contact information about the selected resource. Examples of MAPI-compliant programs include Microsoft Outlook and Microsoft Exchange.

The Resource Information dialog box contains many of the same fields you see on the Resource Sheet view.

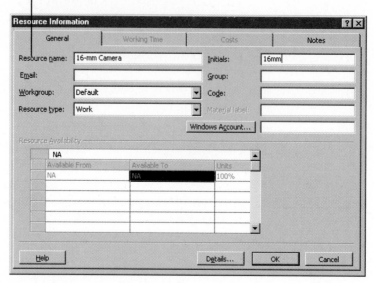

When creating a resource in the Resource Information dialog box, you cannot enter a Max. Units value. However, you can edit this value in the dialog box, as well as on the Resource Sheet, after you create the resource.

7   Click OK to close the Resource Information dialog box and return to the Resource Sheet.

The Max. Units field shows 100% for this resource; next you will change this.

8   In the Max. Units field for the 16-mm camera, type or select **300%** and press Tab.

This means that you plan to have three 16-mm cameras available every workday.

9   Enter the remaining information about equipment resources in the Resource Information dialog box or directly in the Resource Sheet, whichever you prefer. In either case, make sure **Work** is selected in the Type field.

Resource Name	Initials	Max. Units
5000-Watt Light	5000WL	400%
Dolly	Dolly	200%
Crane	Crane	100%
Editing Lab	EL	100%

Your screen should look similar to the following illustration.

	ⓘ	Resource Name	Type	Material Label	Initials	Group	Max. Units	Std. Rate	Ovt. Rate	Cos ▲
1		Garrett R. Vargas	Work		GV		100%	$0.00/hr	$0.00/hr	
2		Electrician	Work		EL		200%	$0.00/hr	$0.00/hr	
3		Jim Hance	Work		JH		100%	$0.00/hr	$0.00/hr	
4		Scott Cooper	Work		SC		100%	$0.00/hr	$0.00/hr	
5		Jo Brown	Work		JB		100%	$0.00/hr	$0.00/hr	
6		Patti Mintz	Work		PM		100%	$0.00/hr	$0.00/hr	
7		Peter Kelly	Work		PK		100%	$0.00/hr	$0.00/hr	
8		John Rodman	Work		JR		100%	$0.00/hr	$0.00/hr	
9		Jonathan Mollerup	Work		JM		50%	$0.00/hr	$0.00/hr	
10		Jon Ganio	Work		JG		75%	$0.00/hr	$0.00/hr	
11		16-mm Camera	Work		16mm		300%	$0.00/hr	$0.00/hr	
12		5000-Watt Light	Work		5000WL		400%	$0.00/hr	$0.00/hr	
13		Dolly	Work		Dolly		200%	$0.00/hr	$0.00/hr	
14		Crane	Work		Crane		100%	$0.00/hr	$0.00/hr	
15		Editing Lab	Work		EL		100%	$0.00/hr	$0.00/hr	

Proj2000-1-6

Adjusting Working Time for Resources

Microsoft Project uses different types of calendars for different purposes. In this section, we will focus on the **resource calendar**. A resource calendar is working and nonworking times of a resource. Microsoft Project uses resource calendars to determine when work for a specific resource can be scheduled. Resource calendars apply only to work resources (people and equipment) and not to material resources.

When you initially create resources in a project, Microsoft Project creates a resource calendar for each resource. The initial working time settings for resource calendars exactly match those of the **Standard base calendar**. If all of the working times of your resource match the working time of the Standard base calendar, you do not need to edit any resource calendars. However, chances are that some of your resources will need exceptions to the working time in the Standard base calendar—such as

- A flex-time work schedule
- Vacation time
- Other times when a resource is not available to work on the project, such as time spent training or attending a conference

Any changes you make to the Standard base calendar are automatically reflected in all resource calendars that are based on the Standard base calendar. Any specific changes you have made to the working time of a resource are not changed, however.

> You can edit a resource calendar in two places: the Working Time tab of the Resource Information dialog box and the Change Working Time dialog box. Editing a resource calendar in either location has the same effect.

> ## tip
>
> If you have a resource who is available to work on your project only part-time, you might be tempted to set the working time of the resource in your project to reflect a part-time schedule—for example, 9:00 A.M. to 1:00 P.M. daily. However, a better approach would be to adjust the availability of the resource as recorded in the **Max. Units** field to 50%, for example. Changing the unit availability of the resource keeps the focus on the capacity of the resource to work on the project, rather than on the specific times of the day when that work might occur. You set the Max. Units for a resource in the Resource Sheet view, which you display by selecting the Resource Sheet command from the View menu. For more information about resource units, see "Setting Up People Resources" earlier.

In this exercise, you specify the working and nonworking times for individual work resources.

1   On the Tools menu, click Change Working Time.

The Change Working Time dialog box appears.

2   In the For box, select Garrett R. Vargas.

Garrett R. Vargas's resource calendar appears in the Change Working Time dialog box. Garrett, the producer of the film, has told you he will not be available to work on Monday and Tuesday, May 21 and 22, 2001.

To quickly select this date range, drag from 21 through 22.

3   In the calendar below the Select Date(s) label, drag the vertical scroll bar or click the up or down arrow buttons until May 2001 appears.

4   Select the dates May 21 and 22.

5   Under Set Selected Date(s) To, click Nonworking Time.

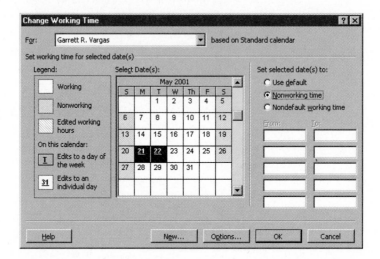

Microsoft Project will not schedule work for Garrett on these dates.

6   Next enter the following working time information for these resources. When asked if you want to save the information for each resource, click Yes.

Resource	Date	Working Time Issue
Patti Mintz	June 4–5, 2001	Patti cannot work on these days; mark as nonworking time.
Jo Brown	July 12–13, 2001	Jo cannot work on these days; mark as nonworking time.

To conclude this exercise, you will set up a "4 by 10" work schedule (that is, 4 days per week, 10 hours per day) for a resource.

7   In the For box, select John Rodman.

8   When prompted to save the resource calendar changes you made for Jo Brown, click Yes.

9   Select the Monday through Thursday column headings.

To quickly select the Monday through Thursday column headings, drag from the M through the Th.

Although you can see only one month at a time in the dialog box, selecting a column heading for a day selects every occurrence of that day of the week—past, present, and future.

10   In the lower To box, select "5:00 PM" and replace it with **7:00 PM**.

11   Select the Friday column heading.

12   Under Set Selected Date(s) To, click Nonworking Time.

Now Microsoft Project can schedule work for John as late as 7:00 P.M. every Monday through Thursday, but it will not schedule work for him on Fridays.

13   Click OK to close the Change Working Time dialog box.

Assigning a Different Base Calendar to a Resource

If you find that you must edit several resource calendars in a similar way (to handle a night shift, for example), it might be easier to assign a different base calendar to a resource or collection of resources. This is more efficient than editing the individual resource calendar for each resource, and it allows you to make project-wide adjustments to a single base calendar if needed. In Lesson 4, you will create a new base calendar.

For example, if your project includes a day shift and a night shift, you can apply the **Night Shift** base calendar to those resources who work the night shift. You change the base calendar of a resource in the Base Calendar box on the Working Time tab of the Resource Information dialog box. You can open this dialog box by selecting the Resource Information command on the Project menu when in a resource view. For collections of resources, you can do this directly in the Base Calendar column on the Entry table in the Resource Sheet view.

Proj2000-1-8

Setting Up Material Resources

Material resources are consumables that you use up as the project progresses. On a construction project, material resources might include nails, lumber, and concrete. On our project, film is the consumable resource that interests us most. You work with material resources in Microsoft Project mainly to track the rate of consumption and the associated cost. Although Microsoft Project is not a complete system for tracking inventory, it can help you stay better informed about how quickly you are consuming your material resources.

Comparing Work and Material Resources

Following are some ways material resources are similar to and different from work resources.

For both material and work resources, you can edit and contour resource assignments, set up multiple pay rates, specify different pay rates to apply at different times, and share resources through a resource pool. In addition, cost calculations for material resources work just about the same way as they do for work resources.

Unlike work resources, however, material resources do not use the following: overtime cost rates, resource calendars, or maximum units. Also, material resources are not affected by resource leveling, and they have no effect on the duration of a task if effort-driven scheduling is enabled.

In this exercise, you enter information about material resources.

1   On the Resource Sheet, click the next empty cell in the Resource Name column.

2   Type **16-mm Film** and press Tab.

3   In the Type field, select Material, and press Tab.

4   In the Material Label field, type **Feet** and press Tab.

Feet is the unit of measure you will use to track film consumption during the project.

5   In the Initials field, type **Film** and press Tab.

You will enter the cost of the material resource later. Your screen should look similar to the following illustration.

		Resource Name	Type	Material Label	Initials	Group	Max. Units	Std. Rate	Ovt. Rate	Cos
1		Garrett R. Vargas	Work		GV		100%	$0.00/hr	$0.00/hr	
2		Electrician	Work		EL		200%	$0.00/hr	$0.00/hr	
3		Jim Hance	Work		JH		100%	$0.00/hr	$0.00/hr	
4		Scott Cooper	Work		SC		100%	$0.00/hr	$0.00/hr	
5		Jo Brown	Work		JB		100%	$0.00/hr	$0.00/hr	
6		Patti Mintz	Work		PM		100%	$0.00/hr	$0.00/hr	
7		Peter Kelly	Work		PK		100%	$0.00/hr	$0.00/hr	
8		John Rodman	Work		JR		100%	$0.00/hr	$0.00/hr	
9		Jonathan Mollerup	Work		JM		50%	$0.00/hr	$0.00/hr	
10		Jon Ganio	Work		JG		75%	$0.00/hr	$0.00/hr	
11		16-mm Camera	Work		16mm		300%	$0.00/hr	$0.00/hr	
12		5000-Watt Light	Work		5000WL		400%	$0.00/hr	$0.00/hr	
13		Dolly	Work		Dolly		200%	$0.00/hr	$0.00/hr	
14		Crane	Work		Crane		100%	$0.00/hr	$0.00/hr	
15		Editing Lab	Work		EL		100%	$0.00/hr	$0.00/hr	
16		16-mm Film	Material	Feet	Film			$0.00		

Here is the material resource you have entered.

The Material Label field only applies to material resources.

Proj2000-1-9

Entering Resource Pay Rates

Almost all projects have some financial aspect, and cost drives the project scope of many projects. Tracking and managing cost information allows the project manager to answer such important questions as:

■   What is the expected total cost of the project, based on our task duration and resource estimates?

■   Are we using expensive resources to do work that less expensive resources could do?

■   How much money will a specific type of resource or task cost over the life of the project?

■   Are we spending money at a rate that we can sustain for the planned duration of the project?

Work and material resources account for the majority of costs in many projects. To take full advantage of the extensive cost management features in Microsoft Project, the project manager should know the costs associated with each work and material resource. For people resources, it might be difficult to get such information. In many organizations, only senior management and human resource specialists know the pay rates of all resources working on a project, and they might consider this information confidential. Depending on your organizational policies and project priorities, you might not be able to track resource pay rates. If you are unable to track this information, your effectiveness as a project manager might be reduced, and the **sponsors** of your projects should understand this.

For our filmmaking project, you have been entrusted with pay rate information for all people resources used in the project. In the information below, note that the fees for the camera, the lights, and the editing lab are rental fees. Because the Industrial Smoke and Mirrors film company already owns the dolly and crane, you will not bill yourself for them. The film rate requires additional explanation, however.

The purpose of assigning a standard pay rate to a material resource is to accurately predict (and later, track) the cost of materials against the project plan. For the material resource named 16-mm Film, you entered a unit of measure of feet in the Material Label field; next you will enter a rate of 20 cents in the Std. Rate field. In other words, you will assign a cost of 20 cents per foot to film. As you consume film over the course of the project, Microsoft Project will calculate the accrued cost of the film you consume. For example, if you shoot 12 minutes of film at 36 feet per minute, you will consume 432 feet of film. Entering that amount shows that you spent $86.40 (12 minutes x 36 feet x $0.20).

In this exercise, you enter cost information for each resource.

1   On the Resource Sheet, click the Std. Rate field for Resource 1, "Garrett R. Vargas."

2   Type **800/w** and press Enter.

Garrett's standard weekly rate appears in the Std. Rate column.

3   In the Std. Rate field for Resource 2, "Electrician," type **22/h** and press Enter.

The electrician's standard hourly rate appears in the Std. Rate column. Your screen should look similar to the following illustration.

	ⓘ	Resource Name	Type	Material Label	Initials	Group	Max. Units	Std. Rate	Ovt. Rate	Cos ▲
1		Garrett R. Vargas	Work		GV		100%	$800.00/wk	$0.00/hr	
2		Electrician	Work		EL		200%	$22.00/hr	$0.00/hr	
3		Jim Hance	Work		JH		100%	$0.00/hr	$0.00/hr	
4		Scott Cooper	Work		SC		100%	$0.00/hr	$0.00/hr	
5		Jo Brown	Work		JB		100%	$0.00/hr	$0.00/hr	
6		Patti Mintz	Work		PM		100%	$0.00/hr	$0.00/hr	
7		Peter Kelly	Work		PK		100%	$0.00/hr	$0.00/hr	
8		John Rodman	Work		JR		100%	$0.00/hr	$0.00/hr	
9		Jonathan Mollerup	Work		JM		50%	$0.00/hr	$0.00/hr	
10		Jon Ganio	Work		JG		75%	$0.00/hr	$0.00/hr	
11		16-mm Camera	Work		16mm		300%	$0.00/hr	$0.00/hr	
12		5000-Watt Light	Work		5000WL		400%	$0.00/hr	$0.00/hr	
13		Dolly	Work		Dolly		200%	$0.00/hr	$0.00/hr	
14		Crane	Work		Crane		100%	$0.00/hr	$0.00/hr	
15		Editing Lab	Work		EL		100%	$0.00/hr	$0.00/hr	
16		16-mm Film	Material	Feet	Film			$0.00		

4   Enter the following standard pay rates for these resources.

Resource Name	Standard Rate
Jim Hance	18.75/h
Scott Cooper	775/w
Jo Brown	18.75/h
Patti Mintz	9.40/h
Peter Kelly	16.75/h
John Rodman	22/h
Jonathan Mollerup	10/h
Jon Ganio	15.50/h
16-mm Camera	250/w
5000-Watt Light	100/w
Dolly	0/h
Crane	0/h
Editing Lab	200/d
16-mm Film	.20

Not all resources are paid a straight standard rate. Some resources require overtime pay for working more than a certain numbers of hours over a certain period of time.

5   On the Resource Sheet, click the Ovt. Rate field for Resource 2, "Electrician."

6   Type **33/h** and press Enter.

Some resources require you to pay a price each time you use them. For example, a consultant or a piece of equipment might have a per-use fee in addition to or instead of an hourly rate. In our project, the Editing Lab has a $25 charge for setting it up and cleaning it every time you use it. You will enter this fee next.

To see the Cost/Use field, you might need to scroll to the right.

7   On the Resource Sheet, scroll to the right, and click the Cost/Use field for Resource 15, "Editing Lab."

8   Type **25** and then press Enter.

Not all resources accrue cost in the same way. For example, a piece of rented equipment might require payment of a rental fee as soon as you rent the equipment, but employees usually accrue pay as time progresses. In the Accrue At field, you specify how Microsoft Project should handle the cost accrual of a resource.

To see the Accrue At field, you might need to scroll to the right.

9   On the Resource Sheet, scroll further to the right, and click the Accrue At field for Resource 11, "16-mm Camera."

Rental fees for the 16-mm cameras must be paid before you use the equipment. To reflect this in your file, you want Microsoft Project to accrue the cost of a resource as soon as the task starts.

10   In the Accrue At field, click Start.

Your screen should look similar to the following illustration.

	Type	Material Label	Initials	Group	Max. Units	Std. Rate	Ovt. Rate	Cost/Use	Accrue At	Base Calen
1	Work		GV		100%	$800.00/wk	$0.00/hr	$0.00	Prorated	Standard
2	Work		EL		200%	$22.00/hr	$33.00/hr	$0.00	Prorated	Standard
3	Work		JH		100%	$18.75/hr	$0.00/hr	$0.00	Prorated	Standard
4	Work		SC		100%	$775.00/wk	$0.00/hr	$0.00	Prorated	Standard
5	Work		JB		100%	$18.75/hr	$0.00/hr	$0.00	Prorated	Standard
6	Work		PM		100%	$9.40/hr	$0.00/hr	$0.00	Prorated	Standard
7	Work		PK		100%	$16.75/hr	$0.00/hr	$0.00	Prorated	Standard
8	Work		JR		100%	$22.00/hr	$0.00/hr	$0.00	Prorated	Standard
9	Work		JM		50%	$10.00/hr	$0.00/hr	$0.00	Prorated	Standard
10	Work		JG		75%	$15.50/hr	$0.00/hr	$0.00	Prorated	Standard
11	Work		16mm		300%	$250.00/wk	$0.00/hr	$0.00	Start	Standard
12	Work		5000ML		400%	$100.00/wk	$0.00/hr	$0.00	Prorated	Standard
13	Work		Dolly		200%	$0.00/hr	$0.00/hr	$0.00	Prorated	Standard
14	Work		Crane		100%	$0.00/hr	$0.00/hr	$0.00	Prorated	Standard
15	Work		EL		100%	$200.00/day	$0.00/hr	$25.00	Prorated	Standard
16	Material	Feet	Film			$0.20		$0.00	Prorated	

Documenting Resource Details in Resource Notes

You might recall from Lesson 1 that you can record any additional information that you want about a task, resource, or assignment in a note. For example, if a resource is not available to work on a specific date range, it is a good idea to record why in a note. That way, the note resides in the Microsoft Project file and can be easily viewed or printed.

In this exercise, you enter resource notes to document why a resource is not available to work on certain dates.

1 In the Resource Name column, select the name of Resource 1, "Garrett R. Vargas."

2 On the Standard toolbar, click the Resource Notes button.

Microsoft Project displays the Resource Information dialog box with the Notes tab visible.

3 In the Notes box, type **Garrett attending West Coast film festival May 21 and 22; unavailable to work on project** and click OK.

A note icon appears in the Indicators column.

4 Point to the note icon.

The note appears in a ToolTip. For notes that are too long to appear in a ToolTip, you can double-click the note icon to display the full text of the note.

Lesson Wrap-Up

In this lesson, you learned how to set up work and material resources, as well as how to record other details, such as cost information.

If you are continuing on to other lessons:

● On the File menu, click Close to close the file. If you are prompted to save changes, click Yes, and then save without a baseline.

If you are not continuing on to other lessons:

1   On the File menu, click Close to close the file. If you are prompted to save changes, click No.

2   On the File menu, click Exit.

Microsoft Project closes.

Lesson Glossary

Max. Units The maximum capacity of a resource to accomplish tasks. A resource that is available to work full time has a maximum units value of 100% or 1.0.

Night Shift A base calendar included with Microsoft Project designed to accommodate an 11:00 P.M. to 8:00 A.M. "graveyard" work shift.

overallocated The condition of a resource when it is assigned to do more work than can be done within the normal work capacity of the resource. In Microsoft Project, the work capacity of a resource is measured in units. One full-time resource has 100% units (recorded in the Max. Units field).

resource calendar The working and nonworking times of an individual work resource.

resources People, equipment, and material (and the associated costs of each) needed to complete the work on a project.

sponsor An individual or organization that provides financial support and champions the project team within the larger organization.

Standard base calendar A base calendar included with Microsoft Project designed to accommodate an 8:00 A.M. to 5:00 P.M. work shift.

work resources The people and equipment that do the work of the project.

Quick Quiz

1   A single resource is available to work on a project full-time. What should the Max. Units value of the resource be in Microsoft Project?

2   Why bother entering equipment resource information into a project plan?

3   What information does a resource calendar contain?

4   What is one difference between work and material resources?

5   True or false: the pay rates for all resources in a project must have the same pay period, for example hourly or weekly.

6   You would like to record some basic information such as contact information and resume details about your resources. What is one way to do this so that the information is saved with the project plan?

Putting It All Together

If necessary, start Microsoft Project. Open the file Putting It All Together 2 in the Lesson 2 folder located in the MS Project Core Practice folder on your hard disk, and save it without a baseline as Music Video 2 in the same folder.

Exercise 1: Set up the following resources for the Music Video project:

- Camera Operator
- Choreographer
- Director
- Editor
- Producer
- Production Staff
- Sound Engineer
- Talent

Exercise 2: Enter the following Max. Units values for these resources:

- Camera Operator, 300%
- Choreographer, 100%
- Director, 100%
- Editor, 100%
- Producer, 100%
- Production Staff, 400%
- Sound Engineer, 300%
- Talent, 800%

LESSON 3

Assigning Resources to Tasks

After completing this lesson, you will be able to:

✔ *Assign a resource to a task.*

✔ *Display duration, unit, and work values simultaneously.*

✔ *Assign multiple resources to a task.*

✔ *Turn off effort-driven scheduling for a task, and assign resources.*

✔ *Assign a material resource to a task.*

In Lesson 1 you created tasks, and in Lesson 2 you created resources. Now you are ready to assign resources to tasks. An **assignment** is the matching of a resource to a task to do **work**. From the perspective of tasks, you might call the process of assigning a resource a task assignment; from the perspective of resources, you might call it a resource assignment. It is the same thing either way: a task plus a resource equals an assignment.

You do not have to assign resources to tasks in Microsoft Project; you could just work with tasks. But there are several good reasons to assign resources in your project plan. If you assign resources to tasks, you can answer questions such as:

■ Who should be working on what tasks and when?

■ Do you have the right number of resources to do the scope of work your project requires?

■ Are you expecting a resource to work on a task at a time when that resource will not be available to work (for example, when the resource will be on vacation)?

■ Have you assigned a resource to so many tasks that you have exceeded the capacity of the resource to work—in other words, have you overallocated the resource?

■ Are you evaluating the performance of the resource against a pre-established plan? A resource who appears to be very busy but takes twice as long as another resource to complete a task might not be as productive as he or she appears.

In this lesson, you use a variety of methods to assign resources to tasks. You assign work resources (people and equipment) and material resources to tasks, and you see where resource assignments should affect task duration and where they should not.

Practice files for the lesson

To complete the procedures in this lesson, you will need to use a file named Wingtip Toys Commercial 3. Open the Lesson 3 folder in the MS Project Core Practice folder located on your hard disk. Open the file 3A, and save it without a baseline as Wingtip Toys Commercial 3 in the Lesson 3 folder.

Proj2000-1-18

Assigning Resources to Tasks

Assigning a resource to a task allows you to track the progress of the resource in working on the task. Microsoft Project also calculates resource and task costs for you, if you enter cost information.

You might recall from Lesson 2 that the capacity of a resource to work is measured in **units** and recorded in the Max. Units field. Overallocating a resource is easy: Just assign a resource to one task with more units than the resource has available. Or assign the resource to multiple tasks with schedules that overlap and with combined units that exceed those of the resource.

Unless you specify otherwise, Microsoft Project assigns 100% of the units for the resource to the task. If the resource has less than 100% maximum units, Microsoft Project assigns the resource's maximum units value.

In this exercise, you assign resources to tasks one at a time.

> **The View Bar appears on the left side of the Microsoft Project window.**

Gantt Chart

1   On the View Bar, click Gantt Chart.

2   On the Standard toolbar, click Assign Resources.

The Assign Resources dialog box appears. In it, you see the resource names you entered in Lesson 2. If the Assign Resources dialog box obscures the Task Name column, drag the dialog box out of the way, to the lower right corner of the screen.

3   In the Task Name column, click Task 9, "Reserve camera equipment."

4   In the Name column in the Assign Resources dialog box, select Ken Bergman, and then click Assign.

A check mark appears next to Ken Bergman's name, indicating that you have assigned him to the task of reserving camera equipment. In the Units column, you can see that he is assigned at 100%.

Next you assign other resources to tasks.

> **You can also assign one or more resources to a task by using the mouse. First, select one resource in the Assign Resources dialog box. To select multiple resources, hold down Ctrl and click the additional resource names. Point to the column to the left of the resource name. When the mouse pointer changes to a resource icon, drag the resource icon to the task name in the Task Name column.**

5   In the Entry table, click the name of Task 8, "Apply for filming permits."

6   In the Assign Resources dialog box, select Patti Mintz, and click Assign.

A check mark appears next to Patti Mintz's name, indicating that you have assigned her to the task you selected.

7   In the Gantt Chart view, click the name of Task 10, "Reserve sound equipment."

8   In the Assign Resources dialog box, select Peter Kelly, and then click Assign.

The names of assigned resources appear next to the Gantt bars.

![Microsoft Project screenshot showing the Gantt Chart view with the Assign Resources dialog box open]

The resources assigned to the selected task...

...have a check mark next to their names in the Assign Resources dialog box.

9 Click Close to close the Assign Resources dialog box.

Proj2000-4-2

The Scheduling Formula: Working with Duration, Units, and Work

After you create a task but before you assign a resource to it, the task has **duration** but no work associated with it. Why no work? Work represents the amount of time a resource or resources will spend to complete a task. If you have one person working full-time, the amount of time measured as work is the same as the amount of time measured as duration. The amount of work differs from the duration only if you assign more than one resource to a task or the one resource you assign is not working full-time.

Microsoft Project calculates work using what is sometimes called the **scheduling formula**:

Duration × Units = Work

Let's look at an example. The duration of Task 9 is one week. For our toy commercial project, a week equals 40 hours. When you assigned Ken Bergman to Task 9, Microsoft Project applied 100% of Ken's working time to this task. The scheduling formula for Task 8 looks like this:

40 hours task duration × 100% resource units = 40 hours work

In other words, with Ken assigned to Task 9 at 100% units, the task should require 40 hours of work. You can verify this in Microsoft Project by displaying the Task Form in the Task Entry view.

> You can see how many hours constitute a week by opening the Tools menu, choosing the Options command, and clicking the Calendar tab.

In this exercise, you display the project in the Task Entry view.

1 In the Gantt Chart, click the name of Task 9, "Reserve camera equipment."

2 On the View menu, click More Views.

3 In the More Views dialog box, click Task Entry, and then click Apply.

The Task Form appears in the lower pane of the Microsoft Project window.

You can drag the split bar to see more or less of the Gantt Chart and Task Form.

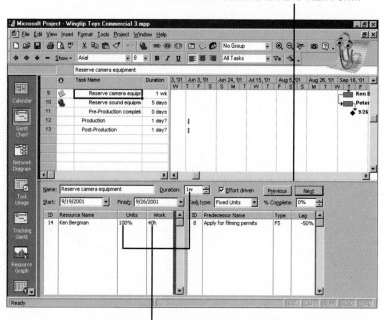

In the Task Form, you see all three variables of the scheduling formula: units, work, and duration.

To quickly display the Task Form below the Gantt Chart, you can also click Split on the Window menu.

The Task Entry view displays the Gantt Chart view in the upper pane of the Microsoft Project window and the Task Form view in the lower pane. The Task Form shows all three variables of the scheduling formula at once: the duration of the task in the Duration field, the units for the resource in the Units column, and the resulting work value for the task assignment in the Work column. We will refer to these values frequently in this lesson so that you will understand how Microsoft Project generates values.

Assigning Multiple Resources to Tasks

Proj2000-1-11

Now you will assign two resources to a single task to see the effect on the overall duration of a task. By default, Microsoft Project uses a scheduling method called **effort-driven scheduling**. This means that the task's work remains constant regardless of the number of resources you assign. Microsoft Project applies effort-driven scheduling only when you assign resources to or remove resources from tasks.

As you saw previously, you define the amount of work a task represents when you initially assign a resource or resources to it. If you later add resources to that task, the amount of work does not change, but the task's duration decreases. Conversely, you might initially assign more than one resource to a task and later remove one of those resources from the task. If you do this with effort-driven scheduling on, the amount of work for the task stays constant. The duration, or time it takes the remaining resource to complete that task, increases.

The following example illustrates the effect of effort-driven scheduling on a task as you assign resources to it. We have inserted the Work column in the Entry table, and we will focus on the Duration and Work columns in that table, as well as the Units and Work columns for the individual resource in the Task Form.

Let's start with a task that has a 24-hour (3-day) duration, to which we have not yet assigned any resources. We want the task's duration to decrease as we add resources to it (after the initial assignment), so we leave effort-driven scheduling on for the task.

Initially this task has a
duration of 24 hours...

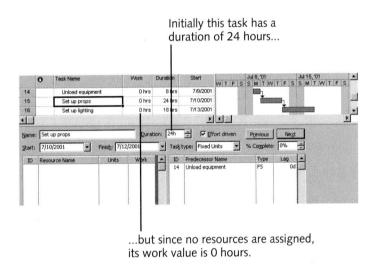

...but since no resources are assigned,
its work value is 0 hours.

Next we will make the initial assignment: one resource at 100% units. You might recall from above that a task has a work value only after you initially assign a resource to the task. After we make the initial resource assignment, the task's duration and work value are both 24 hours.

After one resource is
assigned at 100% units...

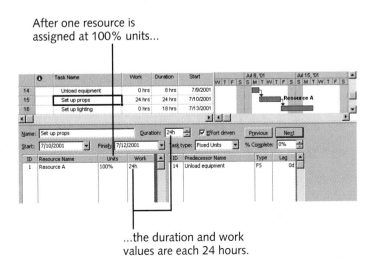

...the duration and work
values are each 24 hours.

tip

If you initially assign two resources to a task with a duration of 24 hours, Microsoft Project schedules each resource to work 24 hours, for a total of 48 hours of work on the task. However, you might initially assign one resource to a task with a duration of 24 hours and later add a second resource. In this case, effort-driven scheduling will cause Microsoft Project to schedule each resource to work 12 hours in parallel, for a total of 24 hours of work on the task. Remember that effort-driven scheduling adjusts task duration only if you add or delete resources from a task.

Next we make the second resource assignment. We will also assign that resource at 100% units. Because effort-driven scheduling is turned on, the task's work remains at 24 hours, but that work is distributed between the two resources. The task's duration, therefore, is reduced from 24 hours to 12.

After a second resource is assigned, total work remains at
24 hours but the duration of the task has decreased to 12 hours.

Effort-driven scheduling is on for this task,
so the work value of the task remains constant.

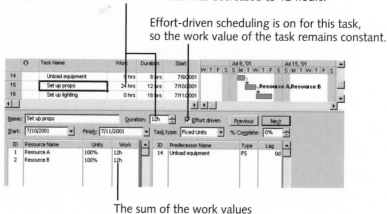

The sum of the work values
of the two resources is equal
to the work value of the task.

The resource unit values determine how Microsoft Project distributes the work between resources. In this example, we have assigned both resources at 100% units, so they share the work equally. If we had assigned either resource at anything other than 100%, the work would be distributed between them proportionally. For example, let's say that we initially assigned Resource A to a 24-hour task at 100% units. If we later added Resource B at 50%, we would expect Resource A to spend 16 hours on that task and Resource B to spend only 8 hours.

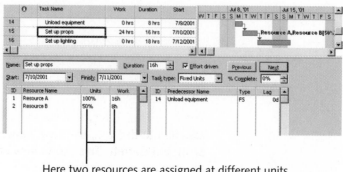

Here two resources are assigned at different units,
so their individual work values differ as well.

You do not need to display the Work column or the Task Form for effort-driven scheduling to take effect; we displayed them here to help illustrate the scheduling calculations. By default, effort-driven scheduling is turned on in Microsoft Project, but you can turn it off for individual tasks or for all new tasks entered in a project.

In this exercise, you assign multiple resources to individual tasks and see how this affects task durations.

1 In the Gantt Chart view, click the name of Task 2, "Review script."

2 In the Resource Name column in the Task Form, click directly below the Resource Name column heading. Then click the small down arrow that appears there.

3 In the Resource Name list, click Scott Cooper, and click OK in the upper-right corner of the Task Form.

Scott Cooper is assigned to Task 2. A quick check of the scheduling formula looks like this:

40 hours (same as 1 week) task duration × 100% resource units
= 40 hours work

Next you will assign a second resource to the task in the Task Form.

4 In the Resource Name column in the Task Form, click directly below Scott Cooper's name, and then click the small down arrow that appears there.

5 Click Garrett R. Vargas, and then click OK.

Garrett R. Vargas is also assigned to Task 2. Your screen should look similar to the following illustration.

The duration of this task decreases as
additional resources are assigned to it.

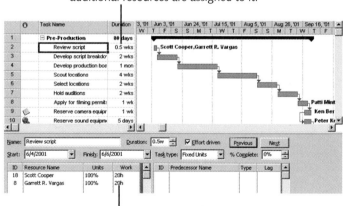

The 40 hours total task work is divided
between the two assigned resources.

As you can see in the Duration field and in the Gantt Chart view, Microsoft Project reduced the duration of Task 2 from one week to one-half week.

The total work required is still 40 hours, as it was when only Scott was assigned to the task, but now the work is distributed evenly between Scott and Garrett. This shows how effort-driven scheduling works. If, after an initial assignment, you add resources to a task, the total work remains constant but is distributed among the assigned resources. Further, the task's duration decreases accordingly. In the Task Form, the check mark in the Effort Driven check box tells you that effort-driven scheduling is turned on for Task 2.

The scheduling formula now looks like this:

20 hours (same as a one-half week) task duration × 200% resource units = 40 hours work

The 200% resource units is the sum of Scott's 100% plus Garrett's 100%, and the 40 work hours is the sum of Scott's 20 hours plus Garrett's 20 hours.

The other important effect of reducing the duration of Task 2 is that the start dates of all successor tasks changed as well. In Lesson 1, you created finish-to-start task relationships for these tasks. In this example, you see the benefit of creating task relationships rather than entering fixed start and finish dates. Microsoft Project adjusts the start dates of successor tasks that do not have a **constraint,** such as a fixed start date or finish date.

Next you assign multiple resources to Task 3.

6 In the Gantt Chart view, click the name of Task 3, "Develop script breakdown and schedule."

7 Click the first row in the Resource Name column in the Task Form. Select Scott Cooper from the list, and click OK.

8 Click directly below Scott Cooper's name.

9 Click Lane Sacksteder, and then click OK.

Microsoft Project reduces the duration of Task 3 from 2 weeks to just over 1 week, and it adjusts the start dates of all successor tasks.

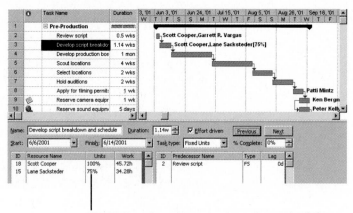

The Units values determine how the work of the task is divided among the assigned resources.

Because the values of the scheduling formula are not whole numbers in this case, let's look at how Microsoft Project came up with these values.

- The task duration of 45.7 hours (same as 1.14 weeks) is the result of dividing 80 hours of work by 175% units.

- Scott's work value of 45.7 hours is the result of multiplying 45.7 hours of task duration by 100% units.

- Lane's work value of 34.28 hours is the result of multiplying 45.7 hours task duration by 75% units.

Is Scott really going to work on this task exactly 45.7 hours, and Lane 34.28 hours? Probably not. Microsoft Project can produce numbers such as these that, while mathematically precise, might be too precise to be practical. That is okay; the important thing is that you understand how the numbers were generated.

To finish this exercise, assign multiple resources to a task with the Assign Resources dialog box.

10 In the Gantt Chart view, click the name of Task 5, "Scout locations."

 11 On the Standard toolbar, click Assign Resources.

The Assign Resources dialog box appears.

12 In the Name column of the Assign Resources dialog box, select Jo Brown, and click Assign.

A check mark appears next to Jo Brown's name, indicating that you have initially assigned her to the task you selected.

13 In the Name column, select Ken Bergman, and click Assign.

The duration of Task 5 is reduced, and the start dates of all successor tasks are adjusted accordingly.

14 Click Close to close the Assign Resources dialog box.

When Should Effort-Driven Scheduling Apply?

You should think through the extent to which effort-driven scheduling should apply to the tasks in your projects. For example, if one resource should take 10 hours to complete a task, could 10 resources complete the task in one hour? How about 20 resources in 30 minutes? Probably not; the resources would likely get in each other's way and require additional coordination to complete the task. If the task is very complicated, it might require significant training before a resource could contribute fully. Overall productivity might even decrease if you assign more resources to the task.

No single rule exists about when you should apply effort-driven scheduling and when you should not. As the project manager, you should analyze the nature of the work required by each task in your project and use your best judgment.

Proj2000-1-10

Assigning Resources with Effort-Driven Scheduling Off

Effort-driven scheduling might not apply to all tasks in a project, and you can turn it off when necessary. For example, let's say you have a task of monitoring wine as it ferments. Regardless of how many resources you assign to that task, it will still take the same amount of time. If you add more resources to a task with effort-driven scheduling turned off, the task's duration will remain constant and the total work for the task will increase. Why is this? Let's look again at the scheduling formula:

Duration × Units = Work

If the task's duration is not affected by the number of resources assigned, adding more resource units to a task must increase the total work. For example, the duration of the task for building a brick wall should decrease if a second bricklayer is assigned to help the initial bricklayer (with effort-driven scheduling on). However, the task's duration should not decrease if a foreman is also assigned to the task (effort-driven scheduling off). The foreman is working, but his or her work does not directly assist the two bricklayers.

In this exercise, you turn off effort-driven scheduling for a task and assign multiple resources to the task.

1   In the Gantt Chart view, click the name of Task 4, "Develop production boards."

2   In the Task Form, clear the Effort Driven check box.

3   Click the first row in the Resource Name column in the Task Form. Select Scott Cooper from the list, and then click OK.

4   Directly below Scott Cooper's name, click Lane Sacksteder, and then click OK.

5   Directly below Lane Sacksteder's name, click Patti Mintz, and then click OK.

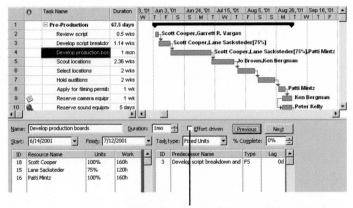

Effort-driven scheduling is off for this task, so the task's duration is not affected and work increases as resources are assigned.

As you can see, the task's duration remains the same regardless of how many resources you assign to it. Microsoft Project allocates each resource its own work amount, which increases the total amount of work on the task. The scheduling formula now looks like this:

160 hours (same as 20 days, or one month) task duration × 275% resource units = 440 hours work

- The 275% resource units is the sum of Scott's 100% plus Lane's 75% plus Patti's 100%.

- The 440 work hours is the sum of Scott's 160 hours plus Lane's 120 hours plus Patti's 160 hours.

To finish this exercise, turn off effort-driven scheduling and assign multiple resources to a task in the Task Information dialog box.

6 In the Gantt Chart view, click the name of Task 6, "Select locations."

7 On the Standard toolbar, click the Task Information button.

The Task Information dialog box appears.

8 Click the Advanced tab.

9 Clear the Effort Driven check box, and then click the Resources tab.

10 Click directly below the Resource Name column heading.

11 In the Resource Name list, click Jo Brown.

12 In the Resource Name column, click directly below Jo Brown's name, and then click Scott Cooper.

13 In the Resource Name column, click directly below Scott Cooper's name, click Garrett R. Vargas, and then press Enter.

14 Click OK to close the Task Information dialog box.

In the Gantt Chart and Task Form views, you can see that you have assigned these three resources to Task 6, for which effort-driven scheduling has been turned off. Turning off effort-driven scheduling and assigning resources in the Task Information dialog box is another example of how you can accomplish the same task in different ways in Microsoft Project, depending on your preference.

Assigning Material Resources to Tasks

In Lesson 2, you created the material resource named "16-mm film." In our film project, we are interested in tracking the use of film and its cost. When assigning a material resource, you can handle cost in one of two ways:

- Assign a fixed unit quantity of the resource to the task. Microsoft Project will multiply the unit cost of this resource by the number of units you consume to determine the total cost.

- Assign a variable rate quantity of the resource to the task. Microsoft Project will adjust the quantity and cost of the resource as the task's duration changes.

In this exercise, you assign the material resource "16-mm film" to a task and enter a fixed unit quantity of consumption.

1   On the Standard toolbar, click Assign Resources.

The Assign Resources dialog box appears. You plan to shoot 60 minutes of film while scouting locations. Because 16-mm film is shot at a rate of 36 feet per minute, 60 minutes equals 2160 feet of film.

2   In the Gantt Chart, click the name of Task 5, "Scout locations."

3   In the Assign Resources dialog box, select the Units field for the 16-mm film resource.

4   Type 2160, and then click Assign.

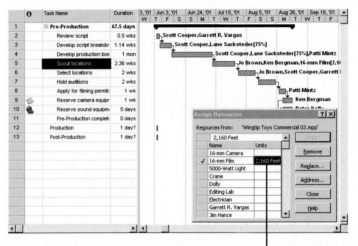

When entering units for a material resource assignment, rather than a percentage you enter a rate of consumption or (in this case) a fixed quantity.

Because 16-mm film is a material resource, it cannot do work. Therefore, assigning that resource does not affect the duration of the task.

Lesson Wrap-Up

In this lesson, you learned how to assign resources to tasks and work with duration, unit, and work values.

If you are continuing on to other lessons:

●   On the File menu, click Close to close the file. If you are prompted to save changes, click Yes, and then save without a baseline.

If you are not continuing on to other lessons:

1   On the File menu, click Close to close the file. If you are prompted to save changes, click No.

2   On the File menu, click Exit.

Microsoft Project closes.

Lesson Glossary

assignment The matching of a work resource (people or equipment) to a task to do work. You can also assign a material resource to a task, but those resources have no effect on work or duration.

constraint A restriction, such as Must Start On or Finish No Later Than, that you can place on the start or finish date of a task.

duration The length of working time you expect it will take to complete a task.

effort-driven scheduling A scheduling method in which the task's work remains constant regardless of the number of resources assigned to it. As resources are added to a task, the duration decreases, but the work remains the same and is distributed among the assigned resources. Effort-driven scheduling is on by default in Microsoft Project, but it can be turned off for any task.

scheduling formula A representation of how Microsoft Project calculates work, based on the task's duration and resource units. The scheduling formula is Duration × Units = Work.

units A standard way of measuring the capacity of a resource to work when you assign the resource to a task in Microsoft Project. Units is one variable in the scheduling formula: Duration × Units = Work.

work The total amount of effort required to accomplish a task. Work is measured in person-hours and might not match the task's duration. Work is one variable in the scheduling formula: Duration × Units = Work.

Quick Quiz

1 If the Max. Units value of a resource is 50%, is that resource available to work on a task full-time or half-time?

2 What is the scheduling formula?

3 With effort-driven scheduling enabled for a task, what is the effect of assigning additional resources on the task's duration?

4 When should you not apply effort-driven scheduling to a task?

5 Why does assigning a material resource not affect the task's duration, even when effort-driven scheduling is enabled for that task?

Putting It All Together

If necessary, start Microsoft Project. Open the file Putting It All Together 3 in the Lesson 3 folder located in the MS Project Core Practice folder on your hard disk, and save it without a baseline as Music Video 3 in the same folder.

Exercise: Assign resources to tasks as shown:

Task ID, Name	Resource Name (Units)
2, Develop script breakdown	Choreographer (100%), Director (100%), Editor (100%), Producer (100%)
3, Develop choreography	Camera Operator (100%), Choreographer (100%), Talent (800%)
5, Rehearsal	Camera Operator (100%), Choreographer (100%), Director (100%), Production Staff (200%), Sound Engineer (100%), Talent (800%)
6, Shoot	Camera Operator (300%), Choreographer (100%), Director (100%), Producer (100%), Production Staff (400%), Sound Engineer (100%), Talent (800%)
8, Fine cut edit	Director (100%), Editor (100%), Producer (100%)
9, Add final music	Director (100%), Editor (100%), Sound Engineer (100%)
10, Clone dubbing master	Sound Engineer (100%)
11, Hand off final video	Producer (100%)

LESSON 4

Fine-Tuning Your Project Plan

After completing this lesson, you will be able to:

✔ *Create a task calendar and apply it to tasks.*

✔ *Change a task type and see the effects this has on how Microsoft Project schedules tasks.*

✔ *Split a task to record an interruption in work.*

✔ *Set up a recurring task in the project schedule.*

✔ *Apply a constraint to a task.*

✔ *Identify the tasks on the critical path.*

✔ *Look at how resources are scheduled to work over the duration of the project.*

In the previous lessons you set up tasks, resources, and assignments—the three elements of a project plan. Now you will fine-tune some details of these elements.

Practice files for the lesson

To complete the procedures in this lesson, you will need to use a file named Wingtip Toys Commercial 4. Open the Lesson 4 folder in the MS Project Core Practice folder located on your hard disk. Open the file 4A, and save it without a baseline as Wingtip Toys Commercial 4 in the Lesson 4 folder.

Proj2000-1-7
Proj2000-1-12

Adjusting Working Time for Tasks

Sometimes you want specific tasks to occur at times that are outside of the **project calendar's** working time. To accomplish this, you apply a **task calendar** to these tasks. As with the project calendar, you specify which **base calendar** to use as a task calendar. You need a task calendar only when you want a task to have different working and nonworking times from the project calendar. Here are some examples of when you might need a task calendar:

■ You are using the **Standard base calendar** as your project calendar, and you have a task that must run overnight.

■ You have a task that must occur over the weekend.

Unlike resources and resource calendars, Microsoft Project does not create task calendars as you create tasks. When you need a custom task calendar, you assign one of the base calendars provided with Microsoft Project (or more likely a new base calendar you have created) to the task.

For example, if you assign the 24 Hours base calendar to a task, Microsoft Project will schedule that task according to a 24-hour workday rather than the working time specified in the project calendar.

tip

When you assign a base calendar to a task, you can choose to ignore resource calendars for all resources assigned to the task. Doing so causes Microsoft Project to schedule the resources to work on the task according to the task calendar and not their own resource calendars (for example, to work 24 hours per day). If this would result in resources working in what would otherwise be their nonworking time, you might want to first discuss this with the affected resources.

In the toy commercial project, one of the scenes must be filmed at night. However, the project calendar does not include working time late enough to cover the filming of this scene. Because this task is really an exception to the normal working time of the project, you do not want to change the project calendar. In this exercise, you create a new base calendar, and you apply it to the appropriate task.

1   On the Tools menu, click Change Working Time.

2   In the Change Working Time dialog box, click the New button.

The Create New Base Calendar dialog box appears.

3   In the Name box, type **Evening Shoot**

4   In the Make A Copy Of box, make sure Standard is selected, and then click OK.

5   In the calendar below the Select Date(s) label, select the column headings for Monday through Friday.

6   In the upper row of the From and To boxes, enter **5:00 PM** and **11:00 PM**, and then delete the values in the second row. Your Change Working Time dialog box should look like this:

This custom base calendar contains unique working times not available in the built-in base calendars.

7   Click OK to close the dialog box.

Next you will apply the Evening Shoot calendar to a task.

8   Select the name of Task 21, "Scene 2 shoot." This scene must be filmed in the evening.

9   On the Standard toolbar, click the Task Information button.

The Task Information dialog box appears.

10   Click the Advanced tab.

11   In the Calendar box, select Evening Shoot from the list.

12   Click the Scheduling Ignores Resource Calendars box, and then click OK to close the dialog box.

Microsoft Project applies the Evening Shoot calendar to Task 21. A calendar icon appears in the Indicators column, reminding you that this task has a task calendar applied to it. Because you chose to ignore resource calendars in the previous step, the resources assigned to these tasks will be scheduled at times that would otherwise be non-working times for them.

Proj2000-1-13
Proj2000-2-7

Understanding task types is essential for controlling how Microsoft Project schedules work and getting the results you want.

Changing Task Types

You might recall from Lesson 3 that Microsoft Project uses the following formula, called the **scheduling formula**, to calculate a task's work value:

Work = Duration × Units

Each value in the scheduling formula corresponds to a **task type**. A task type determines which of the three scheduling formula values remains fixed if the other two values change.

The default task type is **fixed units**: when you change a task's duration, Microsoft Project recalculates work. Likewise, if you change a task's work, Microsoft Project recalculates the duration. In either case, the units value is unchanged. The two other task types are fixed duration and fixed work.

For a **fixed duration** task, you can change the task's units or work value, and Microsoft Project will recalculate the other value. For a **fixed work** task, you can change the units or duration value, and Microsoft Project will recalculate the other value. Note that you cannot turn off **effort-driven scheduling** for this task type.

Which is the right task type to apply to each of your tasks? It depends on how you want Microsoft Project to schedule that task. The following table summarizes the effects of changing any value for any task type. (You read it like a multiplication table.)

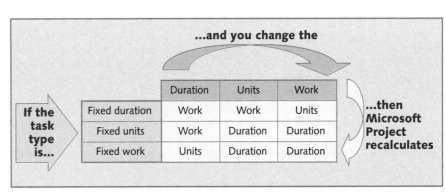

If the task type is...	...and you change the		
	Duration	Units	Work
Fixed duration	Work	Work	Units
Fixed units	Work	Duration	Duration
Fixed work	Units	Duration	Duration

...then Microsoft Project recalculates

To see the task type of the selected task, on the Standard toolbar, click the Task Information button, and then click the Advanced tab. You can also see the task type in the Task Form. (When in the Gantt Chart view, you can display the Task Form by opening the Window menu and clicking the Split command.) You can change a task type at any time. Note that characterizing a task type as "fixed" does not mean that its duration, units, or work values are unchangeable. You can change any value for any task type.

Task Types and Effort-Driven Scheduling

A lot of people misunderstand task types and effort-driven scheduling and conclude that these two issues are more closely related than they really are. Both settings affect work, duration, and units values. However, effort-driven scheduling affects your schedule only when assigning or removing resources from tasks, while changing a task type affects only the resources currently assigned to the task. For more information about effort-driven scheduling, see "Assigning Multiple Resources to a Task" in Lesson 3.

In this exercise, you change the task types of two tasks.

1 In the Gantt Chart view, select the name of Task 2, "Review script."

2 On the Window menu, click Split.

The Task Form appears in the lower pane of the window. In it, you can see that Task 2 is a Fixed Units task with a total work value of 40 hours (that is, 20 hours each for two resources), resource units of 100% each, and a one-half week duration. Next you will change the task's duration to see the effects on the other values.

3 In the Duration field in the Task Form, type or select **1w**, and then click OK in the upper-right corner of the Task Form.

As we would expect, the units value remains fixed at 100% for each resource and the total work value increases to 80 hours (40 hours each).

4 On the Edit menu, click Undo Entry.

Microsoft Project resets Task 2's duration to one-half week.

After a discussion among all the resources who will review the script, all agree that the task's duration should double but the work required to complete the task should remain the same. Next you change the task's type from fixed units to fixed work, and you increase the duration.

5 In the Task Type list on the Task Form, select Fixed Work, and click OK.

Microsoft Project changes the task type of Task 2 to fixed work. Next you will change the task's duration to see the effects on the other values.

6 In the Duration field in the Task Form, type or select **1w**, and click OK.

The units value of each resource decreases to 50%, and the total work remains fixed at 40 hours (20 hours each).

Changing the duration of a fixed work task causes
Microsoft Project to recalculate resource units.

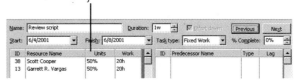

Increasing the duration of a fixed work task decreases the level of effort (measured as units) that resources will apply to the task. Put another way, the resources will put in the same overall effort (measured as work) over a longer time period.

Next you change a task type using the Task Information dialog box.

7 In the Gantt Chart view in the top pane of the window, select the name of Task 39, "Hold formal approval showing."

8 On the Standard toolbar, click the Task Information button.

The Task Information dialog box appears.

9 Click the Advanced tab.

The selected task describes the formal screening of the toy commercial for the customers of the project. The task is scheduled for a full day, although a few of the assigned resources will work for the equivalent of a half-day. To reflect this (and properly manage resource costs for the task), you will make this a fixed duration task and adjust the work values for some of the assigned resources.

10 In the Task Type box, select Fixed Duration.

11 Click the Resources tab.

12 In the Units column, set the Units values for Ken Bergman and David Campbell to 50% each.

> Rather than scrolling through the Gantt Chart view, click anywhere in the Entry table, press Ctrl+G (or click Go To on the Edit menu) to display the Go To dialog box, enter 39 in the ID box, and then click OK.

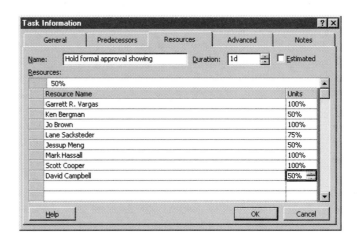

13 Click OK to close the Task Information dialog box.

You can see the updated work values of the two resources in the Task Form in the lower pane. In fact, you could have performed this entire exercise in either the Task Form or the Task Information dialog box, depending on your preference.

14 On the Window menu, click Remove Split.

tip

A summary task always has a fixed-duration task type, and you cannot change it. Because a summary task is based on the earliest start date and the latest finish date of its subtasks, its duration is calculated based on its subtasks and is not directly editable. If you wish to confirm this, double-click Summary Task 33, "Post-Production," and view the Advanced tab in the Task Information dialog box.

Proj2000-1-4

Interrupting Work on Tasks

When initially planning project tasks, you might know that work on a certain task will be interrupted. You can **split** the task to indicate times when the work will be interrupted and when it can resume. Here are some reasons why you might want to split a task:

■   There is an *anticipated* interruption in a task. For example, a resource might be assigned to a week-long task but need to attend an event on Wednesday that is unrelated to the task.

■   There is an *unanticipated* interruption in a task. Once a task is underway, a resource might have to stop work on the task because another task has taken priority. Once the second task is completed, the resource can resume work on the first task.

In this exercise, you split a task.

1   In the Gantt Chart view, select the name of Task 4, "Develop production boards."

You know that work on this task will be interrupted for two days starting June 26.

2   To see Task 4's Gantt bar, on the Standard toolbar, click the Go To Selected Task button.

The timescale is divided into major units (on top) and minor units (below). The granularity of the minor scale determines how you can split tasks. In this example, you can split tasks in one-day increments.

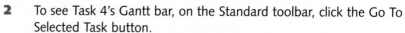

Adjusting the minor scale is important for splitting tasks: the precision of the minor scale determines the smallest time increment into which you can split a task. With the timescale set at the Days level, you must split a task by at least a day. If you wanted to split a task at the hourly level, you would have to adjust the minor timescale further (through the Timescale command on the Format menu).

3   On the Standard toolbar, click the Split Task button.

A ToolTip appears, and the mouse pointer changes.

4   Move the mouse pointer over the Gantt bar of Task 4.

Use the ToolTip to help you accurately split tasks.

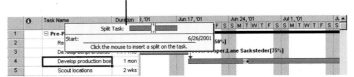

This ToolTip is essential for accurately splitting a task; it contains the date at which you would start the second segment of the task if you dragged the mouse pointer from its current location on the Gantt bar. As you move the mouse pointer along the Gantt bar, you see the start date in the ToolTip change.

5   Move the mouse pointer over the Gantt bar of Task 4 until the start date of Tuesday, 6/26/01, appears in the ToolTip.

6   Click and drag the mouse pointer to the right until the start date of Thursday, 6/28/01, appears in the ToolTip, and then release the mouse button.

Microsoft Project inserts a task split, represented in the Gantt Chart as a dotted line, between the two segments of the task.

The split appears as a dotted line connecting the segments of the task.

Here are a few more things to keep in mind when splitting tasks:

■   You can split a task into as many segments as you want.

■   You can drag a segment of a split task left or right to change the duration of the split.

■   The time of the task split itself, represented by the dotted line, is not counted in the duration of the task unless the task is fixed duration. No work occurs during the split.

■   If the duration of a split task changes, the last segment of the task is increased or decreased.

■   If a split task is rescheduled (for example, if its start date changes), the entire task, splits and all, is rescheduled. The task keeps the same pattern of segments and splits.

■   To rejoin two segments of a split task, drag one segment of the task until it touches another segment.

■   If you do not want to display splits as a dotted line, you can remove them. On the Format menu, click Layout, and then clear the Show Bar Splits check box.

Proj2000-1-3

Setting up a Recurring Task

Most projects require repetitive tasks, such as staff meetings, creating and publishing status reports, or quality inspections. Although it is easy to overlook the scheduling of such events, you should account for them in your project plan. After all, staff meetings and similar events that indirectly support the project require time from resources. And, that is time away from their other assignments.

To help account for such events in your project plan, create a **recurring task**. As the name suggests, a recurring task repeats at a specified frequency, such as daily, weekly, monthly, or yearly. When you create a recurring task, Microsoft Project creates a series of tasks with "start no earlier than" **constraints**, no task relationships, and effort-driven scheduling turned off.

In this exercise, you create a recurring task.

1   In the Gantt Chart view, select the name of Task 12, "Production."

You want the recurring tasks to be inserted into the project as the last items in the Pre-Production phase, directly above Task 12.

2   On the Insert menu, click Recurring Task.

The Recurring Task Information dialog box appears.

3   In the Task Name box, type **Staff planning meeting**

4   In the Duration box, type **2h**

5   Under Recurrence Pattern, make sure Weekly is selected, and then select the Friday check box.

Next you specify the date of its first occurrence; by default, it is the project start date.

6   In the Start box, type **6/8/2001 3:00 PM**

Next you specify the number of recurrences. You do this by entering either an exact number of recurrences or a date by which the task should end.

7   Select End After, and then type or select **12** occurrences.

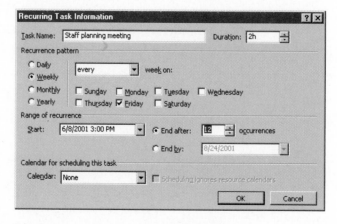

8   Click OK to create the recurring task.

Microsoft Project inserts the recurring tasks, nested within the Pre-Production phase. Initially the summary task is collapsed. A recurring task icon appears in the Indicators column.

Unlike other summary tasks, the summary recurring task shows only the individual occurrences of the task.

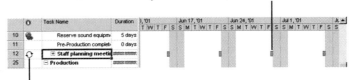

This icon indicates a recurring task.

Note that the summary Gantt bar for the recurring task does not look like the other summary Gantt bars in the Gantt Chart. A summary Gantt bar for a recurring task shows only the occurrences or "roll-ups" of the individual occurrences of the task.

Next you assign resources to the recurring task.

9 On the Standard toolbar, click Assign Resources.

10 In the Assign Resources dialog box, select Garrett R. Vargas. Then hold down the Ctrl key while selecting Jo Brown, Lani Ota, Patti Mintz, and Scott Cooper.

11 Click Assign, and then click Close.

The Assign Resources dialog box closes, and Microsoft Project assigns the selected resources to the recurring task. Next you will view the individual occurrences of the recurring task.

12 Click the plus sign next to the summary recurring task's title "Staff planning meeting." Your screen should look similar to the following illustration:

Recurring tasks are numbered sequentially. You can also see resource assignments for the individual tasks.

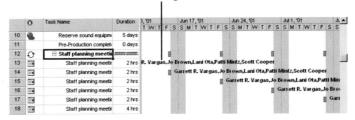

As you can see, each occurrence of the summary task is sequentially numbered, and the resource assignments appear for the subtasks.

13 Click the minus sign next to the summary recurring task's title, "Staff planning meeting," to hide the subtasks.

Here are a few more things to keep in mind when creating recurring tasks:

■ When you schedule a recurring task to end on a specific date, Microsoft Project suggests the current project end date. If you use this date, be sure to manually change it if the project end date changes later.

- Microsoft Project alerts you if you create a recurring task that would occur during nonworking time (a holiday, for example). You then have the options of not creating that occurrence or scheduling it for the next working day.

- You should always assign resources to recurring tasks with the Assign Resources dialog box. Entering resource names in the Resource Name field of the summary recurring task assigns the resources to the summary task, not to the individual occurrences.

Setting Task Constraints

Proj2000-1-15

Every task you enter into Microsoft Project has some type of constraint applied to it. A constraint controls the start or finish date of a task and the degree to which that task can be rescheduled. There are three categories of constraints:

- **Flexible constraints.** Microsoft Project can change the start and finish dates of a task, but it cannot change its duration. For example, the task "Selecting locations to film" can start as soon as possible. No constraint date is associated with flexible constraints.

- **Semi-flexible constraints.** A task has a start or finish date boundary. However, within that boundary, Microsoft Project has the scheduling flexibility to change start and finish dates (but not the duration) of a task. For example, a task such as "Install props" must finish no later than 3/26/01. However, the task could finish before this date. Semi-flexible constraints are sometimes called soft constraints.

- **Inflexible constraints.** A task must begin or end on a certain date. For example, a task such as "Set up lighting" must end on 4/10/01. Inflexible constraints are sometimes called hard constraints.

In all, there are eight types of task constraints.

This Constraint Type	Means
As Soon As Possible (ASAP)	Microsoft Project will schedule a task to occur as soon as it can occur. This is the default constraint type applied to all new tasks when scheduling from the project start date. This is a flexible constraint.
As Late As Possible (ALAP)	Microsoft Project will schedule a task to occur as late as it can occur without delaying successor tasks or changing the project finish date. This is the default constraint type applied to all new tasks when scheduling from the project finish date. This is a flexible constraint.
Start No Earlier Than (SNET)	Microsoft Project will schedule a task to start on or after the constraint date you specify. Use this constraint type to ensure that a task will not start before a specific date. This is a semi-flexible constraint.

This Constraint Type	Means
Start No Later Than (SNLT)	Microsoft Project will schedule a task to start on or before the constraint date you specify. Use this constraint type to ensure that a task will not start after a specific date. This is a semi-flexible constraint.
Finish No Earlier Than (FNET)	Microsoft Project will schedule a task to finish on or after the constraint date you specify. Use this constraint type to ensure that a task will not finish before a specific date. This is a semi-flexible constraint.
Finish No Later Than (FNLT)	Microsoft Project will schedule a task to finish on or before the constraint date you specify. Use this constraint type to ensure that a task will not finish after a specific date. This is a semi-flexible constraint.
Must Start On (MSO)	Microsoft Project will schedule a task to start on the constraint date you specify. Use this constraint type to ensure that a task will start on an exact date. This is an inflexible constraint.
Must Finish On (MFO)	Microsoft Project will schedule a task to finish on the constraint date you specify. Use this constraint type to ensure that a task will finish on an exact date. This is an inflexible constraint.

These eight types of constraints have very different effects on the scheduling of tasks:

■ Flexible constraints, such as As Soon As Possible, allow tasks to be scheduled without any limitations other than their predecessor and successor relationships. No fixed start or end dates are imposed by these constraint types. Use these constraint types whenever possible.

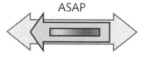

■ Semi-flexible constraints, such as Start No Earlier Than or Start No Later Than, limit the rescheduling of a task within the date boundary you specify.

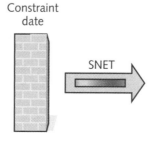

■ Inflexible constraints, such as Must Start On, completely prevent the rescheduling of a task. Use these constraint types only when absolutely necessary.

The type of constraint you apply to the tasks in your projects depends on what you need from Microsoft Project. You should use inflexible constraints only if the start or finish date of a task is fixed by factors beyond the control of the project team. Examples of such tasks include handoffs to clients and the end of a funding period. For tasks without such limitations, you should use flexible constraints. Flexible constraints give you the most discretion in adjusting start and finish dates, and they allow Microsoft Project to adjust dates if your project plan changes. For example, if you have used ASAP constraints and the duration of a predecessor task changes from 4 days to 2 days, Microsoft Project adjusts or "pulls in" the start and finish dates of all successor tasks. However, if a successor task had an inflexible constraint applied, Microsoft Project could not adjust its start or finish dates.

In this exercise, you apply a Start No Earlier Than constraint to a task.

1 In the Gantt Chart view, select Task 37, "Scene 3 setup."

This scene must be shot at a location that is not available to the film crew until September 27, 2001.

2 Drag the vertical divider bar to the right to show the Start column.

3 Select the Start field for Task 37, and then click the down arrow button to display the calendar box.

4 In the calendar box, click September 27.

If the Start column displays only pound signs (####), the column is too narrow to display its contents. To widen the column, move the mouse pointer to the divider between the Start and Finish columns at the top of the table.

When the mouse pointer changes to a two-headed arrow, double-click the divider. Microsoft Project widens the column to fit the content.

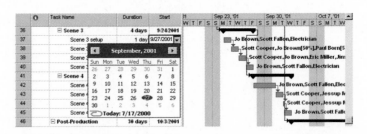

Microsoft Project applies an SNET constraint to the task, and a constraint icon appears in the Indicators column. You can point to the icon to see the constraint details in a ToolTip.

Point your mouse at a constraint indicator (or any icon in the Indicators column) to see more details.

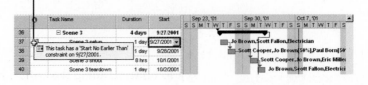

5 Drag the vertical divider bar back to the right edge of the Duration column.

All tasks that depend on Task 37 are also rescheduled.

Here are a few more things to keep in mind when applying constraints to tasks:

■ Selecting a date in the Finish column applies an FNET constraint.

■ You can create an SNET constraint by dragging a Gantt bar directly on the Gantt Chart.

■ To remove a constraint, open the Project menu, click Task Information, and then click the Advanced tab. In the Constraint Type box, select As Soon As Possible or (if scheduling from the project finish date) As Late As Possible.

■ If you need to apply semi-flexible or inflexible constraints to tasks in addition to task relationships, you might create what is called negative slack. For example, you can create a finish-to-start relationship before applying a Must Start On constraint that forces the successor task to start before the predecessor task has finished. This would result in negative slack and a scheduling conflict. By default, the constraint date applied to the successor task will override the relationship. However, if you prefer, you can set Microsoft Project to honor relationships over constraints. On the Tools menu, click Options, and then click the Schedule tab. Clear the Tasks Will Always Honor Their Constraint Dates check box. This setting applies only to the current project file.

■ If you must schedule a project from a finish date rather than a start date, some constraint behaviors change. For example, the ALAP (rather than the ASAP) constraint type becomes the default for new tasks. You should pay close attention to constraints when scheduling from a finish date to make sure they have the effects you intend.

Proj2000-4-1

Viewing the Project's Critical Path

A **critical path** is the series of tasks that will push out the project's end date if the tasks are delayed. The word "critical" has nothing to do with how important these tasks are to the overall project. The word refers only to how their scheduling will affect the project's finish date. However, the project finish date is of great importance in most projects. If you want to shorten the duration of a project to bring in the finish date, you must begin by shortening the critical path.

Over the life of a project, the project's critical path is likely to change from time to time as tasks are completed ahead of or behind schedule. Schedule changes, such as assigning resources to tasks, can also change the critical path. After a task on the critical path is completed, it is no longer critical, because it cannot affect the project finish date.

Microsoft Project constantly recalculates the critical path, even if you never see it.

A key to understanding the critical path is to understand **slack**, also known as float. There are two types of slack: free and total. **Free slack** is the amount of time a task can be delayed before it delays another task.

Total slack is the amount of time a task can be delayed before it delays the finish of the project. A task is on the critical path if its total slack is less than a certain amount—normally, if it is zero.

In contrast, **noncritical tasks** have slack, meaning they can start or finish earlier or later within their slack time without affecting the completion date of a project.

In this exercise, you view the project's critical path.

1   On the View menu, select More Views.

2   In the More Views dialog box, select Detail Gantt, and then click Apply.

The project appears in the Detail Gantt view.

3   On the Edit menu, select Go To.

4   In the ID box, type **31**, and then click OK.

Microsoft Project displays Task 31, the "Scene 2" summary task.

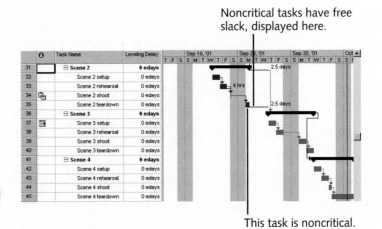

Noncritical tasks have free slack, displayed here.

This task is noncritical.

The tasks subsequent to Scene 3 are critical tasks. In the Detail Gantt view, Microsoft Project distinguishes between critical and noncritical tasks. Critical task bars are red, but noncritical task bars are blue. In this view, you can also see tasks with free slack.

Notice the Gantt bar of Task 35, "Scene 2 teardown." The blue bar represents the duration of the task. The thin teal line and the number next to it represent free slack for this task. As you can see, this particular task has quite a bit of free slack and is, therefore, a noncritical task. (Remember that the term "critical" in this sense has nothing to do with how important the task is compared to other tasks, only with how much or little total slack the task has.)

5   On the View menu, select Gantt Chart.

Working with the critical path is the most important way to manage a project's overall duration. In later lessons, you will make adjustments that might extend the project's duration. Checking the project's critical path and, when necessary, shortening the overall project duration is an important project management skill.

Proj2000-2-5
Proj2000-5-10

Examining Resource Allocations over Time

In this exercise, you will focus on resource allocation—how the task assignments you've made affect the workloads of the people and equipment resources of the project. How a resource's time is managed over time is called **allocation**, and specifically the resource is in one of three states:

- **Underallocated:** The resource's maximum capacity is not filled by the resource's assignments. For example, a full-time resource who has only 25 hours of work assigned in a 40-hour workweek is underallocated.

- **Fully allocated:** The resource's maximum capacity is just filled by assignments. For example, a full-time resource who has 40 hours of work assigned in a 40-hour workweek is fully allocated.

- **Overallocated:** The resource's maximum capacity is exceeded by assignments. For example, a full-time resource who has 65 hours of work assigned in a 40-hour workweek is overallocated.

You might recall from Lesson 3 that in Microsoft Project a resource's capacity to work is measured in units; the maximum capacity of a given resource is called maximum units. Units are measured either as numbers (for example, 3 units) or as a percentage (for example, 300% units).

It is tempting to say that fully allocating all resources all the time is every project manager's goal—but that would be an oversimplification. Depending on the nature of your project and the resources working on it, some underallocations might be perfectly fine. Overallocation might not always be a problem either, depending on the scope of the overallocation. If one resource is overallocated for just a half hour, Microsoft Project will alert you, but such a minor overallocation might not be a problem you need to solve, depending on the resource involved and the nature of the assignment. Severe overallocation—for example, a resource being assigned twice the work he or she could possibly accomplish in one day—is always a problem, however, and you should know how to identify it and have strategies for addressing it.

In this exercise, you look at resource allocations and focus on two resources who are overallocated.

1   On the View bar, click Resource Usage.

The Resource Usage view appears.

On the left side of the Resource Usage view is a table (the Usage table by default) that shows assignments grouped per resource, the total work assigned to each resource, and each assignment's work. This information is organized into an outline that you can expand or collapse.

The right side of the view contains assignment details (work, by default) arranged on a **timescale**. You can scroll the timescale horizontally to see different time periods. You can also change the **major scale** or **minor scale** to display data in units of weeks, days, hours, and so on.

Next, you will collapse the outline in the table to see total work per resource over time.

2   In the Usage table, click the Resource Name column heading.

3   On the Formatting toolbar, click Hide Subtasks.

Microsoft Project collapses the Resource Usage view to show just resource names in the Usage Table, and their total work values over time in the timescaled grid on the right.

Notice the name of the first resource, "Unassigned." Who is this resource named "Unassigned," you might be wondering? Actually, it is nobody. "Unassigned" refers to all tasks to which no specific resources are assigned.

Another unusual resource here is named "16-mm Film." This is a material resource, and its value in the Work column contains the number of feet of film to be consumed based on the tasks to which this material resource is assigned. The work values of all the other resources are measured in hours.

Next you will look at two people resources and their allocations.

4   In the Resource Name column, select the name of Resource 4, "Anne L. Paper."

5   On the Standard toolbar, click the Go To Selected Task button.

Microsoft Project scrolls the timescaled grid to show Anne L. Paper's earliest assignment: 3 hours on a Friday.

6   Point to the F column heading at the top of the timescaled grid.

In any timescaled view you can get details about dates by hovering your mouse pointer over the timescale.

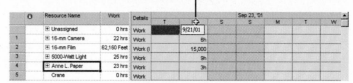

A ToolTip appears with the date of the assignment: 9/21/01. Such ToolTips are handy in any timescaled view such as the Resource Usage view and the Gantt Chart.

Currently the timescale is set to display weeks in the major scale and days in the minor scale. Now, change the timescale to see the work data summarized more broadly.

7   On the Format menu, click Timescale.

The Timescale dialog box appears.

8   In the Units box under Major Scale, select Years. In the Units box under Minor Scale, select Months. Be sure that 1 is the Count value for both scales.

9   Click OK to close the Timescale dialog box.

Microsoft Project changes the timescaled grid to show work values per month.

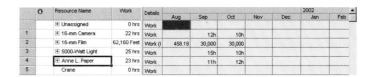

As you can see in the timescaled grid, Anne L. Paper is underallocated in each of the two months in which she has assignments in the project: July and August. Anne is one of the actors assigned to the scenes in which her character is needed, so this underallocation is really not a problem we need to address.

Notice the exclamation mark indicators next to the names of Garrett R. Vargas, Jo Brown, and other resources. Also note that their names are formatted in red. The indicators and the red formatting mean that these resources are overallocated: at one or more points in the schedule their assigned tasks exceed their capacity to work. We will focus on Garrett R. Vargas, first by changing the timescale settings.

10 On the Format menu, click Timescale.

The Timescale dialog box appears.

11 In the Units box under Major Scale, select Weeks. In the Units box under Minor Scale, select Days.

12 Click OK to close the Timescale dialog box.

13 In the Resource Name column, select the name of Resource 13, "Garrett R. Vargas."

14 On the Standard toolbar, click the Go To Selected Task button.

Microsoft Project scrolls the timescaled grid to show Garrett R. Vargas's earliest assignments. You can see that on Friday, June 8, Garrett's 6 hours of work are formatted in red, indicating that he is overallocated on that day.

Given that Garrett works full-time, how could he be overallocated with just six hours of work? To determine this, you will need to get a closer look at his assignments.

15 Click the plus sign next to Garrett R. Vargas's name in the Resource Name column.

Microsoft Project expands the Resource Usage view to show Garrett R. Vargas's individual assignments.

Even though this resource's assignments on this day don't exceed his capacity to work, they have been scheduled at times that overlap, resulting in an hour-by-hour overallocation.

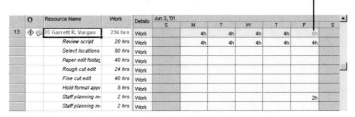

Only two assignments are on June 8: the four-hour task "Review script" and the two-hour task "Staff planning meeting 1." These two tasks have been scheduled at times that overlap between the hours of 3:00 P.M. and 5:00 P.M. (If you wish to see this, format the timescale to display days in the major scale and hours in the minor scale.) This is a real overallocation: Garrett probably cannot complete both tasks simultaneously. However, it is a relatively minor overallocation given the scope of the project, and we are not too concerned about resolving this level of overallocation.

Other overallocations are also in the schedule, however, none look too serious at this time.

Here are a few more things to keep in mind when viewing resource allocation:

- By default, the Resource Usage view displays the Usage table. You can display different tables, however. On the View menu, click Table: Usage, and then select the table you want displayed.

- By default, the Resource Usage view displays work values in the timescaled grid. However, you can display additional assignment values such as cost and remaining availability. On the Format menu, click Details, and then select the value you want displayed.

- Instead of using the Timescale command on the Format menu to change the major and minor scales of the timescale, you can click the Zoom In and Zoom Out buttons on the Standard toolbar. However, this method might not produce the exact level of detail you want. If it does not, use the Timescale command on the Format menu.

- To see allocations for each resource graphed against a units scale, you can display the Resource Graph by selecting the Resource Graph command on the View menu or you can click the Resource Graph button on the View bar. Use the arrow keys or horizontal scroll bar to switch between resources in this view.

Lesson Wrap-Up

In this lesson, you learned how to apply a variety of important task-related tools after creating your project plan, as well as how to view resource allocations over time.

If you are continuing on to other lessons:

- On the File menu, click Close to close the file. If you are prompted to save changes, click Yes, and then save without a baseline.

If you are not continuing on to other lessons

1   On the File menu, click Close to close the file. If you are prompted to save changes, click No.

2   On the File menu, click Exit.

Microsoft Project closes.

Lesson Glossary

allocation The portion of a resource's capacity devoted to work on a specific task. A full-time resource assigned to work full-time on a task is fully allocated to that task. In Microsoft Project, a resource's work capacity is measured in units. One full-time resource has 100% units (recorded in the Max. Units field).

base calendar A calendar that can serve as the project calendar or a task calendar. Microsoft Project includes three base calendars, named Standard, 24 Hours, and Night Shift. You can customize these, or you can use them as a basis for your own base calendar.

constraint A restriction, such as Must Start On (MSO) or Finish No Later Than (FNLT), that you can place upon the start or finish date of a task.

critical path A series of tasks that will push out the project's end date if the tasks are delayed.

effort-driven scheduling A scheduling method in which a task's work remains constant regardless of the number of resources assigned to it. As resources are added to a task, the duration decreases, but the work remains the same and is distributed among the assigned resources. Effort-driven scheduling is on by default in Microsoft Project, but it can be turned off for any task.

fixed duration A task type in which the duration value is fixed. If you change the amount of work you expect a task to require, Microsoft Project recalculates units for each resource. If you change duration or units, Microsoft Project recalculates work.

fixed units A task type in which the units value is fixed. If you change the task's duration, Microsoft Project recalculates the amount of work scheduled for the task. If you change units or work, Microsoft Project recalculates duration.

fixed work A task type in which the work value is fixed. If you change the task's duration, Microsoft Project recalculates units for each resource. If you change units or work, Microsoft Project recalculates duration.

flexible constraint A constraint type that gives Microsoft Project the flexibility to change the start and finish dates (but not the duration) of a task. As Soon As Possible (ASAP) and As Late As Possible (ALAP) are both flexible constraints.

free slack The amount of time that a task can be delayed without delaying the start date of a successor task.

fully allocated The condition of a resource when the total work of its task assignments is exactly equal to that resource's work capacity. For example, a full-time resource assigned to work 40 hours per week is fully allocated. In Microsoft Project, a resource's work capacity is measured in units. One full-time resource has 100% units (recorded in the Max. Units field).

inflexible constraint A constraint type that forces a task to begin or end on a certain date. Must Start On (MSO) and Must Finish On (MFO) are both inflexible constraints.

major scale In the timescale, the major scale appears above the minor scale and contains larger units of time, such as months or weeks.

minor scale In the timescale, the minor scale appears below the major scale and contains smaller units of time, such as weeks or days.

noncritical tasks Tasks that have slack. Noncritical tasks can finish later within the slack time without affecting the project completion date.

overallocated The condition of a resource when it is assigned to do more work than can be done within the resource's normal work capacity. In Microsoft Project, a resource's work capacity is measured in units. One full-time resource has 100% units (recorded in the Max. Units field).

project calendar The base calendar that is used by the entire project. The project calendar defines normal working and nonworking time.

recurring task A task that repeats at established intervals. You can create a recurring task that repeats for a fixed number of times or ends by a specific date.

scheduling formula A representation of how Microsoft Project calculates work, based on the duration and resource units of an assignment. The scheduling formula is Duration × Units = Work.

semi-flexible constraint A constraint type that gives Microsoft Project the flexibility to change the start and finish dates (but not the duration) of a task within one date boundary. Start No Earlier Than (SNET), Start No Later Than (SNLT), Finish No Earlier Than (FNET), and Finish No Later Than (FNLT) are all semi-flexible constraints.

slack The amount of time that a task can be delayed without delaying the start date of a successor task (free slack) or the project end date (total slack).

split An interruption in a task, represented in the Gantt bar as a dotted line between two segments of a task. You can split a task multiple times.

Standard base calendar A base calendar included with Microsoft Project designed to accommodate an 8:00 A.M. to 5:00 P.M. work shift.

task calendar The base calendar that is used by a single task. A task calendar defines working and nonworking times for a task, regardless of settings in the project calendar.

task type A setting applied to a task that determines how Microsoft Project schedules the task, based on which of the three scheduling formula values (units, duration, or work) is fixed. The three task types are fixed units, fixed duration, and fixed work.

timescale In views such as the Gantt Chart view and the Resource Usage view, the timescale appears as a band across the top of the grid and denotes units of time. The timescale is divided into a major scale (such as weeks) and a minor scale (such as days). You can customize the timescale in the Timescale dialog box, which you can open from the Format menu.

total slack The amount of time that a task can be delayed without delaying the project end date.

underallocated When the work assigned to a resource is less than the resource's maximum capacity. For example, a full-time resource who has only 25 hours of work assigned in a 40-hour workweek is underallocated. In Microsoft Project, a resource's work capacity is measured in units. One full-time resource has 100% units (recorded in the Max. Units field).

Quick Quiz

1   What is the difference between how task calendars and resource calendars are created?

2   What are the three task types?

3   Why might you want to split a task?

4   Why might you want to set up a recurring task?

5   What are the three categories of task constraints, and which should you use whenever possible?

6   A task is on the project's critical path. What can we conclude about this task?

7   What are the three types of resource allocation?

Putting It All Together

Open the file Putting It All Together 4 in the Lesson 4 folder located in the MS Project Core Practice folder on your hard disk, and save it without a baseline as Music Video 4 in the same folder.

Exercise 1: Within each summary task, link the subtasks with finish-to-start relationships. Then link the three summary tasks with finish-to-start relationships.

Exercise 2: Apply a Start No Earlier Than constraint to the Summary Task 7, "Post-Production." This phase of work must start no earlier than June 25, 2001, due to limited access to video editing rooms.

LESSON 5

Sorting, Grouping, and Filtering Project Information

After completing this lesson, you will be able to:

✔ *Sort task and resource data.*

✔ *Display task and resource data in groups.*

✔ *Filter or highlight task and resource data.*

In this lesson, you use some of the tools in Microsoft Project to change the way your data is organized. Microsoft Project includes powerful features that allow you to organize and analyze data that otherwise would require such separate tools as a spreadsheet application.

Practice files for the lesson

To complete the procedures in this lesson, you will need to use a file named Wingtip Toys Commercial 5. Open the Lesson 5 folder in the MS Project Core Practice folder located on your hard disk. Open file 5A, and save it without a baseline as Wingtip Toys Commercial 5 in the Lesson 5 folder.

Proj2000-5-6

Sorting Data in a View

Sorting is the simplest way to reorganize task or resource data in Microsoft Project. You can sort tasks or resources by predefined criteria, or you can create your own sort order with up to three levels of nesting. For example, you can sort resources by resource group and then sort by cost within each resource group.

Like grouping and filtering, which you will work with in later sections, sorting does not (with one exception) change the underlying data of your project plan; it simply reorders the data you have. The one exception is the option it offers to renumber Task or Resource IDs after sorting. Once tasks or resources are renumbered, you cannot restore their original numbered sequence.

However, it is fine to permanently renumber tasks or resources if that is what you intend to do. For example, when building a resource list, you might enter resource names in the order in which the resources join your project. Later, when the list is complete, you might want to sort them alphabetically by name and permanently renumber them. Once this is done, the resource names will appear in alphabetical order in the Assign Resources dialog box and in resource views.

In planning your project's budget, you would like to see all resources sorted by resource group field. Further, within each group, resources should be sorted by cost from most to least expensive. In this exercise, you sort a resource view to see the data arranged this way.

1   On the View bar, click Resource Sheet.

The Resource Sheet view appears. By default, the Entry table appears in the Resource Sheet view; however, the Entry table does not display the cost field per resource. You will switch to the Summary table instead.

2   On the View menu, point to Table: Entry, and then click Summary.

The Summary table appears. Your screen should look similar to the following illustration.

	Resource Name	Group	Max. Units	Peak	Std. Rate	Ovt. Rate	Cost	Work
1	16-mm Camera	Equipment	300%	300%	$250.00/wk	$0.00/hr	$137.50	22 hrs
2	16-mm Film	Film and Lat		eet/hr	$0.20		$12,432.00	62,160 Feet
3	5000-Watt Light	Equipment	400%	400%	$100.00/wk	$0.00/hr	$62.50	25 hrs
4	Anne L. Paper	Talent	100%	100%	$75.00/day	$0.00/hr	$215.63	23 hrs
5	Crane	Equipment	100%	0%	$0.00/hr	$0.00/hr	$0.00	0 hrs
6	Daniel Penn	Talent	100%	0%	$75.00/day	$0.00/hr	$0.00	0 hrs
7	David Campbell	Talent	100%	100%	$75.00/day	$0.00/hr	$853.13	91 hrs
8	Dolly	Equipment	200%	100%	$0.00/hr	$0.00/hr	$0.00	8 hrs
9	Editing Lab	Filem and La	100%	100%	$200.00/day	$0.00/hr	$1,675.00	64 hrs
10	Electrician	Crew	200%	200%	$22.00/hr	$33.00/hr	$2,200.00	100 hrs
11	Eric Lang	Production	100%	0%	$15.50/hr	$0.00/hr	$0.00	0 hrs
12	Eric Miller	Talent	100%	100%	$75.00/day	$0.00/hr	$281.25	30 hrs
13	Garrett R. Vargas	Production	100%	200%	$800.00/wk	$0.00/hr	$4,720.00	236 hrs
14	Jessup Meng	Production	50%	50%	$10.00/hr	$0.00/hr	$305.00	30.5 hrs
15	Jim Hance	Talent	100%	100%	$75.00/day	$0.00/hr	$75.00	8 hrs
16	Jo Brown	Production	100%	200%	$18.75/hr	$0.00/hr	$5,362.50	286 hrs
17	John Rodman	Production	100%	100%	$22.00/hr	$0.00/hr	$528.00	24 hrs
18	Jon Ganio	Crew	100%	100%	$14.00/hr	$0.00/hr	$266.00	19 hrs
19	Jonathan Mollerup	Crew	50%	0%	$10.00/hr	$0.00/hr	$0.00	0 hrs
20	Joseph Matthews	Talent	100%	100%	$75.00/day	$0.00/hr	$206.25	22 hrs
21	Ken Bergman	Production	100%	100%	$18.75/hr	$0.00/hr	$3,168.75	169 hrs
22	Lane Sacksteder	Production	75%	75%	$15.50/hr	$0.00/hr	$2,647.18	170.78 hrs
23	Lani Ota	Production	100%	100%	$22.00/hr	$0.00/hr	$528.00	24 hrs

Now you are ready to sort the Resource Sheet view.

3   On the Project menu, point to Sort, and click Sort By.

The Sort dialog box appears.

4   Under Sort By, select Cost from the drop-down list, and next to that click Descending.

5   Make sure that the Permanently Renumber Resources check box is cleared.

6   Make sure that the Sort Resources By Project check box is selected.

7   Click Sort.

The summary table in the Resource Sheet view is sorted by the Cost column, in descending order. Your screen should look similar to the following illustration.

The Permanently Renumber Tasks (or when in a resource view, the Permanently Renumber Resources) check box in the Sort dialog box is a Microsoft Project–level setting; if checked, it permanently renumbers tasks or resources in any Microsoft Project file in which you sort. Because you might not want to permanently renumber tasks or resources every time you sort, it is a good idea to clear this check box.

When you sort data, the sort order applies to the active view, regardless of the specific table currently displayed in the view. For example, if you sort the Gantt Chart view by start date while displaying the Entry table and then switch to the Cost table, you will see the tasks sorted by start date.

The values in the resource group field have been entered for you.

The Summary table is now sorted by Cost, in descending order.

	Resource Name	Group	Max. Units	Peak	Std. Rate	Ovt. Rate	Cost	Work
2	16-mm Film	Film and Lat		eet/hr	$0.20		$12,432.00	62,160 Feet
38	Scott Cooper	Production	100%	200%	$775.00/wk	$0.00/hr	$8,190.09	422.72 hrs
16	Jo Brown	Production	100%	200%	$18.75/hr	$0.00/hr	$5,362.50	286 hrs
13	Garrett R. Vargas	Production	100%	200%	$800.00/wk	$0.00/hr	$4,720.00	236 hrs
21	Ken Bergman	Production	100%	100%	$18.75/hr	$0.00/hr	$3,168.75	169 hrs
22	Lane Sacksteder	Production	75%	75%	$15.50/hr	$0.00/hr	$2,647.18	170.78 hrs
10	Electrician	Crew	200%	200%	$22.00/hr	$33.00/hr	$2,200.00	100 hrs
39	Scott Fallon	Crew	100%	100%	$24.00/hr	$0.00/hr	$1,824.00	76 hrs
33	Peter Kelly	Production	100%	100%	$18.75/hr	$0.00/hr	$1,742.00	104 hrs
9	Editing Lab	Filem and La	100%	100%	$200.00/day	$0.00/hr	$1,675.00	64 hrs
36	Richard Lum	Production	100%	100%	$625.00/wk	$0.00/hr	$1,625.00	104 hrs
42	Suki White	Production	100%	100%	$700.00/wk	$0.00/hr	$1,540.00	88 hrs
31	Patti Mintz	Production	100%	100%	$9.40/hr	$0.00/hr	$977.60	104 hrs
7	David Campbell	Talent	100%	100%	$75.00/day	$0.00/hr	$853.13	91 hrs
35	Richard Kaplan	Production	100%	100%	$9.00/hr	$0.00/hr	$720.00	80 hrs
17	John Rodman	Production	100%	100%	$22.00/hr	$0.00/hr	$528.00	24 hrs
23	Lani Ota	Production	100%	100%	$22.00/hr	$0.00/hr	$528.00	24 hrs
32	Paul Born	Production	50%	50%	$200.00/day	$0.00/hr	$350.00	14 hrs
14	Jessup Meng	Production	50%	50%	$10.00/hr	$0.00/hr	$305.00	30.5 hrs
27	Megan Sherman	Crew	100%	100%	$18.00/hr	$0.00/hr	$288.00	16 hrs
12	Eric Miller	Talent	100%	100%	$75.00/day	$0.00/hr	$281.25	30 hrs
18	Jon Ganio	Crew	100%	100%	$14.00/hr	$0.00/hr	$266.00	19 hrs
30	Patricia Brooke	Crew	100%	100%	$14.00/hr	$0.00/hr	$266.00	19 hrs

This arrangement is fine for looking at resource costs for the entire project, but you would like to see this data organized by resource group. To see this, you will apply a two-level sort order.

8   On the Project menu, point to Sort, and then click Sort By.

The Sort dialog box appears, in which you can apply up to three nested levels of sort criteria.

9   Under Sort By, select Group from the drop-down list, and next to that click Ascending.

10   Under Then By (in the center of the dialog box), select Cost from the drop-down list, and next to that click Descending.

11   Make sure that the Permanently Renumber Resources check box is cleared.

The Sort Resources By Project check box should be selected.

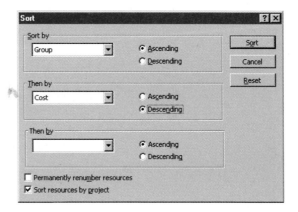

12   Click Sort.

Microsoft Project sorts the Resource Sheet view to display resources by group and then by cost within each group. Your screen should look similar to the following illustration.

Now the Summary table is sorted first by Resource Group and then within each group by Cost.

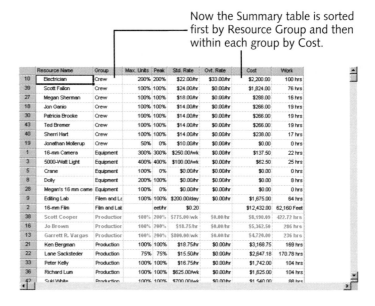

This is an easy way to identify the most expensive resources in each functional group working on the short film project.

To conclude this exercise, re-sort the resource information to return it to its original order.

13   On the Project menu, point to Sort, and then click By ID.

Microsoft Project re-sorts the resource list by Resource ID.

Note that there is no visual indicator that a task or resource view has been sorted other than the order in which the rows of data appear. Unlike grouping and filtering, you cannot save custom sort settings that you have specified. However, the sort order you most recently specified will remain in effect until you re-sort the view.

Proj2000-5-3
Proj2000-5-4
Proj2000-5-11

In some respects, grouping in Microsoft Project is similar to the Subtotals feature in Microsoft Excel. In fact, grouping allows you to reorganize and analyze your Microsoft Project data in ways that previously would have required you to export your Microsoft Project data to a spreadsheet program.

Grouping Data in a View

As you develop a project plan, the default views available in Microsoft Project give you several ways of viewing and analyzing your data. One important feature you can apply to task and resource views is **grouping**. Grouping allows you to organize task or resource information according to criteria you choose. For example, rather than viewing the task list in the Gantt Chart view sorted by Task ID, you can view it sorted by task duration. Grouping goes a step beyond just sorting, however. Grouping adds summary values, or "roll-ups," at intervals that you can customize. For example, you can group resources by their cost with a $1,000 interval between groups.

Grouping can significantly change the way you view your task or resource data, allowing for a more refined level of data analysis and presentation. Grouping does not change the underlying structure of your project plan, however; it simply reorganizes and summarizes the data. As with sorting, when you group data in a view, the grouping applies to all tables you can display in the view.

Microsoft Project includes several predefined task and resource groups, such as grouping tasks by duration or resources by standard pay rate. You can also customize any of the built-in groups or create your own.

In this exercise, you group by the Resource Group field and show summary costs. This is similar to the sorting you did in the previous section, but you are adding summary cost values.

1   On the Project menu, point to Group By: No Group, and then click Resource Group.

Microsoft Project reorganizes the resource data into resource groups, adds summary cost values per group, and presents the data in an expanded outline form. Your screen should look similar to the following illustration.

After grouping by the Resource Group field, Microsoft Project adds summary values per group. The summary values are formatted in yellow.

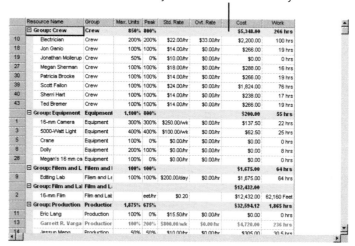

	Resource Name	Group	Max. Units	Peak	Std. Rate	Ovt. Rate	Cost	Work
	⊟ **Group: Crew**	**Crew**	**850%**	**800%**			**$5,348.00**	**266 hrs**
10	Electrician	Crew	200%	200%	$22.00/hr	$33.00/hr	$2,200.00	100 hrs
18	Jon Ganio	Crew	100%	100%	$14.00/hr	$0.00/hr	$266.00	19 hrs
19	Jonathan Mollerup	Crew	50%	0%	$10.00/hr	$0.00/hr	$0.00	0 hrs
27	Megan Sherman	Crew	100%	100%	$18.00/hr	$0.00/hr	$288.00	16 hrs
30	Patricia Brooke	Crew	100%	100%	$14.00/hr	$0.00/hr	$266.00	19 hrs
39	Scott Fallon	Crew	100%	100%	$24.00/hr	$0.00/hr	$1,824.00	76 hrs
40	Sherri Hart	Crew	100%	100%	$14.00/hr	$0.00/hr	$238.00	17 hrs
43	Ted Bremer	Crew	100%	100%	$14.00/hr	$0.00/hr	$266.00	19 hrs
	⊟ **Group: Equipment**	**Equipment**	**1,100%**	**800%**			**$200.00**	**55 hrs**
1	16-mm Camera	Equipment	300%	300%	$250.00/wk	$0.00/hr	$137.50	22 hrs
3	5000-Watt Light	Equipment	400%	400%	$100.00/wk	$0.00/hr	$62.50	25 hrs
5	Crane	Equipment	100%	0%	$0.00/hr	$0.00/hr	$0.00	0 hrs
8	Dolly	Equipment	200%	100%	$0.00/hr	$0.00/hr	$0.00	8 hrs
28	Megan's 16 mm ca	Equipment	100%	0%	$0.00/hr	$0.00/hr	$0.00	0 hrs
	⊟ **Group: Filem and L**	**Filem and l**	**100%**	**100%**			**$1,675.00**	**64 hrs**
9	Editing Lab	Filem and La	100%	100%	$200.00/day	$0.00/hr	$1,675.00	64 hrs
	⊟ **Group: Film and La**	**Film and L**					**$12,432.00**	
2	16-mm Film	Film and Lab		eet/hr	$0.20		$12,432.00	62,160 Feet
	⊟ **Group: Production**	**Production**	**1,875%**	**675%**			**$32,594.12**	**1,865 hrs**
11	Eric Lang	Production	100%	0%	$15.50/hr	$0.00/hr	$0.00	0 hrs
13	Garrett R. Varga	Production	100%	200%	$800.00/wk	$0.00/hr	$4,720.00	236 hrs
14	Jessun Menq	Production	50%	50%	$10.00/hr	$0.00/hr	$305.00	30.5 hrs

Microsoft Project applies colored formatting to the summary data rows, in this case, a yellow background. Because the summary data is derived from subordinate data, you cannot edit it directly. Displaying these summary values has no effect on the cost or schedule calculations of the project plan.

This arrangement of the resource cost information is similar to the sorting you did in the previous section. However, you would like to have more control over how Microsoft Project organizes and presents the data. To accomplish this, you create a group.

2   On the Project menu, point to Group By: Resource Group, and then click More Groups.

The More Groups dialog box appears. In it, you can see all of the predefined groups for tasks and resources available to you. Your new group will be most similar to the Resource Group, so you will start by copying it.

3   Ensure Resource Group is selected, and then click Copy.

The Group Definition dialog box appears.

4   In the Name box, type **Resource Groups by Cost**

5   In the Field Name column, click the first empty cell below "Group."

6   Type or select **Cost**

7   In the Order column, select Descending for the Cost field name.

The resources will be sorted within their groups by cost from highest to lowest values.

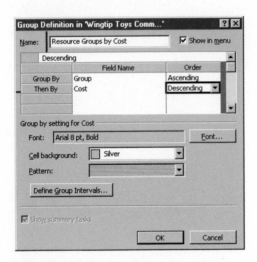

Next you will fine-tune the cost intervals at which Microsoft Project will group the resources.

8   Click the Define Group Intervals button.

The Define Group Interval dialog box appears.

9   In the Group On box, select Interval.

10   In the Group Interval box, type **1,000** and then click OK.

11   Click OK again to close the Group Definition dialog box.

Resource Groups By Cost appears as a new group in the More Groups dialog box.

12   Click Apply.

Microsoft Project applies the new group to the Resource Sheet view. Your screen should look similar to the following illustration.

After Microsoft Project applies a two-level group,
information is grouped first by Resource Group
and then within each group by Cost.

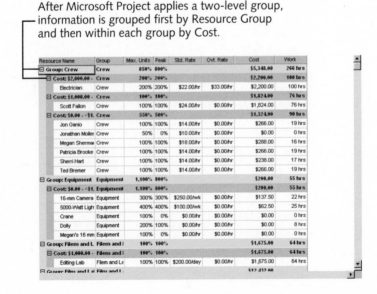

r group value (the yellow bands)
ues at $1,000 intervals (the gray

ove the grouping.

No Group ▾   13   up By: Resource Groups By Cost,

mary values and outline structure,
g or removing a group has no ef-

A   os you create are available to you
t   dard toolbar. The name of the active
g   embles a box with a drop-down list.
C   n to see other group names. If no
g   No Group" appears on the button.

Fil

Anot   way you view Microsoft Project
task   . As the name suggests, filtering
hides   t meet the criteria you specify, dis-
playi   in. Like grouping, filtering does
not c   roject file, only how it appears.

There are two ways to use filters: apply predefined filters to a view, or apply an **AutoFilter** to a view.

■ Apply a predefined or custom filter to see or highlight just the task or resource information that meets the criteria of the filter. For example, the Critical Task filter displays only the tasks that are critical. Some predefined filters, such as the Task Range filter, prompt you to enter specific criteria, for example, a range of Task IDs.

■ Use AutoFilters for more ad hoc filtering in any table in Microsoft Project. When the AutoFilter feature is turned on, small down arrows appear next to the names of column headings. Clicking the arrow displays a list of criteria by which you can filter the data. The criteria you see depend on the type of data contained in the column—for example, AutoFilter criteria in a date column include choices like "Today" and "This month," as well as a "Custom" option with which you can specify your own criteria. You use Auto-Filter in Microsoft Project in the same way you might use AutoFilter in Microsoft Excel.

Both types of filters hide rows in task or resource sheet views that do not meet the criteria you specify. If a task or resource sheet view has a filter applied, the filter name appears in the Filter button on the Formatting toolbar. You might see gaps in the task or Resource ID numbers after applying a filter. The "missing" data is only hidden and not deleted. As with sorting and grouping, when you filter data in a view, the filtering applies to all tables you can display in the view.

A commonly used format for communicating schedule information on a film project is called a shooting schedule. In this exercise, you create a filter that displays only the uncompleted film shoot tasks. In later exercises, you will combine this filter with a custom table and a custom view to create a complete shooting schedule that will keep everyone on the film project informed.

1   On the View bar, click Gantt Chart.

The Gantt Chart view appears. Before you create a custom filter, you can quickly see the tasks you are interested in by applying an AutoFilter.

2   On the Formatting toolbar, click the AutoFilter button.

Microsoft Project displays arrows to the right of the column headings. Your screen should look like the following illustration.

After turning on AutoFilters, these arrows appear next to column headings. Click them to choose the AutoFilter criteria you want.

3   Click the down arrow in the Task Name column heading, and then select (Custom).

The Custom AutoFilter dialog box appears. You would like to see just the tasks that contain the word "shoot."

4   Under Name, make sure "Contains" appears in the first box.

5   In the adjacent box, type **shoot**

6   Click OK to close the Custom AutoFilter dialog box.

Microsoft Project filters the task list to show only the tasks that contain the word "shoot" and their summary tasks. Your screen should look similar to the following illustration.

After applying an AutoFilter,
the filtered column name and its
AutoFilter arrow are formatted blue.

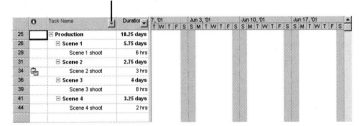

Note the blue formatting of the Task Name column heading and arrow. These are visual indicators that an AutoFilter has been applied to this view.

Next you turn off the AutoFilter and create a custom filter.

   7   On the Formatting toolbar, click the AutoFilter button.

Microsoft Project toggles the AutoFilter off, redisplaying all tasks in the project. Now you are ready to create a custom filter.

8   On the Project menu, point to Filtered For: All Tasks and then click More Filters.

The More Filters dialog box appears. In it, you can see all of the predefined filters for tasks (when in a task view) and resources (when in a resource view) available to you.

9   Click the New button.

The Filter Definition dialog box appears.

10 In the Name box, type **Uncompleted Shoots**

11 In the first row in the Field Name column, type or select **Name**

12 In the first row in the Test column, type or select **contains**

13 In the first row in the Value(s) column, type **shoot**

That covers the first criterion for the filter; next you will add the second criterion.

14 In the second row in the And/Or column, type or select **And**

15 In the second row in the Field Name column, type or select **Actual Finish**

16 In the second row in the Test column, type or select **equals**

17   In the second row in the Value(s) column, type **NA**

NA means "not applicable" and is the way Microsoft Project marks some fields that have no value yet. In other words, any shooting task that does not have an actual finish date must be uncompleted.

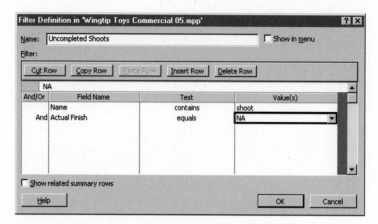

18   Click OK to close the Filter Definition dialog box.

The new filter appears in the More Filters dialog box.

19   Click Apply.

Microsoft Project applies the new filter to the Gantt Chart view. Your screen should look similar to the following illustration.

Ater applying a filter, Microsoft Project hides information that does not meet the filter's criteria. Note the gaps in the Task IDs; this is one visual clue that a filter has been applied.

Now the tasks are filtered to show only the uncompleted shooting tasks. Because we have not started tracking actual work yet, all of the shooting tasks are uncompleted at this time.

To conclude this exercise, you will remove the filtering.

tip

Rather than hiding tasks that do not meet the filter criteria, you can highlight those that do in blue formatting without hiding the tasks that do not. Click the Highlight button instead of the Apply button in the More Filters dialog box.

All Tasks ▼

20   On the Project menu, point to Filtered For: Uncompleted Shoots, and then click All Tasks.

Microsoft Project removes the filter. As always, displaying or removing a filter has no effect on the original data.

tip

All filters are also available to you in the Filter button on the Formatting toolbar. The name of the active filter appears in this button; click the arrow next to the filter name to see other filters. If no filter is applied to the current view, "All Tasks" or "All Resources" appears on the button, depending on the type of view currently displayed.

Lesson Wrap-Up

In this lesson, you learned how to sort, group, and filter task and resource data in a project.

If you are continuing on to other lessons:

● On the File menu, click Close to close the file. If you are prompted to save changes, click Yes, and then save without a baseline.

If you are not continuing on to other lessons

1 On the File menu, click Close to close the file. If you are prompted to save changes, click No.
2 On the File menu, click Exit.
   Microsoft Project closes.

Lesson Glossary

AutoFilter A quick way to view only the task or resource information in a table that meets the criteria you choose. To turn on AutoFilter, click the AutoFilter button on the Formatting toolbar. To filter a table with AutoFilter, click the arrow next to a column heading, and choose the criteria you want.

filter A way to see or highlight only the task or resource information in a table that meets the criteria you choose.

group A way to reorder task or resource information in a table and to display summary values for each group. You can specify up to three nested levels of groups. (The term "group" is also used to refer to the Resource Group field, which is unrelated.)

sort A way of ordering task or resource information in a view by the criteria you choose.

Quick Quiz

1 Microsoft Project can sort with up to three levels of nesting. What does this mean?
2 When you group data in Microsoft Project, you cannot edit the group summary row values. Why not?
3 What are two visual indicators that an AutoFilter has been applied to a table?

Putting It All Together

If necessary, start Microsoft Project. Open the Putting It All Together 5 file in the Lesson 5 folder located in the MS Project Core Practice folder on your hard disk, and save it without a baseline as Music Video 5 in the in the same folder.

Exercise: Leonard Zuvela, manager of the band Fourth Coffee, has asked you for some specific cost information. First, he would like to see the resource costs listed from highest to lowest. Leonard has to secure management approval for any resources with a planned cost greater than $5,000, so he would like to see who those resources are.

Sort the Resource sheet by cost, and then use AutoFilter to display only the resources with a cost greater than $5,000.

LESSON 6

Formatting Your Project Plan

After completing this lesson, you will be able to:

✔ *Change the formatting of items in the Gantt Chart view.*

✔ *Draw a text box on the chart portion of the Gantt Chart view.*

✔ *Display additional information about your resources in a text field.*

✔ *Create a custom table.*

✔ *Create a custom view.*

In this lesson, you use some of the formatting features in Microsoft Project to change the way your data appears.

Practice files for the lesson

To complete the procedures in this lesson, you will create a file named Wingtip Toys Commercial 6. Open the Lesson 6 folder in the MS Project Core Practice folder located on your hard disk. Open file 6A, and save it without a baseline as Wingtip Toys Commercial 6 in the Lesson 6 folder.

Proj2000-5-5

Formatting the Gantt Chart

For many people, a Gantt Chart is synonymous with a project plan. In Microsoft Project, the default **view** is the Gantt Chart. You are likely to spend a lot of your time in Microsoft Project in this view.

The Gantt Chart view consists of two parts: a **table** on the left and a **timescaled** bar chart on the right. The bars on the chart graphically represent the tasks on the table in terms of start and finish dates, duration, and status (for example, if work on the task has started or not). Other elements on the chart, such as link lines, represent relationships between tasks. In short, the Gantt Chart is a popular and widely understood representation of project information throughout the project management world.

The default formatting applied to the Gantt Chart view works well for onscreen viewing, sharing with other programs, or printing. However, you can change the formatting of just about any element on the Gantt Chart that you choose. In this exercise, you will focus on Gantt Chart bars. There are three distinct ways to format Gantt Chart bars:

■ Format whole categories of items in the Bar Styles dialog box, which you can open by selecting the Bar Styles command on the Format menu. In this case, the formatting changes you make to a type of item (a milestone, for example) apply to all such items in the Gantt Chart.

■ Format whole categories of items in the GanttChartWizard, which is available on the Format menu. This wizard contains a series of dialog boxes in which you select formatting options for the most-used items on the Gantt Chart. The Gantt ChartWizard has fewer choices than the Bar Styles command.

■ Format individual bars directly. The formatting changes you make have no effect on other elements in the Gantt Chart. You can double-click a bar on the Gantt Chart to see its formatting options.

In this exercise, you change a variety of items on the Gantt Chart through the Format Bar Styles dialog box.

1   On the Format menu, click Bar Styles.

The Bar Styles dialog box appears.

The first item you would like to change is the shape of the milestones on the Gantt Chart. Because many of the toy commercial's resources are aspiring movie stars, a star shape seems appropriate.

2   In the Name column, select Milestone.

3   In the Shape box under the Start label, select the star shape, which is the last item in the drop-down list.

You can see the effect of your choice in the Appearance column of the dialog box. The star shape appears for the sample milestone.

┌─The options you choose in the lower portion of the dialog box...

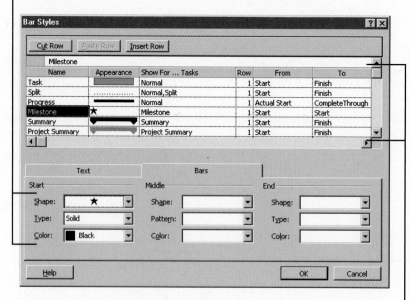

...are reflected in the upper portion of the dialog box. ──┘

The next change you would like to make is to display resource initials instead of full names next to the task bars.

4   Click the Text tab.

5   In the Name column at the top of the dialog box, select Task.

6   In the Text tab, select Resource Names in the Right box, click the down arrow, and then select Resource Initials.

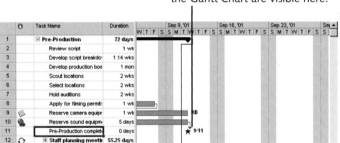

7   Click OK to close the Bar Styles dialog box.

Microsoft Project applies your formatting changes to the Gantt Chart. To get a better look at the formatting changes you made, you will view a milestone.

8   Select the name of Task 11, "Pre-Production complete!" On the Standard toolbar, click the Go To Selected Task button.

The format changes you made to the Gantt Chart are visible here.

You can see the reformatted milestone and resource initials on the Gantt Chart.

Drawing on a Gantt Chart

Proj2000-3-1

Microsoft Project includes a Drawing toolbar with which you can draw objects directly on a Gantt Chart. If you wish, you can link a drawn object to either end of a Gantt bar or to a specific date on the timescale. For example, if you would like to note a particular event or graphically call out a specific item, you can draw text boxes, arrows, and other items directly on a Gantt Chart. If the Drawing toolbar does not have the type of item you would like to add, you can add bitmap images or documents as well.

In this exercise, you display the Drawing toolbar and add a text box to the Gantt Chart describing a film festival. Because you will use the standard Gantt Chart view for other purposes later, you will add text to the Detail Gantt view.

1   On the View menu, click More Views.

The More Views dialog box appears.

2   In the Views box, select Detail Gantt, and then click Apply.

The Detail Gantt view appears.

3   On the View menu, point to Toolbars and then select Drawing.

The Drawing toolbar appears.

> You can also right-click any toolbar to see the Toolbars shortcut menu and then display or hide a toolbar listed on that menu.

> You can also double-click the border of the text box to view its properties.

4   On the Drawing toolbar, click the Text Box button, and then drag a small square anywhere on the chart portion of the Detail Gantt view.

5   Type **Film festival June 4 and 5**

6   On the Format menu, point to Drawing and then click Properties.

The Format Drawing dialog box appears.

7   Click the Line & Fill tab.

8   In the Color box under the Fill label, select Yellow.

9   Click the Size & Position tab.

You want to attach the text box to a specific date rather than to a specific Gantt bar.

10   Make sure that Attach To Timescale is selected, and in the Date box, select June 4, 2001.

11   In the Vertical box, type **1** and then click OK to close the Format Drawing dialog box.

Microsoft Project formats the text box with yellow fill and positions it below the timescale where you specified. Depending on the portion of the Detail Gantt view that is visible on screen, you might not see the text box. To see it, go to the date you specified.

12   On the Edit menu, click Go To.

The Go To dialog box appears.

13   In the Date box, select June 4, 2001, and then click OK.

Microsoft Project scrolls the Detail Gantt view to display the date you specified. Your screen should look similar to the following illustration.

Double-click the border of a drawn object
to change its formatting or other properties.

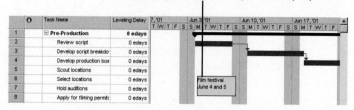

Because you attached the text box to a specific date on the timescale, it will always appear near this date even if you zoom the timescale in or out. Had you attached the text box to a Gantt bar, it would move with the Gantt bar if the task were rescheduled.

To conclude this exercise, you will hide the Drawing toolbar using the shortcut menu.

14   Right-click any of the visible toolbars, and in the shortcut menu that appears, click Drawing.

Microsoft Project hides the Drawing toolbar.

Proj2000-5-13

Displaying Additional Resource Information in a Text Field

You can display **fields** other than those that appear by default in tables. Some of these additional fields, such as the Email Address field, have specific uses. Others are general purpose, and you can customize them to suit your needs. For example, job titles are so important in the film industry that film credits are organized by job titles. To record the resources' job titles, you will enter them into a custom **text field**. You can add whatever information you want in as many as 30 text fields for each of your resources.

> There are additional custom fields available for other types of information, such as numbers, costs, and dates.

The default resource fields describe many aspects of your resources, but you might have additional needs. In this exercise, you will insert a column into the Resource Sheet, and you will enter the job titles of some of the resources.

1   On the View bar, click Resource Sheet.

2   On the Resource Sheet, click the Type column heading.

3   On the Insert menu, click Column.

The Column Definition dialog box appears. Here you choose the field you want to display and how you want it to appear.

> To insert a column, you can also select a column heading and press Insert.

4   In the Field Name list, click **Text1**

5   In the Title box, enter **Title**

Because the Title field will contain text, you will align it to the left to match the other text fields in the Resource Sheet.

> Type a letter to scroll to the field names that start with that letter in the Field Name list. In this case, typing t scrolls the field name list to Text1, which is the first item in the list that starts with "t."

6   In the Align Title and Align Data drop-down lists, select Left.

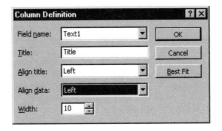

7   Click OK to close the Column Definition dialog box and return to the Resource Sheet.

8   Enter the following titles for these resources in the Title field.

Resource Name	Title
Garrett R. Vargas	Producer
Jo Brown	Production manager
Jonathan Mollerup	2nd Assistant director
Ken Bergman	Director of photography
Lane Sacksteder	1st Assistant director
Patti Mintz	Production assistant
Peter Kelly	Sound technician
Scott Cooper	Director

Your screen should look similar to the following illustration.

Here is the resource text field you have inserted and named "Title."
Text fields are useful for any type of information you want to record
about resources that are not addressed by the default fields.

	ⓘ	Resource Name	Title	Type	Material Label	Initials	Group	Max. Units	Std. Rate	
22		Lane Sacksteder	1st Assistar	Work		LS	Production	75%	$15.50/hr	
23		Lani Ota		Work		LO	Production	100%	$22.00/hr	
24		Mark Hassall		Work		MH	Production	100%	$950.00/wk	
25		Mary Anne Kobylka		Work		MAK	Talent	100%	$12.00/hr	
26		Matthew Dunn		Work		MD	Production	100%	$200.00/wk	
27		Megan Sherman		Work		MS	Crew	100%	$18.00/hr	
28		Megan's 16 mm camera		Work		16	Equipment	100%	$0.00/hr	
29		Pat Kirkland		Work		PK	Production	100%	$45.00/day	
30		Patricia Brooke		Work		PB	Crew	100%	$14.00/hr	
31		Patti Mintz	Production ɛ	Work		PM	Production	100%	$9.40/hr	
32		Paul Born		Work		PB	Production	50%	$200.00/day	
33		Peter Kelly	Sound techr	Work		PK	Production	100%	$16.75/hr	
34		Ray Zambroski		Work		RZ	Production	100%	$24.00/hr	
35		Richard Kaplan		Work		RK	Production	100%	$9.00/hr	
36		Richard Lum		Work		RL	Production	100%	$625.00/wk	
37		Salman Mughal		Work		SM	Production	100%	$18.00/hr	
38	◈	Scott Cooper	Director	Work		SC	Production	100%	$775.00/wk	
39		Scott Fallon		Work		SF	Crew	100%	$24.00/hr	

Proj2000-5-8

Editing and Creating Tables

A table is a spreadsheet-like presentation of project data, organized into vertical columns and horizontal rows. Each column represents one of the many fields in Microsoft Project, and each row represents a single task or resource. The intersection of a column and a row is called a cell (for those of you more oriented towards spreadsheets) or a field (for those of you who think in database terms).

Microsoft Project includes 15 predefined task tables and 10 resource tables that can be applied in views. You have already used some of these tables, such as the Entry table and the Summary table. Chances are that these tables will contain the fields you want most of the time. However, you can modify any predefined table, or you can create your own table with just the data you want.

In this exercise, you create a table to display the information found on a shooting schedule, a common format for presenting schedule information in film and video projects.

1   On the View menu, click More Views.

The More Views dialog box appears.

2   Select Task Sheet, and then click Apply.

Microsoft Project displays the Task Sheet view. This view does not include the chart portion of the Gantt Chart view, so it is easier to see more columns in the active table.

3   On the View menu, point to Table: Entry, and then click More Tables.

The More Tables dialog box appears. Based on the type of view (task or resource) currently displayed, you can see all of the predefined tables for tasks or resources available to you.

4   Ensure that Task is the active option and that Entry is the selected table, and then click Copy.

The Table Definition dialog box appears.

5   In the Name box, type **Shooting Schedule Table**

Next you will remove several fields, add others, and then put the remaining fields in the order you want.

6   In the Field Name column, select each of the following field names and then click Delete Row after selecting each field name:

Indicators

Duration

Finish

Predecessors

Resource Names

After you have deleted these fields, your screen should look similar to the following illustration.

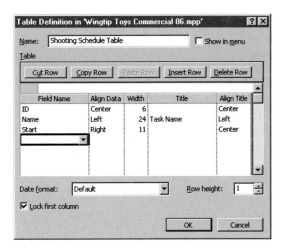

Next you will add some fields to this table definition.

7   In the Field Name column, click the down arrow in next empty cell below "Start," and then select Cast (Text9) from the drop-down list.

8   In the Align Data column in the same row, select Left.

As soon as Left is selected, Microsoft Project automatically completes row entries for the Cast field name by adding data to the Width column and to the Align Title column.

9   In the Width column, type or select **25**

10   In the Field Name column in the next empty row below "Cast," select Location (Text10) from the drop-down list.

11   In the Align Data column, select Left.

The two customized text fields Cast (Text9) and Location (Text10) contain the character names and locations for the shooting tasks. These were previously added to the project plan.

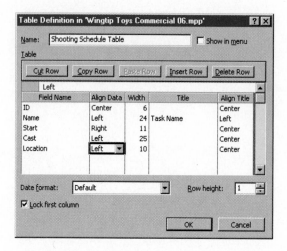

The remaining work to complete this table definition is to reorder the fields to match the order commonly found on a shooting schedule.

12   In the Field Name column, select Start, and then click Cut Row.

13   In the Field Name column, select Name, and then click Paste Row.

After you have reordered these fields, your screen should look similar to the following illustration.

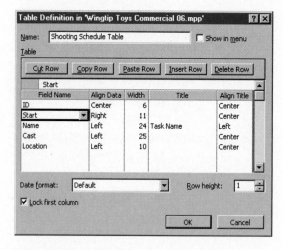

This matches the order in which information is commonly listed on a film shooting schedule.

14   In the Date Format box, select 1/31/00 12:33 PM.

15   Click OK to close the Table Definition dialog box.

The new table appears in the More Tables dialog box.

16   Click Apply.

Microsoft Project applies the new table to the Task Sheet view. If the Start column displays pound signs (###), double-click the column heading's right edge to widen it. Your screen should look similar to the following illustration.

	Start	Task Name	Cast	Location
1	6/4/01 8:00 AM	⊟ Pre-Production		
2	6/4/01 8:00 AM	Review script		
3	6/11/01 8:00 AM	Develop script breakdo		
4	6/18/01 2:43 PM	Develop production boa		
5	7/18/01 2:43 PM	Scout locations		
6	8/3/01 1:00 PM	Select locations		
7	8/17/01 1:00 PM	Hold auditions		
8	8/31/01 1:00 PM	Apply for filming permit:		
9	9/5/01 8:00 AM	Reserve camera equipr		
10	9/5/01 8:00 AM	Reserve sound equipm		
11	9/11/01 5:00 PM	Pre-Production complet		
12	6/8/01 3:00 PM	⊞ Staff planning meetii		
25	9/12/01 8:00 AM	⊟ Production		
26	9/12/01 8:00 AM	⊟ Scene 1		
27	9/12/01 8:00 AM	Scene 1 setup		
28	9/17/01 8:00 AM	Scene 1 rehearsal		
29	9/18/01 8:00 AM	Scene 1 shoot	Garth, Man on street, Store cle	Street corne
30	9/18/01 3:00 PM	Scene 1 teardown		
31	9/19/01 3:00 PM	⊟ Scene 2		
32	9/19/01 3:00 PM	Scene 2 setup		
33	9/20/01 3:00 PM	Scene 2 rehearsal		
34	9/21/01 5:00 PM	Scene 2 shoot	Garth, Shelly	Shelly's livin
35	9/24/01 8:00 AM	Scene 2 teardown		

Next you will combine the custom filter you created in Lesson 5, section "Filtering Data in a View," with this custom table to create a shooting schedule view for the film project.

Defining Custom Views

Proj2000-5-9

In nearly all of the lessons in this book, you have switched between various predefined views in Microsoft Project. A view might contain elements such as tables, **groups**, and **filters**. You can combine these with other elements (such as a timescaled grid in a usage view) or with graphic elements (such as the graphic representation of tasks in the chart portion of the Gantt Chart view).

Microsoft Project includes 23 views, which organize information for specific purposes. You might find that you need to see your project information in some way not available in the predefined views. Should this happen, you can edit an existing view or create your own view.

In this exercise, you create a film shooting schedule view that combines the custom filter and custom table you created earlier. The view you create will more closely match the standard format used in the film industry.

1   On the View menu, click More Views.

The More Views dialog box appears. In it, you can see all of the predefined views available to you.

2   Click the New button.

The Define New View dialog box appears. Most views occupy a single pane, but a view can consist of two separate panes.

3   Make sure Single View is selected, and then click OK.

The View Definition dialog box appears.

4   In the Name box, type **Shooting Schedule View**

5   In the Screen box, select Task Sheet from the drop-down list.

6 In the Table box, select Shooting Schedule Table from the drop-down list.

7 In the Group box, select No Group from the drop-down list.

8 In the Filter box, select Uncompleted Shoots from the drop-down list.

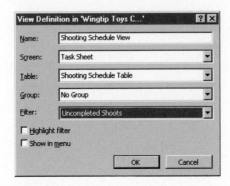

Here you see all the elements that can make up a view.

9 Select the Show In Menu check box.

10 Click OK to close the View Definition dialog box.

The new view appears in the More Views dialog box.

11 Click Apply.

Microsoft Project applies the new view. Your screen should look similar to the following illustration.

The custom view is like a shooting schedule,
a standard format in the film industry.

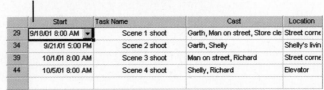

Now only uncompleted shoots are displayed, and the fields appear in an order consistent with a standard shooting schedule for a film project. Also, Microsoft Project added the Shooting Schedule view to the View bar. This view will be saved with this Microsoft Project data file, and you can use it whenever you wish.

Lesson Wrap-Up

In this lesson, you learned how to format the Gantt Chart, use text fields, and create custom tables and views.

If you are continuing on to other lessons:

● On the File menu, click Close to close the file. If you are prompted to save changes, click Yes, and then save without a baseline.

If you are not continuing on to other lessons:

1 On the File menu, click Close to close the file. If you are prompted to save changes, click No.

2 On the File menu, click Exit.

Microsoft Project closes.

Lesson Glossary

field The lowest-level information about a task, resource, or assignment; also called a cell.

filter A way to see or highlight only the task or resource information in a table that meets the criteria you choose.

group A way to reorder task or resource information in a table and to display summary values for each group. You can specify up to three nested levels of groups. (The term "group" is also used to refer to the Resource Group field, which is unrelated.)

table A spreadsheet-like presentation of project data, organized in vertical columns and horizontal rows. Each column represents one of the many fields in Microsoft Project, and each row represents a single task or resource.

text fields Columns or fields in forms in which you can enter any information you want about a resource. Microsoft Project allows up to 30 text fields for each resource.

timescale In views such as the Gantt Chart view and the Resource Usage view, the timescale appears as a band across the top of the grid and denotes units of time. The timescale is divided into a major scale (such as weeks) and a minor scale (such as days). You can customize the timescale in the Timescale dialog box, which you can open from the Format menu.

view The primary way you see data in Microsoft Project. The three categories of views are charts, sheets, and forms.

Quick Quiz

1 The Gantt Chart view, like some (but not all) other views in Microsoft Project, is composed of two major elements. What are they?

2 You can draw objects right on the bar chart portion of the Gantt Chart view. What are two items to which you can anchor a drawn object?

3 For the resources in your project, you have some additional information to record and it does not match any of the predefined fields in Microsoft Project. What should you do?

4 What makes up a table in Microsoft Project?

5 What are the three items that can appear in or be applied to a view?

Putting It All Together

If necessary, start Microsoft Project. Open the file Putting It All Together 6 in the Lesson 6 folder located in the MS Project Core Practice folder on your hard disk, and save it without a baseline as Music Video 6 in the same folder.

Exercise: You have probably noticed that people like to mark up project schedules such as Gantt Charts with related information. One way to record information is in a task or resource note. However, for maximum visibility when the Gantt Chart is printed, you will draw a text box directly on the chart portion of the Gantt Chart.

Draw a text box that contains the text "Requires Bob's Steadicam" and attach it directly below Task 6.

LESSON 7

Printing Project Information

After completing this lesson, you will be able to:

✔ *Change the page setup options for a view, then preview what you intend to print.*

✔ *View and edit reports designed for printing project data.*

In this lesson, you work with some of the many views and reports in Microsoft Project to print your project plan. One of the most important tasks of any project manager is communicating project information to **stakeholders**, and that often means printing on paper. You can use the pre-defined views and reports as is, or customize them to better suit your needs.

Practice files for the lesson

To complete the procedures in this lesson, you will need to use a file named Wingtip Toys Commercial 7. Open the Lesson 7 folder in the MS Project Core Practice folder located on your hard disk. Open the file 7A, and save it without a baseline as Wingtip Toys Commercial 7 in the Lesson 7 folder.

Proj2000-3-10

Customizing and Printing Views

Printing a **view** allows you to get on paper just about whatever you see on your screen. Any customization you apply to a **view**, such as applying different **tables** or **groups**, will print as well. With a few exceptions, you can print any view you see in Microsoft Project. Here are the exceptions:

■ You cannot print the Relationship Diagram view or form views, such as the Task Form.

■ If you have two views displayed in a combination view (one view in the top pane and the other view in the bottom pane), only the view in the active pane will print.

Keep in mind that the part of your project plan you see on your screen at one time might be a relatively small portion of the full project, which might require a large number of pages to print. For example, the Gantt Chart of a six-month project with 85 tasks can require 14 or more letter-size pages to print in its entirety. Printing Gantt Chart or Network Diagram views can use quite a bit of paper. In fact, some heavy-duty Microsoft Project users print poster-size printouts of their project plans using plotters.

Whether you have a printer or a plotter, it is a good idea to preview any views you intend to print. By using the Page Setup dialog box in conjunction with the Print Preview window, you can control many aspects of the view to be printed. For example, you can control the number of pages on which the view will be printed, apply headers and footers, and determine content that appears in the legend of the Gantt Chart and some other views.

tip

Projects with several hundred tasks won't fit on a single letter-size or legal-size page in a legible form. If you have a project that large, you might get better results by printing just summary or filtered data. For example, a collapsed view showing only summary tasks and milestones might be more informative for people who just want an overall sense of the project plan. If you are interested in a specific time period, you can print just that portion of the timescale. Or you might apply a filter to display only the information that is of greatest interest to a particular audience: late or overbudget tasks, for example.

In this exercise, you preview a Gantt Chart view and change options in the Page Setup dialog box.

1   On the File menu, click Print Preview.

Microsoft Project displays the Gantt Chart view in the Print Preview window. Your screen should look similar to the following illustration.

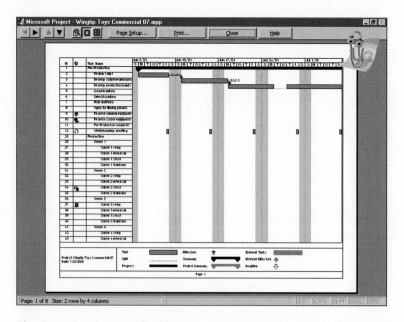

The Print Preview window has several options to explore. Let's start with the page navigation buttons.

2   On the Print Preview toolbar, click the Page Right button several times to display different pages.

3 Click the Page Down button once.

To get a broader view of the output, you will switch to a multi-page view.

4 Click the Multiple Pages button.

The entire Gantt Chart appears in the Print Preview window. Your screen should look similar to the following illustration.

The Multi-Page Print Preview shows you the entire printed output laid out on separate sheets (the paper size is determined by your printer settings).

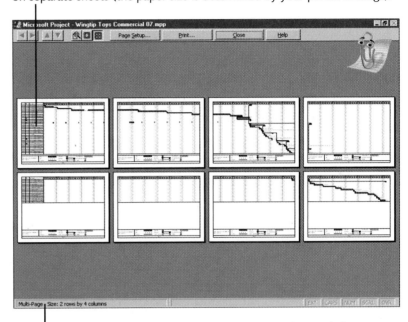

This status bar message refers to rows and columns of printed sheets, as they are laid out in the multi-page Print Preview.

The status bar shows "2 rows by 4 columns." We refer to rows and columns in the Gantt Chart and in other views in Microsoft Project. In the Print Preview window, however, these terms denote rows and columns of *pages*—in this case, two rows of pages by four columns of pages, for a total of eight pages. The status bar text can help you quickly determine the size (in pages) your printed view will be.

Next you will change some options in the Page Setup dialog box.

5 On the Print Preview toolbar, click the One Page button.

Microsoft Project displays the first page of the Gantt Chart.

6 Click the Page Setup button.

The Page Setup dialog box appears. This is the same dialog box you would see if you selected the Page Setup command on the File menu. The first change we will make to the printed Gantt Chart is to add the current date to the header that prints on every page.

7 Click the Header tab.

8   On the Header tab are Alignment tabs. Make sure that Center is selected, and then click the Insert Current Date button.

Microsoft Project inserts the &[Date] code into the header and displays a preview in the Preview window of the Page Setup dialog box. Next you will change the content of the Gantt Chart legend.

9   Click the Legend tab.

10   On the Legend tab are Alignment tabs. Click the Left tab.

With the current settings, Microsoft Project will print the project title and the current date on the left side of the legend. Instead of the current date, you would like to print the start date and the duration of the project.

11   In the Alignment window, select the "Date: &[Date]" code, and type **Start date:**

The text you type replaces the text that was selected.

12   In the General box, select Project Start Date from the drop-down list, and then click the Add button.

Microsoft Project adds the label and code for the project start date to the legend.

13   Press the Enter key to add a third line to the legend and then type **Duration:**

14   In the Project Fields box, select Duration from the drop-down list, and then click the Add button.

Microsoft Project adds the label and code for project duration to the legend.

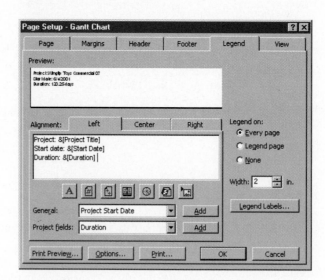

15   Click OK to close the Page Setup dialog box.

Microsoft Project applies the changes you specified to the legend. To get a closer look, zoom in on the legend.

16   In the Print Preview window, click the lower left corner of the page with the magnifying-glass pointer.

Microsoft Project zooms in to show the page at a legible resolution. Your screen should look similar to the following illustration.

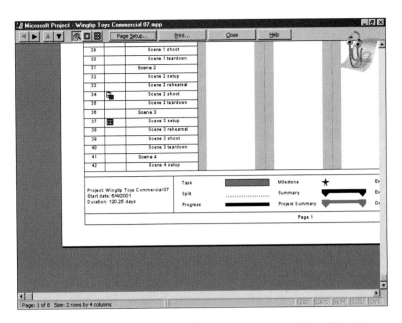

You can see the data you added to the legend, which will print on every page of the printed output.

17 On the Print Preview toolbar, click Close.

The Print Preview window closes, and the Gantt Chart view appears. Although you did not print, your changes to the header and the legend will be saved when you save the project file.

tip

You can print the project plan now if you wish, but previewing the project plan is adequate for the purposes of the lesson. When printing in Microsoft Project, you have additional options in the Print dialog box, which you can open by choosing the Print command on the File menu. For example, you can choose to print a specific date range of a timescaled view, such as the Gantt Chart, or you can print a specific page range.

Proj2000-3-11
Proj2000-3-6

Customizing and Printing Reports

Reports are predefined formats intended for printing Microsoft Project data. Unlike views, which you can either print or work with online, reports are designed only for printing or for viewing in the Print Preview window. You do not enter data directly into a report. Microsoft Project includes several predefined task, resource, and assignment reports you can edit to get the information you want.

In this exercise, you view a report in the Print Preview window, and then you edit its format to include additional information.

1 On the View menu, click Reports.

The Reports dialog box appears, showing the six broad categories of reports available in Microsoft Project.

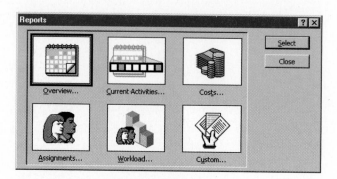

2   Click Custom, and then click the Select button.

The Custom Reports dialog box appears, listing all predefined reports in Microsoft Project and any custom reports that have been added.

3   In the Reports box, select Task, and then click the Preview button.

Microsoft Project displays the Task report in the Print Preview window. Your screen should look similar to the following illustration.

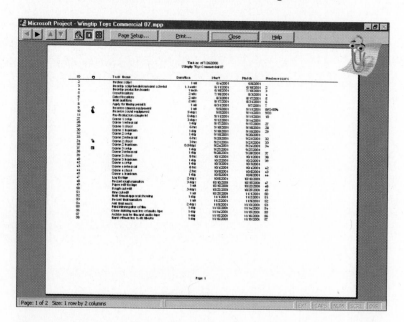

This report is a complete list of project tasks (except for summary tasks), similar to what you would see in the Entry table of the Gantt Chart view. You would like to see this data presented in a different way, so you will edit this report.

4   On the Print Preview toolbar, click the Close button.

The Print Preview window closes, and the Custom Reports dialog box reappears.

5   In the Reports box, ensure that Task is still selected, and then click the Copy button.

The Task Report dialog box appears.

6   In the Name box, select the displayed text, and then type **Custom Task Report**

7   In the Period box, select Months from the drop-down list.

8   In the Table box, select Summary from the drop-down list.

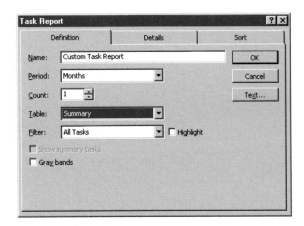

tip

The tables listed in the Task Report dialog box are the same as those you can apply to a view. In fact, the "Shotting Schedule Table" you created in Lesson 6 appears in the list here. When editing a report format, you can apply built-in or custom tables and filters, choose which additional details to include in the report, and apply a sort order to the information—all in the dialog box for the report you are editing.

9 Click OK to close the Task Report dialog box.

10 In the Custom Reports dialog box, make sure that Custom Task Report is selected in the Reports box, and then click the Preview button.

Microsoft Project applies the custom report settings you chose, and the report appears in the Print Preview window. Your screen should look similar to the following illustration.

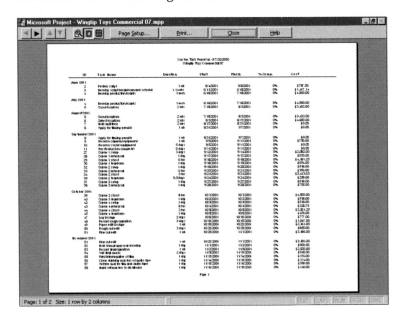

This custom report shows the fields displayed on the Summary Task table but divides the tasks by month.

11 On the Print Preview toolbar, click the Close button.

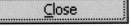

12 In the Custom Reports dialog box, click Close.

13 Click Close again to close the Reports dialog box. The Gantt Chart view reappears.

Lesson Wrap-Up

In this lesson, you learned how to set printing options for views, as well as how to preview and customize a report before printing.

If you are continuing on to other lessons:

● On the File menu, click Close to close the file. If you are prompted to save changes, click Yes, and then save without a baseline.

If you are not continuing on to other lessons:

1   On the File menu, click Close to close the file. If you are prompted to save changes, click No.

2   On the File menu, click Exit. Microsoft Project closes.

Lesson Glossary

group A way to reorder task or resource information in a table and to display summary values for each group. You can specify up to three nested levels of groups. (The term "group" is also used to refer to the Resource Group field, which is unrelated.)

report A format designed for printing. Microsoft Project includes several predefined reports, each focusing on specific aspects of your project data. You can also define your own reports.

stakeholders All people or organizations that might be affected by project activities (those who "have a stake" in its success). These also include those resources working on the project, as well as others (such as customers) external to the project work.

table A spreadsheet-like presentation of project data, organized in vertical columns and horizontal rows. Each column represents one of the many fields in Microsoft Project, and each row represents a single task or resource.

view The primary way you see data in Microsoft Project. The three categories of views are charts, sheets, and forms.

Quick Quiz

1   What is a quick way to determine how many sheets of paper a Gantt Chart view will require when printed?

2   What is a report, and how does it differ from a view?

Putting It All Together

If necessary, start Microsoft Project. Open the file Putting It All Together 7 in the Lesson 7 folder located in the MS Project Core Practice folder on your hard disk, and save it without a baseline as Music Video 7 in the same folder.

Exercise: On many projects, it is common for the work resources and others involved to have limited or no knowledge of traditional project management documents such as Gantt Charts. To properly communicate project details to others involved with the music video project, you will need to print the "Who Does What" report.

LESSON 8

Tracking Progress Against the Project Plan

After completing this lesson, you will be able to:

✔ *Save current values in the schedule as a baseline.*

✔ *Record actual work completed through a specific date.*

✔ *Record tasks as being a particular percent complete.*

✔ *Enter daily actual work values for tasks and assignments.*

✔ *Determine which tasks and resource assignments have cost more than originally planned.*

✔ *Reschedule the remaining work for a task that has been interrupted.*

Up to now, the lessons you have completed have focused on project **planning**—developing and communicating the details of a project before actual work begins. After work begins, so does the next phase of project management: tracking progress. **Tracking** means recording project details such as who did what work, when the work was done, and at what cost. These details are often called **actuals**.

Tracking actuals is essential to properly managing, as opposed to just planning, a project. The project manager must know how well the project team is performing and when to take corrective action. Properly tracking project performance and comparing it against the original plan lets you answer such questions as:

■ Are tasks starting and finishing as planned, and, if not, what will be the impact on the project's finish date?

■ Are resources spending more or less time than planned to complete tasks?

■ Are tasks costing more or less money than planned?

Microsoft Project supports several ways to track progress, depending on the level of detail or control required by you, your project **sponsor**, and other **stakeholders**. Tracking the fine details of a project requires more work from you and, possibly, from the resources working on the project. So before you begin tracking progress, you should determine the level of detail you need. The different levels of tracking described in this lesson include the following:

■ Record project work as scheduled. This works best if everything in the project occurs exactly as planned. Hey, it could happen!

■ Record each task's percentage of completion, either at precise values or at increments such as 25%, 50%, 75%, or 100%.

■ Track work by time period. This is the most detailed level of tracking. Here you record actual work values per day, week, or other interval.

You may find that you need to apply a combination of these approaches within a single project because different portions of a project may have different tracking needs. For example, you might want to track high-risk tasks more closely than low-risk ones. Each of these approaches to tracking progress is described in this lesson.

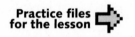
Practice files for the lesson

To complete the procedures in this lesson, you will begin with a file named Wingtip Toys Commercial 8. Open the Lesson 8 folder in the MS Project Core Practice folder located on your hard disk. Open the file 8A, and save it without a baseline as Wingtip Toys Commercial 8 in the Lesson 8 folder. Later in the lesson, you will open different versions of this file that have more actuals already entered for you.

Proj2000-2-10

Saving a Project Baseline

One of the most important activities of a project manager after developing a project plan is to record actuals and evaluate project performance. To judge project performance properly, you will need to compare it against your original plan. This original plan is called the baseline plan, or just the **baseline**. A baseline is a collection of important values in a project plan, such as the planned start dates, finish dates, and costs of the various tasks and assignments. When you save a baseline, Microsoft Project takes a "snapshot" of the existing values and saves it in the Microsoft Project file for future comparison.

> Timephased values are spread over time. For example, the value of a task's work field might be 40 hours, but its timephased values might be 8 hours per day spread over 5 days. You can view timephased values in the timescale grid on the right side of views such as those for Task Usage or Resource Usage. Timephased values are always organized in a grid with the timescale at the top of the grid.

The specific values saved in a baseline include the task, resource, and assignment **fields** and **timephased fields** listed in the following table.

Task	Resource	Assignment
Start field	Work and time-phased work fields	Start field
Finish field	Cost and time-phased cost fields	Finish field
Duration field		Work and timephased work fields
Work and time-phased work fields		Cost and timephased cost fields
Cost and time-phased cost fields		

You should save the baseline when:

■ You have developed the project plan as fully as possible. (However, this does not mean you cannot add tasks, resources, or assignments to the project after work has started. Usually this is unavoidable.)

■ You have not yet started entering actual values, such as for work completed.

The toy commercial project plan is now fully developed, and actual work is to begin on the project shortly. In this exercise, you save the baseline for the toy commercial project and then view various task, resource, and assignment baseline values.

1   On the Tools menu, point to Tracking and click Save Baseline.

The Save Baseline dialog box appears.

2   Click OK.

Microsoft Project saves the baseline, even though there's no indication in the Gantt Chart view that anything has changed. You will now see some of the changes caused by saving the baseline.

3   On the View menu, click More Views.

The More Views dialog box appears.

4   In the Views box, select Task Sheet and click Apply.

In the Task Sheet view, you have more room to see the fields in the table because it does not include the Gantt Chart. Now switch to a different table in the Task Sheet view.

5   On the View menu, point to Table: Entry, and click Work.

The Work table appears. This table includes both the Work and Baseline columns, shown side by side for easy comparison.

Your screen should look similar to the following illustration.

> If necessary, double-click the right edge of any column names that display pound signs (###) to see all of the field values.

	Task Name	Work	Baseline	Variance	Actual	Remaining	% W. Comp.
1	⊟ Pre-Production	1,100 hrs	1,100 hrs	0 hrs	0 hrs	1,100 hrs	0%
2	Review script	40 hrs	40 hrs	0 hrs	0 hrs	40 hrs	0%
3	Develop script breakdo	80 hrs	80 hrs	0 hrs	0 hrs	80 hrs	0%
4	Develop production boa	280 hrs	280 hrs	0 hrs	0 hrs	280 hrs	0%
5	Scout locations	160 hrs	160 hrs	0 hrs	0 hrs	160 hrs	0%
6	Select locations	240 hrs	240 hrs	0 hrs	0 hrs	240 hrs	0%
7	Hold auditions	40 hrs	40 hrs	0 hrs	0 hrs	40 hrs	0%
8	Apply for filming permit:	60 hrs	60 hrs	0 hrs	0 hrs	60 hrs	0%
9	Reserve camera equipr	40 hrs	40 hrs	0 hrs	0 hrs	40 hrs	0%
10	Reserve sound equipm	40 hrs	40 hrs	0 hrs	0 hrs	40 hrs	0%
11	Pre-Production complete	0 hrs	0 hrs	0 hrs	0 hrs	0 hrs	0%
12	⊞ Staff planning meetir	120 hrs	120 hrs	0 hrs	0 hrs	120 hrs	0%
25	⊟ Production	742 hrs	742 hrs	0 hrs	0 hrs	742 hrs	0%
26	⊞ Scene 1	284.5 hrs	284.5 hrs	0 hrs	0 hrs	284.5 hrs	0%
31	⊞ Scene 2	120.5 hrs	120.5 hrs	0 hrs	0 hrs	120.5 hrs	0%
36	⊞ Scene 3	250 hrs	250 hrs	0 hrs	0 hrs	250 hrs	0%
41	⊞ Scene 4	87 hrs	87 hrs	0 hrs	0 hrs	87 hrs	0%
46	Production complete!	0 hrs	0 hrs	0 hrs	0 hrs	0 hrs	0%
47	⊟ Post-Production	810 hrs	810 hrs	0 hrs	0 hrs	810 hrs	0%
48	Log footage	32 hrs	32 hrs	0 hrs	0 hrs	32 hrs	0%
49	Record rough narration	72 hrs	72 hrs	0 hrs	0 hrs	72 hrs	0%
50	Paper edit footage	160 hrs	160 hrs	0 hrs	0 hrs	160 hrs	0%
51	Rough cut edit	48 hrs	48 hrs	0 hrs	0 hrs	48 hrs	0%

At this point, because no actual work has occurred yet and no changes to the scheduled work have been made, the values in the Work and Baseline fields are identical. Once actual work has been recorded, the scheduled Work values might differ from the Baseline values, in which case you would see the differences displayed in the Variance column.

What you see in the table are task-level values, which are closely related to but not the same as resource-level or assignment-level values. For example, in the table you see the total Work and Baseline values of each task, but you cannot tell which resources will contribute work to each task.

Next you will view resource-level and assignment-level baseline values.

Resource Sheet

6   On the View bar, click Resource Sheet.

The Resource Sheet view appears.

7   On the View menu, point to Table: Entry, and click Work.

The Work table appears. Again you see the Work and Baseline fields, but this time for resources. Your screen should look similar to the following illustration.

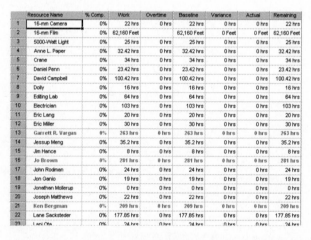

	Resource Name	% Comp.	Work	Overtime	Baseline	Variance	Actual	Remaining
1	16-mm Camera	0%	22 hrs	0 hrs	22 hrs	0 hrs	0 hrs	22 hrs
2	16-mm Film	0%	62,160 Feet		62,160 Feet	0 Feet	0 Feet	62,160 Feet
3	5000-Watt Light	0%	25 hrs	0 hrs	25 hrs	0 hrs	0 hrs	25 hrs
4	Anne L. Paper	0%	32.42 hrs	0 hrs	32.42 hrs	0 hrs	0 hrs	32.42 hrs
5	Crane	0%	34 hrs	0 hrs	34 hrs	0 hrs	0 hrs	34 hrs
6	Daniel Penn	0%	23.42 hrs	0 hrs	23.42 hrs	0 hrs	0 hrs	23.42 hrs
7	David Campbell	0%	100.42 hrs	0 hrs	100.42 hrs	0 hrs	0 hrs	100.42 hrs
8	Dolly	0%	16 hrs	0 hrs	16 hrs	0 hrs	0 hrs	16 hrs
9	Editing Lab	0%	64 hrs	0 hrs	64 hrs	0 hrs	0 hrs	64 hrs
10	Electrician	0%	103 hrs	0 hrs	103 hrs	0 hrs	0 hrs	103 hrs
11	Eric Lang	0%	20 hrs	0 hrs	20 hrs	0 hrs	0 hrs	20 hrs
12	Eric Miller	0%	30 hrs	0 hrs	30 hrs	0 hrs	0 hrs	30 hrs
13	Garrett R. Vargas	0%	263 hrs	0 hrs	263 hrs	0 hrs	0 hrs	263 hrs
14	Jessup Meng	0%	35.2 hrs	0 hrs	35.2 hrs	0 hrs	0 hrs	35.2 hrs
15	Jim Hance	0%	8 hrs	0 hrs	8 hrs	0 hrs	0 hrs	8 hrs
16	Jo Brown	0%	281 hrs	0 hrs	281 hrs	0 hrs	0 hrs	281 hrs
17	John Rodman	0%	24 hrs	0 hrs	24 hrs	0 hrs	0 hrs	24 hrs
18	Jon Ganio	0%	19 hrs	0 hrs	19 hrs	0 hrs	0 hrs	19 hrs
19	Jonathan Mollerup	0%	0 hrs	0 hrs	0 hrs	0 hrs	0 hrs	0 hrs
20	Joseph Matthews	0%	22 hrs	0 hrs	22 hrs	0 hrs	0 hrs	22 hrs
21	Ken Bergman	0%	209 hrs	0 hrs	209 hrs	0 hrs	0 hrs	209 hrs
22	Lane Sacksteder	0%	177.85 hrs	0 hrs	177.85 hrs	0 hrs	0 hrs	177.85 hrs
23	Lani Ota	0%	24 hrs	0 hrs	24 hrs	0 hrs	0 hrs	24 hrs

In the Work table, you see resource-level values. You can identify the total Work and Baseline values for each resource, but you cannot view the specific tasks to which each resource will contribute work. To conclude this exercise, you will view assignment-level baseline values.

Task Usage

8   On the View bar, click Task Usage.

The Task Usage view appears.

9   On the Format menu, point to Details, and click Baseline Work.

tip

You can also right-click anywhere in the timephased grid. In the submenu that appears, click Baseline Work.

Microsoft Project displays the *baseline* work timephased values below each scheduled *work* timephased value.

10   On the Standard toolbar, click the Go To Selected Task button.

Your screen should look similar to the following illustration.

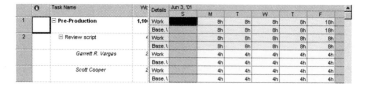

This time you see assignment-level values for Task 2, "Review script." As you might expect, because no actual work or changes to the schedule have been recorded, the schedule and baseline values are the same. These values are organized per task in the timescaled grid. On the left side of the view, you can see that resources are organized according to the task to which they are assigned.

Now that you have had a look at some task, resource, and assignment baseline fields and timephased values, it is time to enter some actuals!

Tracking a Project as Scheduled

The simplest approach to tracking progress is to report that the actual work is proceeding exactly as planned. For example, if the first month of a five-month project has elapsed and all of its tasks have started and finished as scheduled, you can quickly record this in the Update Project dialog box.

In the toy commercial project, some time has now passed since saving the baseline, and so far so good. In this exercise, you record project actuals by updating work to the current date.

1   On the View bar, click Gantt Chart.

The Gantt Chart view appears.

2   On the Tools menu, point to Tracking, and click Update Project.

The Update Project dialog box appears.

> The default date that appears here is the latter of either the current date or the status date, as recorded in the Project Information dialog box.

3   Make sure the Update Work As Complete Through option is selected. In the adjacent date list, type or select **June 19, 2001**, and click OK.

Microsoft Project records the actual work for the tasks that were scheduled to start before June 19. Then it displays that progress by drawing **progress bars** in the Gantt bars for those tasks. Your screen should look similar to the following illustration.

Check marks appear in the Indicators column for tasks that have been completed.

This progress bar indicates the portion of the task that has been completed.

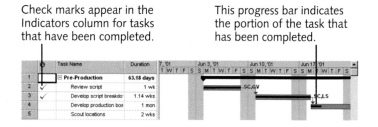

In the Gantt Chart view, the progress bar shows how much of each task has been completed. Because Tasks 2 and 3 have been completed, a check mark appears in the Indicators column for those tasks, and the progress bar extends through the full length of the task's Gantt bars. By June 19, only a portion of Task 4 has been completed, however, so the progress bar for that task extends only to June 19.

Some of the recurring staff planning meetings have also been completed as scheduled by June 19, so these progress bars appear in the summary Gantt bars before June 19.

Entering Percent Complete of Tasks

Proj2000-2-4

Once work has begun on a task, you can quickly record progress on it as a percentage. There are different ways to do this, depending on your needs:

- Record that a task is 25%, 50%, 75%, or 100% complete by clicking a button on the Tracking toolbar.

- Enter an exact percent complete, for example, in the Task Information dialog box, which you can open by selecting the Task Information command on the Project menu.

In either case, when you enter a percentage other than 0% complete, Microsoft Project changes the task's actual start date to match its scheduled start date. It then calculates actual duration, remaining duration, actual costs, and other values, based on the percentage you enter. For example, if you specify that a four-day task is 50% complete, Microsoft Project calculates that it has had two days of actual duration and has two days of remaining duration.

In this exercise, you record percentages of tasks complete. You begin by displaying the Tracking toolbar.

1   On the View menu, point to Toolbars and click Tracking.

The Tracking toolbar appears. This toolbar contains several buttons relating to tracking activities, but the buttons that interest us now are the 0% through 100% complete buttons.

2   In the Task Name column, select Task 4, "Develop production boards."

3   On the Standard toolbar, click the Go To Selected Task button.

4   On the Tracking toolbar, click the 100% Complete button.

Microsoft Project records the actual work for the task as scheduled, and then it extends a progress line through the length of the Gantt bar.

Your screen should look similar to the following illustration.

Remember that you can also right-click any toolbar. In the shortcut menu that appears, click Tracking.

You can use the percent complete buttons with an individual task or with a range of tasks selected.

Next, you will enter a percent complete value for a different task.

5   In the Task Name column, select the name of Task 5, "Scout Locations."

6   On the Standard toolbar, click the Go To Selected Task button.

7   On the Standard toolbar, click the Task Information button.

The Task Information dialog box appears.

8   Click the General tab.

9   In the Percent Complete box, type or select **35** and click OK.

Microsoft Project records the actual work for the task as scheduled, and then it draws a progress line through 35% of the Gantt bar.

So far you have recorded actual work that started and finished on schedule. While this may prove true for some tasks, often you need to record actuals per task or resource, or account for tasks that lasted longer or shorter than planned. This is the subject of the next section.

> The ToolTip that appears when you point to a progress line in a Gantt bar tells you the percent complete of a task.

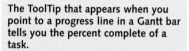

Proj2000-2-9

Tracking Work by Time Period

When you need to track actual work at the most detailed level possible, use the timescaled grid in the Task Usage or the Resource Usage view. In either, you can enter actual work values for individual assignments daily, weekly, or as frequently as you wish. For example, if a task has three resources assigned to it and you know that two resources worked on the task for eight hours one day and the third for six hours, you enter these as three separate values on a timescaled grid.

Entering timephased values requires more work on the part of the project manager and may require more work from resources to inform the project manager of their daily actuals. However, doing so gives you far more detail about task and resource status than the other methods of entering actuals described in this lesson. Entering timephased values might be the best approach to take if you have a group of tasks or entire projects that have the following qualities:

■   High-risk tasks.

■   Relatively short-duration tasks where a **variance** of even a single day could put the overall project at risk.

■   Tasks in which sponsors or other stakeholders have an especially strong interest.

■   Tasks that require hourly billing for labor.

Practice files for the lesson

Some time has passed since you completed the previous exercise. To continue with this lesson, you will use an updated version of Wingtip Toys Commercial 8. First close the open file in Microsoft Project. If prompted to save changes, click No. Next, open the Lesson 8 folder in the MS Project Core Practice folder located on your hard disk. Open the file 8B, and save it as Wingtip Toys Commercial 8 in the Lesson 8 folder. If prompted to overwrite the original file, click Yes.

At this point in the toy commercial project, the Pre-Production phase is complete. It took a few days longer than planned, mainly because of interruptions to work. Now the Production phase has begun, and the filming of scenes is under way. Because of the large number of resources involved, the high setup and teardown costs, and the limited availability of sites at which some scenes must be filmed, these tasks are the riskiest ones of the project. In this exercise, you enter daily actuals for Production tasks in the Task Usage view.

Task Usage

1 On the View bar, click Task Usage.

The Task Usage view appears. On the left is the Usage table, and on the right, the timescaled grid.

2 Click the minus sign next to Task 1, "Pre-Production," to collapse this phase of the project.

3 Select Task 25, "Production," and then on the Standard toolbar, click the Go To Selected Task button.

Microsoft Project scrolls the timescaled grid to display the first scheduled work values of the Production phase.

4 Click the plus sign next to Task 26, "Scene 1," to expand this summary task.

5 On the Format menu, point to Details and click Actual Work.

Microsoft Project displays the Actual Work timephased fields for each assignment. Your screen should look similar to the following illustration.

	ⓞ	Task Name	Work	Details	Sep 2, '01 S	M	T	W	T	F
1	✓	⊞ Pre-Production	1,002	Work		4h				
				Act. W		4h				
25		⊟ Production	742	Work		16h	32h	32h	44h	97h
				Act. W						
26		⊟ Scene 1	284.5	Work		16h	32h	32h	44h	97h
				Act. W						
27		⊟ Scene 1 setup	96	Work		16h	32h	32h	16h	
				Act. W						
		Jo Brown	24	Work		4h	8h	8h	4h	
				Act. W						
		Scott Fallon	24	Work		4h	8h	8h	4h	
				Act. W						
		Electrician	48	Work		8h	16h	16h	8h	
				Act. W						
28		⊟ Scene 1 rehearsal	56	Work					28h	28h
				Act. W						
		Scott Cooper	8	Work					4h	4h
				Act. W						
		Jessup Meng	4	Work					2h	2h
				Act. W						
		Paul Born	4	Work					2h	2h
				Act. W						
		David Campbell	8	Work					4h	4h

The first actual value to enter is for Task 27, "Scene 1 setup." This task was completed after several days of work, although you do not know (or for this task, care) what the individual's actual work values were.

6 In the timescale grid, select the Act. Work field for "Scene 1 setup" on Monday, September 3, 2001.

tip
If you point to the name of a day on the timescale, Microsoft Project will display the full date of that day in a ToolTip.

7 Type **14h** and press the Right Arrow key.

Your screen should look similar to the following illustration.

When entering values in the Actual Work field in the timescaled grid, you can see how Microsoft Project distributes the actual work among assigned resources, and rolls up the value to summary tasks.

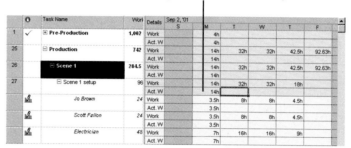

As soon as you enter this value, several things happen:

- The actual work value for Monday rolls up to the "Scene 1" summary task and then to the "Production" summary task.

- Because you entered the actual work value for the task and not for the individual resource assignments, Microsoft Project split up the actual work value among the assigned resources, in proportion to their scheduled work values.

8 In the Act. Work field for "Scene 1 setup" on Tuesday, September 4, 2001, type **35h** and press the Right Arrow key.

Again Microsoft Project rolls up the actual work value to the summary tasks and splits up the actual work value among the assigned resources. Your screen should look similar to the following illustration.

Entering an actual work value at the task level causes Microsoft Project to distribute the actual work among the assigned resources in the same proportion as their scheduled work.

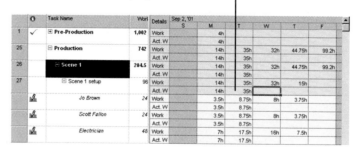

9 In the Act. Work field for "Scene 1 setup" on Wednesday, type **32h**. For Thursday, type **15h**. This completes the task.

For Task 28, "Scene 1 rehearsal," you have individual resources' actual work values for Thursday and Friday, September 6 and 7, 2001.

10 Enter the following actual work values in the timescale grid.

Resource Name	Thursday's Actual Work	Friday's Actual Work
Scott Cooper	2.5h	5.5h
Jessup Meng	2h	2h
Paul Born	1.5h	3h
David Campbell	5h	4.5h
Eric Miller	5h	4.5h
Sue Jackson	4h	5h
Ken Bergman	3h	5h
Daniel Penn	3h	5h

When you are finished, your screen should look similar to the following illustration.

Entering an actual work value at the resource level
causes Microsoft Project to add up the individual values
and record it as the actual work value for the task.

	O	Task Name	Work	Details	Sep 2, '01 S	M	T	W	T	F
28	✓	⊟ Scene 1 rehearsal	60.5	Work					26h	34.5h
				Act. W					26h	34.5h
	📝	Scott Cooper	8	Work					2.5h	5.5h
				Act. W					2.5h	5.5h
	📝	Jessup Meng	4	Work					2h	2h
				Act. W					2h	2h
	📝	Paul Born	4.5	Work					1.5h	3h
				Act. W					1.5h	3h
	📝	David Campbell	9.5	Work					5h	4.5h
				Act. W					5h	4.5h
	📝	Eric Miller	9.5	Work					5h	4.5h
				Act. W					5h	4.5h
	📝	Sue Jackson	9	Work					4h	5h
				Act. W					4h	5h
	📝	Ken Bergman	8	Work					3h	5h
				Act. W					3h	5h
	📝	Daniel Penn	8	Work					3h	5h
				Act. W					3h	5h

This time, the individual resources' actual work values were rolled up to the tasks' actual work values. Also, you may have noticed that as soon as you entered an actual work value for Thursday, Microsoft Project recalculated the scheduled work for Friday.

To finish this exercise, you can quickly record that the remaining tasks for Scene 1 were completed as scheduled.

11 In the Task Name column, hold down the Ctrl key and select Tasks 29 and 30. You may have to scroll vertically to select these tasks.

12 On the Tracking toolbar, click the 100% Complete button.

Microsoft Project records the actual work values for all the assignments of these tasks.

Proj2000-2-8

Identifying Tasks and Resources That Are over Budget

The schedule ("Did tasks start and finish on time?"), while critical to nearly all projects, is only one indicator of overall project health. For projects that include cost information, another critical indicator is cost variance: Are tasks running over or under budget? Task costs in Microsoft Project consist either of fixed costs applied directly to tasks or of resource costs derived from assignments, or both. Evaluating cost variance allows you to make incremental budget adjustments for individual tasks to avoid exceeding your project's overall budget.

Practice files for the lesson

Some time has passed since you completed the previous exercise. To conclude this lesson, you will use an updated version of Wingtip Toys Commercial 8. First close the open file in Microsoft Project. If prompted to save changes, click No. Next, open the Lesson 8 folder in the MS Project Core Practice folder located on your hard disk. Open the file 8C, and save it as Wingtip Toys Commercial 8 in the Lesson 8 folder. If prompted to overwrite the original file, click Yes.

In this exercise, you view cost variance first for tasks and then for resources. Although tasks and resources are directly related, it is informative to evaluate each individually.

1   On the View menu, click More Views.

The More Views dialog box appears.

2   In the Views list, select Task Sheet and click Apply.

Microsoft Project displays the Task Sheet view. Next, you will switch to the Cost table.

Collecting Actuals from Resources

The table you use in Step 10 of the previous section is similar to a time card. In fact, to enter assignment-level actual work values, you need some form of paper time card or its electronic equivalent. Several methods can be used to collect such data from resources, assuming you need to track actuals at this level of detail. Some collection methods include the following:

■   Collect actual values yourself. This method is feasible if you communicate with only a small group of resources on a frequent basis. It is also a good opportunity to talk directly to the resources about any surprises they may have encountered (either positive or negative) while performing the work.

■   Collect actuals through a formal status reporting system. This technique may work through the already existing hierarchy of your organization and serve additional purposes besides project status reporting.

■   Use Microsoft Project's e-mail–based collaboration features to collect assignment status data.

■   Use Microsoft Project Central. This companion product for Microsoft Project enables intranet-based team communication, tracking, and status reporting.

The best solution for collecting actuals will depend greatly on your organization's existing policies and practices, and on what information your organization needs.

You also can right-click on the upper left corner of the active table, and in the shortcut menu that appears, click Cost.

3   On the View menu, point to Table: Work, and click Cost.

The Cost table appears in the Task Sheet view. Your screen should look similar to the following illustration.

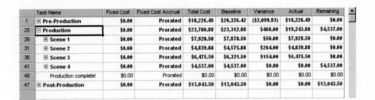

	Task Name	Fixed Cost	Fixed Cost Accrual	Total Cost	Baseline	Variance	Actual	Remaining
1	☐ Pre-Production	$0.00	Prorated	$18,226.49	$20,326.42	($2,099.93)	$18,226.49	$0.00
2	Review script	$0.00	Prorated	$787.50	$787.50	$0.00	$787.50	$0.00
3	Develop script breakdo	$0.00	Prorated	$1,417.14	$1,417.14	$0.00	$1,417.14	$0.00
4	Develop production bos	$0.00	Prorated	$4,960.00	$4,960.00	$0.00	$4,960.00	$0.00
5	Scout locations	$0.00	Prorated	$3,432.00	$3,432.00	$0.00	$3,432.00	$0.00
6	Select locations	$0.00	Prorated	$2,441.25	$4,650.00	($2,208.75)	$2,441.25	$0.00
7	Hold auditions	$0.00	Prorated	$716.00	$421.18	$294.82	$716.00	$0.00
8	Apply for filming permit:	$0.00	Prorated	$874.00	$1,060.00	($186.00)	$874.00	$0.00
9	Reserve camera equipr	$0.00	Prorated	$750.00	$750.00	$0.00	$750.00	$0.00
10	Reserve sound equipm	$0.00	Prorated	$700.00	$700.00	$0.00	$700.00	$0.00
11	Pre-Production complet	$0.00	Prorated	$0.00	$0.00	$0.00	$0.00	$0.00

In this table, you can see each task's baseline cost, scheduled cost (in the Total Cost column), actual cost, and variance. The variance is the difference between baseline cost and the scheduled cost. (Of course, costs are not scheduled in the same sense that work is scheduled. However, because costs other than fixed costs are derived directly from the scheduled work, you can think of the costs as being scheduled.)

Next, you will focus on summary level costs.

4   Click the Task Name column heading.

5   On the Formatting toolbar, click Hide Subtasks.

Microsoft Project displays only the top three summary tasks, which in this project correspond to the major phases of the project. Because we are currently working on tasks in the Production phase, we will direct our attention there.

6   Click the plus sign next to Task 25, "Production."

Microsoft Project expands the Production summary task to show the summary tasks for the individual scenes. Your screen should look similar to the following illustration.

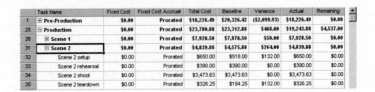

	Task Name	Fixed Cost	Fixed Cost Accrual	Total Cost	Baseline	Variance	Actual	Remaining
1	⊞ Pre-Production	$0.00	Prorated	$18,226.49	$20,326.42	($2,099.93)	$18,226.49	$0.00
25	⊟ Production	$0.00	Prorated	$23,780.88	$23,312.88	$468.00	$19,243.88	$4,537.00
26	⊞ Scene 1	$0.00	Prorated	$7,928.50	$7,878.50	$50.00	$7,928.50	$0.00
31	⊞ Scene 2	$0.00	Prorated	$4,839.88	$4,575.88	$264.00	$4,839.88	$0.00
36	⊞ Scene 3	$0.00	Prorated	$6,475.50	$6,321.50	$154.00	$6,475.50	$0.00
41	⊞ Scene 4	$0.00	Prorated	$4,537.00	$4,537.00	$0.00	$0.00	$4,537.00
46	Production complete!	$0.00	Prorated	$0.00	$0.00	$0.00	$0.00	$0.00
47	⊞ Post-Production	$0.00	Prorated	$13,043.50	$13,043.50	$0.00	$0.00	$13,043.50

Looking at the Variance column, you can see that Scene 1 had some variance, Scene 3 had more, and Scene 2 significantly more. Next you will focus on Scene 2 details.

7   Click the plus sign next to summary Task 31, "Scene 2."

Microsoft Project expands the Scene 1 summary task to show the individual tasks. Your screen should look similar to the following illustration.

	Task Name	Fixed Cost	Fixed Cost Accrual	Total Cost	Baseline	Variance	Actual	Remaining
1	⊞ Pre-Production	$0.00	Prorated	$18,226.49	$20,326.42	($2,099.93)	$18,226.49	$0.00
25	⊟ Production	$0.00	Prorated	$23,780.88	$23,312.88	$468.00	$19,243.88	$4,537.00
26	⊞ Scene 1	$0.00	Prorated	$7,928.50	$7,878.50	$50.00	$7,928.50	$0.00
31	⊟ Scene 2	$0.00	Prorated	$4,839.88	$4,575.88	$264.00	$4,839.88	$0.00
32	Scene 2 setup	$0.00	Prorated	$650.00	$518.00	$132.00	$650.00	$0.00
33	Scene 2 rehearsal	$0.00	Prorated	$390.00	$390.00	$0.00	$390.00	$0.00
34	Scene 2 shoot	$0.00	Prorated	$3,473.63	$3,473.63	$0.00	$3,473.63	$0.00
35	Scene 2 teardown	$0.00	Prorated	$326.25	$194.25	$132.00	$326.25	$0.00

Looking at the Variance column, you can see that the Scene 2 setup and teardown tasks account for all of the variance for the Scene 2 summary task. You would like to find out what is contributing to these variance amounts. Because cost values in the toy commercial project are almost entirely derived from the costs of resource assignments, you will next look at resource cost variance.

8   On the View bar, click Resource Sheet.

The Resource Sheet view appears.

9   On the View menu, point to Table: Work, and then click Cost.

The Cost table appears.

10   On the Project menu, point to Sort, and click Sort By.

The Sort dialog box appears.

Remember that you also can right-click the Select All button in the upper left corner of the active table to switch to a different table.

11   In the Sort By box, select Cost Variance, and click Descending.

12   Make sure the Permanently Renumber Resources box is cleared, and then click Sort.

Microsoft Project sorts the Cost table by cost variance per resource, from highest to lowest amount. Your screen should look similar to the following illustration.

	Resource Name	Cost	Baseline Cost	Variance	Actual Cost	Remaining
10	Electrician	$2,684.00	$2,266.00	$418.00	$2,376.00	$308.00
22	Lane Sacksteder	$2,833.18	$2,756.59	$76.59	$2,740.18	$93.00
7	David Campbell	$1,017.19	$941.36	$75.82	$379.69	$637.50
4	Anne L. Paper	$365.63	$303.86	$61.77	$328.13	$37.50
6	Daniel Penn	$281.25	$219.49	$61.76	$281.25	$0.00
14	Jessup Meng	$385.00	$352.06	$32.94	$235.00	$150.00
12	Eric Miller	$295.31	$281.25	$14.06	$295.31	$0.00
32	Paul Born	$362.50	$350.00	$12.50	$362.50	$0.00
41	Sue Jackson	$140.63	$131.25	$9.38	$140.63	$0.00
1	16-mm Camera	$137.50	$137.50	$0.00	$125.00	$12.50
2	16-mm Film	$12,432.00	$12,432.00	$0.00	$9,432.00	$3,000.00
3	5000-Watt Light	$62.50	$62.50	$0.00	$57.50	$5.00
5	Crane	$0.00	$0.00	$0.00	$0.00	$0.00
8	Dolly	$0.00	$0.00	$0.00	$0.00	$0.00
9	Editing Lab	$1,675.00	$1,675.00	$0.00	$0.00	$1,675.00
15	Jim Hance	$75.00	$75.00	$0.00	$75.00	$0.00
17	John Rodman	$528.00	$528.00	$0.00	$0.00	$528.00
18	Jon Ganio	$266.00	$266.00	$0.00	$238.00	$28.00
19	Jonathan Mollerup	$0.00	$0.00	$0.00	$0.00	$0.00
20	Joseph Matthews	$206.25	$206.25	$0.00	$150.00	$56.25
21	Ken Bergman	$3,918.75	$3,918.75	$0.00	$3,731.25	$187.50

With the data arranged this way, you can see that several resources have cost variances, but the Electrician has the highest variances of all. This is a specific cost issue to investigate and mitigate for the remaining tasks in the project.

Proj2000-2-6

Troubleshooting Time and Schedule Problems

Schedule variance is almost certainly going to appear in any complex project. Maintaining control over the schedule requires that the project manager (a) know when variance has occurred and to what extent, and (b) take timely corrective action to stay on track.

It is common for some corrective actions you take to cause new problems later in the schedule. If you have set up your project plan properly, you should be able to see such ripple effects. For example, in this exercise you delay work on a task because of an unanticipated event, but in doing so you further delay successor tasks and, ultimately, the project's finish date.

Gantt
Chart

25%

In this exercise, you report some work for the next scheduled task and troubleshoot a delay in work caused by a problem at the studio.

1   On the View bar, click Gantt Chart.

The Gantt Chart view appears.

2   Click the plus sign next to Task 41, "Scene 4," to expand this summary task.

3   In the Task Name column, select Task 42, "Scene 4 setup."

4   On the Standard toolbar, click the Go To Selected Task button.

5   On the Tracking toolbar, click the 25% Complete button.

Microsoft Project records progress for the task and displays a progress bar in a portion of the task Gantt bar. Your screen should look similar to the following illustration.

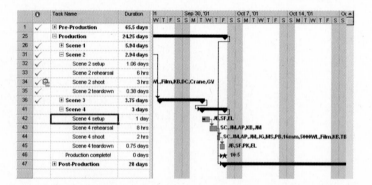

You have learned that on the evening of Tuesday, October 2, a water pipe burst in the studio where Scene 4 was to be shot. None of the project equipment was damaged, but the cleanup will delay work until the following Monday, October 8. This effectively stops work on the production tasks for a few days. Next you will reschedule uncompleted work so the project can start again on Monday.

6   On the Tools menu, point to Tracking and then click Update Project.

The Update Project dialog box appears.

7   Click Reschedule Uncompleted Work To Start After, and in the Date box select Sunday, October 7, 2001.

8   Click OK to close the Update Project dialog box.

Microsoft Project splits Task 42 so that the uncompleted portion of the task is delayed until Monday. Your screen should look similar to the following illustration.

Progress bars indicate the portion of the task that has been completed.

	0	Task Name	Duration	1	Sep 30, 01	Oct 7, '01	Oct 14, '01	Ox
1	✓	⊞ Pre-Production	65.5 days					
25		⊟ Production	27.25 days					
26	✓	⊞ Scene 1	5.94 days					
31	✓	⊟ Scene 2	2.94 days					
32	✓	Scene 2 setup	1.06 days					
33	✓	Scene 2 rehearsal	6 hrs					
34	✓	Scene 2 shoot	3 hrs	W..Film,KB,DC,Crane,GV				
35	✓	Scene 2 teardown	0.38 days					
36	✓	⊞ Scene 3	3.75 days					
41		⊟ Scene 4	6 days					
42		Scene 4 setup	1 day		JB,SF,EL			
43		Scene 4 rehearsal	8 hrs		SC,JM,AP,KB,JM			
44		Scene 4 shoot	2 hrs		SC,JM,AP,JM,JG,MS,PB,16mm,500			
45		Scene 4 teardown	0.75 days		JB,SF,PK,EL			
46		Production complete!	0 days		★ 10-10			
47		⊞ Post-Production	28 days					

The task's remaining work has been rescheduled to start after
October 7. The dotted line represents the resulting split in the task.

As you can see, although the duration of Task 42 remains at one day, its finish date and subsequent start dates for successor tasks have been pushed out. So although we have addressed a specific problem, we have created other problems in the remainder of the project. This is what makes project management an iterative process—time, cost, or scope changes in one part of the schedule affect the schedule elsewhere.

Lesson Wrap-Up

In this lesson, you learned how to save a baseline, enter actuals, and troubleshoot some tracking problems.

If you are continuing on to other lessons:

●   On the File menu, click Close to close the file. If you are prompted to save changes, click Yes, and then save without a baseline.

If you are not continuing on to other lessons:

1   On the File menu, click Close to close the file. If you are prompted to save changes, click No.

2   On the File menu, click Exit.

Microsoft Project closes.

Lesson Glossary

actuals Project work completed and recorded in a Microsoft Project file. Prior to recording actuals, the project plan contains scheduled or planned information. Comparing planned project information with actuals helps the project manager better control project execution.

baseline The original project plan, saved for later comparison. The baseline includes the planned start and finish dates of tasks and assignments, and their planned costs. Microsoft Project files can have no more than one baseline.

field The lowest-level information about a task, resource, or assignment; also called a cell.

planning The initial major phase of project management work. Planning includes all the work in developing a project schedule, up to the point where the tracking of actual work begins.

progress bar A graphical representation on a bar in the Gantt Chart view that shows how much of a task has been completed.

sponsor An individual or organization that provides financial support and champions the project team within the larger organization.

stakeholders All people or organizations that might be affected by project activities (those who "have a stake" in its success). These also include those resources working on the project, as well as others (such as customers) external to the project work.

timephased field Task, resource, or assignment values that are distributed over time. The values of timephased fields appear in the timescale grid on the right side of views such as the Task Usage or Resource Usage views.

tracking The second major phase of project management work. Tracking includes all the collecting, entering, and analyzing of actual project performance values such as work on tasks and actual durations.

variance Any deviation from the schedule or budget established by the baseline plan.

Quick Quiz

1   When is the best time to save a baseline for a project plan?

2   Two weeks after work has started on a project, all tasks have been completed as scheduled. What is one quick way to record this in Microsoft Project?

3   What are two different ways of recording a percentage of a task complete?

4   What are timephased values, and when should you work with them?

5   If you are tracking costs in a project plan, what are two sources of task costs?

6   Why is identifying variance so important to properly managing a project?

Putting It All Together

If necessary, start Microsoft Project. Open the file Putting It All Together 8 in the Lesson 8 folder located in the MS Project Core Practice folder on your hard disk, and save it without a baseline as Music Video 8 in the same folder.

Exercise 1: The Pre-Production phase of the project has been completed, and the Production phase has started. Things have gotten off to a bad start, however, as some of the tasks took longer than planned to complete. Record the following information in the project plan:

- Task 2, "Develop script breakdown," started as scheduled and was completed with an 11-day duration.
- Task 3, "Develop choreography," was completed as scheduled.
- Task 5, "Rehearsal," started as currently scheduled, was interrupted Wednesday and Thursday, June 13 and 14, and is 100% complete.

Exercise 2: The schedule variance is acceptable to the project sponsors, but you are concerned about the high cost variance. You have developed a prioritized list of scope cuts to reduce the final cost. Complete the following activities:

- Reduce the duration of Task 8, "Fine cut edit," to 3 days.
- Reduce the duration of Task 9, "Add final music," to 4 days.
- Check the project's current total cost, and verify that it is less than $35,000.

LESSON 9

Managing a Project Team Online

After completing this lesson, you will be able to:

✔ *Configure Microsoft Project to share project data with Microsoft Project Central.*

✔ *Log in to Project Central, and view a TeamAssign message.*

✔ *Report actual hours worked on a task in Project Central, and submit them to the project manager.*

✔ *Create a new task in Project Central, and report it to the project manager.*

✔ *Accept resource submissions in Project Central, and update Microsoft Project from Project Central.*

✔ *Delegate a task from one resource to another in Project Central.*

This lesson introduces you to the Microsoft Project companion product, Microsoft Project Central. Project Central offers a broad range of collaborative planning and tracking capabilities for all **stakeholders** in a project.

Practice files for the lesson

To complete the procedures in this lesson, you will need to use a file named Parnell Aerospace Promo 9. Open the Lesson 9 folder in the MS Project Core Practice folder located on your hard disk. Open the file 9A, and save it as Parnell Aerospace Promo 9 in the Lesson 9 folder.

Proj2000-3-9
Proj2000-2-3

Enabling Workgroup Features in Microsoft Project

For many project managers, communicating project details is one of the most important, time-consuming tasks they perform. While many project teams enjoy computer-based collaboration systems such as local area networks (LANs), e-mail, and access to intranets and the World Wide Web, critical project information might seem "locked up" in Microsoft Project files under the control of the project manager.

You can use workgroup features to bring information into Microsoft Project, as well as publish information out of Microsoft Project. Taking full advantage of the workgroup features of Microsoft Project allows the entire project team and other interested stakeholders to communicate online when performing essential tasks such as building project plans, **tracking** progress, reporting status, and viewing a wide range of project details.

Microsoft Project supports two primary means of collaborating online. These are e-mail based communication and Microsoft Project Central. The specific workgroup solution that is best for you depends on your project team's network infrastructure, technical resources, and information needs. E-mail–based communication has relatively few setup requirements, but it is limited in what it can do for the project manager and **resources**. Project Central requires more setup effort but offers far more capabilities and benefits.

important

E-mail–based communication requires a MAPI-compliant e-mail client such as Microsoft Outlook, Microsoft Outlook Express, or Lotus Notes. This approach is limited to reporting task assignments, status, and updates. E-mail–based communication is generally not addressed in this courseware.

Both the e-mail–based and the Project Central workgroup solutions require you to configure Microsoft Project to use them. In this exercise, you enable Microsoft Project Central communication within Microsoft Project.

1 On the Tools menu, click Options.

2 Click the General tab.

3 In the User Name box, type **Clair Hector**

For the purposes of completing this exercise, you will play the role of Clair Hector, project manager of the Parnell Aerospace Promo project. Later you will also play the roles of two different resources working on this project.

4 Click the Workgroup tab.

5 In the Default Workgroup Messages For box, Select Web.

The option you choose here will be the default workgroup communication method used for the resources who have assignments in the open Microsoft Project file.

6 In the Microsoft Project Central Server box, type the URL that has been set up for this lesson. Your instructor should be able to provide this for you.

tip

Your instructor has previously determined the URL for this lesson. The URL might take the form *http://<machine name>/projectcentral*

7 Under Identification For Microsoft Project Central Server, click Microsoft Project User Name 'Clair Hector'

8 Click the Create Account button.

Your screen should look similar to the following illustration, though the specific URL in the Microsoft Project Central Server box will differ.

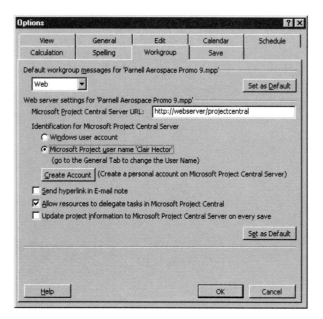

9   Click OK to close the Options dialog box.

10 On the Tools menu, point to Workgroup and then click TeamAssign.

11 In the Workgroup Mail dialog box, make sure that All Tasks is selected, and then click OK.

12 If the Planning Wizard appears with a message about Windows user accounts, click OK.

Microsoft Project creates a TeamAssign message with the names of the assigned resources, a boilerplate message, and the list of tasks to which the resources are assigned. Your screen should look similar to the following illustration, though the specific Date shown might differ:

Not all resources with assignments in this project appear on the To line of the TeamAssign message. Some resources that do not represent individual people, such as the Madrona Community Orchestra, have previously had their Workgroup field's value set to None. This causes Microsoft Project to exclude them from workgroup communications.

The TeamAssign message is sent to resources who have assignments in the project.

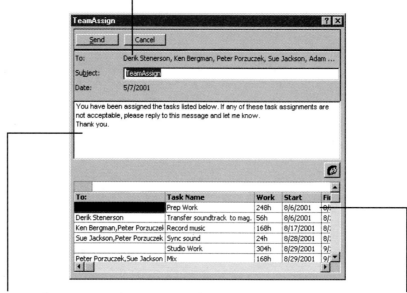

Microsoft Project provides boilerplate text for the TeamAssign message, but you can edit it as needed.

The assignment list includes details about all summary and subtasks, but the individual resources will see only their assignments when they open the TeamAssign message.

13 Click Send.

Microsoft Project sends the TeamAssign message to Project Central. In the next exercises, you will log into Project Central both as a resource and as a project manager.

Introducing Microsoft Project Central

Project Central is a companion product that works with Microsoft Project to allow a broad range of workgroup collaboration. Project Central consists of two major components:

■ The server component, which runs on Microsoft Windows NT Server 4.0 or on Windows 2000 Server running Microsoft Internet Information Services (IIS). IIS controls a database of Project Central information, which, upon the project manager's approval, is synchronized with Microsoft Project files.

■ The client component, which runs in Microsoft Internet Explorer (or the Browser Module included with Project Central) on the desktops of the project manager, the resources, and other stakeholders you have enabled to connect to the Project Central server component and to specific projects.

Together, Microsoft Project and the Project Central client and server components provide a complete intranet-based communication and collaboration tool for project teams and stakeholders. Project Central facilitates the following important activities:

■ Project managers can publish project and portfolio (multiproject) status and other details in one central location.

■ Resources can view personal task assignments and Gantt charts, report actual work and other status, and, if enabled by the project manager, create new tasks and delegate tasks to other resources.

■ Other stakeholders such as **resource managers,** upper management, and customers can view whatever project details they are most interested in and the project manager has made available.

■ All involved in a project or portfolio of projects use one standard tool to communicate project information.

important

Microsoft Project includes one license for Project Central Server. Before you can use Project Central in a workgroup, you must secure the appropriate client access licenses. For more information, see the end-user license agreement in Microsoft Project's online Help or click the License Agreement link on the Project Central logon screen.

In this exercise, you log on to Project Central as a resource, view a TeamAssign message, and then delete it.

1   Open Internet Explorer or the Browser Module.

2   In the Address box, type the URL of your Project Central server.

The Microsoft Project Central login screen appears. Your screen should
look similar to the following illustration, though your specific URL in
the Address box will differ.

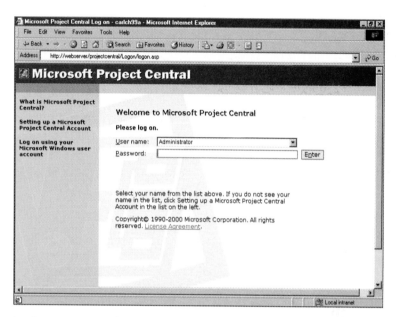

3   In the User Name box, select Derik Stenerson and then click Enter.

4   If a message box about your password being blank appears, click No.

Project Central logs you in as Derik Stenerson, a resource assigned to
the first task in the project, and displays the Home screen. Your screen
should look similar to the following illustration:

The Actions pane gives you quick access to most of the commands on
the Project Central menu bar. If you prefer, you can hide it by clicking
this collapse button.

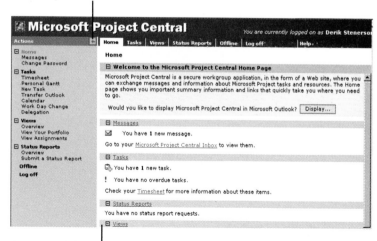

A resource's Home screen contains links to and details about the four
main resource areas of Project Central: Messages, Tasks, Status Reports,
and Views.

Next, you will view the TeamAssign message sent from Microsoft Project to Project Central. You will view the specific message sent to Derik Stenerson, though a similar message was sent to other resources as well.

5 On the Home menu, click Messages.

The Messages: Inbox appears. Your screen should look similar to the following illustration.

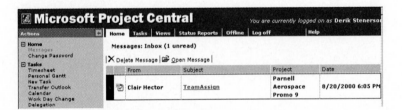

Derik has just one message: the TeamAssign message from Clair Hector, the project manager of the Parnell Aerospace project.

6 In the Subject column, click TeamAssign to display the message.

The TeamAssign message appears. Your screen should look similar to the following illustration:

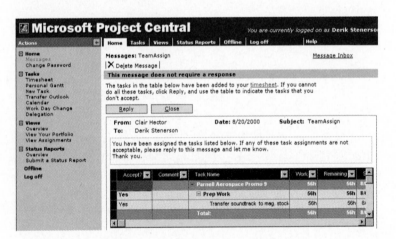

By default TeamAssign assignments are accepted (you can see this in the Accept? column of the message), so no response is needed for this message.

7 In the table in the message, use the scroll bars to see the full content of the table.

The table includes the project name, the summary task name, and the specific subtask to which Derik has been assigned. (In this case, he has been assigned to just one task in the Parnell Aerospace Project.)

The details of this task look fine, so no reply is needed; you will close and delete the message.

8 Click Close.

The Messages: area appears.

9 Click Delete Message.

For the next two exercises, you will play the role of the resource Derik Stenerson and perform other activities in Project Central.

Recording Actuals via Project Central

For resources and other stakeholders involved in a project, Project Central can serve as their single tool both for getting information from the project and for submitting information (such as **actuals**) to the project (each subject to the project manager's approval). Project Central can replace or augment a variety of communication methods such as e-mail, paper-based status reports, timesheets, and the ubiquitous (but often out-of-date) Gantt chart on the bulletin board.

In this exercise, while playing the role of the resource Derik Stenerson you will enter actual values for the task to which you are assigned.

1 On the Tasks menu click Timesheet.

The Timesheet screen appears.

2 Under Show on the View Options tab, make sure that Scheduled Work and Summary Tasks are checked.

Your screen should look similar to the following illustration:

The specific dates displayed in the timesheet table are determined by the settings here. If the date range you want is not visible, enter it here.

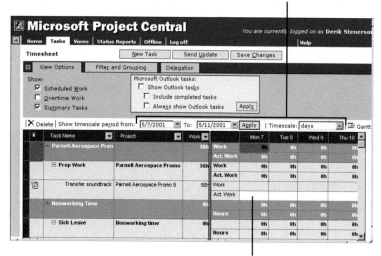

In the Timesheet table, you enter actual work in this row. Notice that the row you can edit is formatted white, while the other rows in this table are gray.

Here in the Timesheet table you see the tasks to which Derik is assigned (only one in this case).

3 On the left side of the Timesheet table, scroll horizontally to display the Start and Finish columns.

Derik's task is scheduled to begin on August 6, 2001, and finish by August 23. Today is August 10, and Derik is ready to enter the first week's actuals for this task. Next you will display this date range on the right side of the Timesheet table.

4 In the Show Timescale Period From box at the top of the Timescale table, type or select **8/6/2001**

5 In the To box next to this, type or select **8/10/2001** and then click Apply.

Project Central displays the week's scheduled work for this task. This is in the row labeled "Work" for the subtask. It also appears "rolled up" for the summary task and project rows, but you can edit only actual work values for the subtask. You will do this next.

6   Select the task's Actual Work cell for Monday, August 6.

tip
Editable cells in the Timesheet table are white; noneditable cells are various shades of gray.

7   Type **4h**, and then press the Right Arrow key.

8   Enter the following values for the remaining days:

For This Day	Enter This Actual Value
Tuesday	0h
Wednesday	6h
Thursday	4h
Friday	2h

Now you are ready to submit the week's actuals to the project manager.

9   At the top of the Timesheet screen, click Send Update.

Project Central displays a message stating that it has sent the information to Clair, the project manager.

10   Click OK to close the message box.

Creating Tasks in Project Central

Allowing resources to create new tasks in Project Central can serve two important purposes:

■   Allow resources to document tasks that were not in the initial project plan. This can help account for more of the work required to execute the project, which might be significantly more work than was initially identified in the Microsoft Project plan.

■   Record lower-level work that might be associated with a summary task in the Microsoft Project file. This ability allows for **bottom-up planning**, where the project manager can plan at the summary level and leave it to the resources to fill in the required subtasks. Even after project work has begun, capturing such details might be useful for billing purposes or developing metrics for future projects, or simply as an accurate historical record of work performed.

Regardless of why resources create tasks in Project Central, these tasks can later be updated to the Microsoft Project file at the project manager's discretion.

In this exercise, you create a new task in Project Central. Still playing the role of the resource Derik, you have determined that a new task should be added to the project.

1 On the Tasks menu, click New Task.

The New Task screen appears.

2 In the Project box, select Parnell Aerospace Promo 9.

3 Under What Outline Level Do You Want To Create The New Task In, make sure that Create The New Task At The Top Outline Level is selected.

4 Under Task Information, enter the following values:

5 In the Name box, type **Music practice session**

6 In the Comment box, type **Requested by musicians**

7 In the Start Date box, type or select **8/16/2001**

8 In the Work box, type **4h**

9 At the top of the New Task screen, click Create Task.

Project Central switches to the Timesheet view. In it, you can see the task you created.

10 At the top of the Timesheet page, click Send Update.

Project Central reports that one new task has been sent to the Project Central database.

11 Click OK to close the message box.

To conclude this exercise, you will log off as Derik.

12 On the Project Central menu bar, click Log Off.

The Project Central login screen appears.

> Hover the mouse pointer over the plus sign next to the new task name "Music practice session." The ToolTip that appears explains that the task has been created by you (Derik) but not yet sent to Clair, the project manager.

> Notice the new indicator next to the new task name "Music practice session." Hover the mouse pointer over the indicator. The ToolTip that appears explains that the task has been sent to Clair but not yet updated in the project.

Managing Resource Submissions in Project Central

Project Central is designed so that the Project Manager must approve all resource submissions such as actual work or new tasks before it updates Microsoft Project. You can either do this manually or set up rules to approve submissions from some or all resources.

In this exercise, you log into Project Central as a project manager and manage the two submissions from the resource Derik.

1 In the User Name box, select Clair Hector, and then click Enter. If the Change Password dialog box appears, click No.

The Home screen appears.

2 On the Home menu, click Messages.

3 In the Subject column of the Messages table, click the Task Update message from Derik.

Project Central displays the Task Update message. Here you can see the actual values Derik reported on his task. Your screen should look similar to the following illustration:

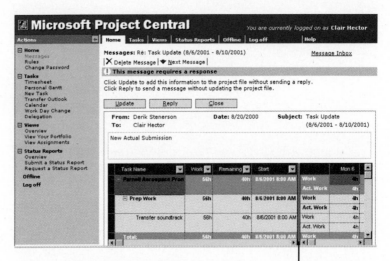

The TaskUpdate table is divided into two separate regions, each with its own scroll bars. You might also need to adjust the scroll bars of the browser to see more of the table. You can drag this divider bar to see more of either region.

These actuals look fine, so you will update the Microsoft Project file with them.

4   Click Update.

Microsoft Project appears, and if you look quickly you can see the progress bar and a split appear in the Gantt bar of Task 2. Next, a message box appears in Project Central.

5   Click Yes to delete the message from Clair's Project Central inbox.

Next, you will approve the new task submitted by Derik.

6   In the Subject column of the Messages table, click the New Tasks message from Derik.

The details of the new task appear.

7   Click Update.

Microsoft Project appears and displays the new task, and then Project Central reappears.

8   Project Central reports that Microsoft Project was successfully updated. Click Yes to delete the new task message from Clair's Project Central inbox.

9   On the Project Central menu bar, click Log Off.

To conclude this exercise, you will switch back to Microsoft Project and view the updated actuals for Task 2 and the new task you approved.

10   On the Windows Task Bar, click the Microsoft Project icon.

Microsoft Project appears. In it you can see the new actuals for Task 2 and the new task. Your screen should look similar to the following illustration:

The actuals reported by the resource in Project Central appear here. These actuals have the same effects on the scheduling of tasks as if they'd been entered via a usage view in Microsoft Project.

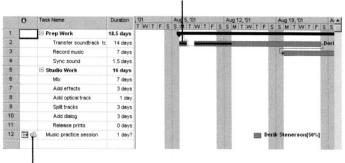

The comment the resource typed in Project Central appears as a task note. Resource-created tasks have hard constraints applied to them in Microsoft Project, and the project manager might wish to remove the constraint and link the new task to other tasks in the project.

If you wanted, you could link the new task to the proper predecessor task, move it to the proper phase, or change resource assignments. Any of these activities might cause Microsoft Project to alert you to send a TeamUpdate message in Project Central to the affected resources.

To conclude this exercise, you will switch back to Project Central.

11   On the Windows Task Bar, click the Internet Explorer icon.

The Project Central login screen appears.

Proj2000-2-1

Delegating Tasks in Project Central

If the Microsoft Project user or the Project Central administrator has enabled task delegation for the active project, any resource can delegate, or reassign, a task in Project Central. When a resource delegates a task, he or she must specify the following:

■   To whom the task is to be delegated.

■   To whom the actuals should be sent—to them or directly to the project manager.

■   Whether the delegated task and its subsequent actuals should appear on their own timesheet.

> In Microsoft Project, you enable task delegation on the Workgroup tab of the Options dialog box (Tools menu). It is enabled by default.

The project manager must approve task delegations before updating the Microsoft Project file.

In this exercise, you delegate a task to another resource. This time you will play the role of the resource Stephanie Hooper.

1   In the User Name box, select Stephanie Hooper, and then click Enter.

2   If a message box about your password being blank appears, click No.

3   On the Tasks menu, click Delegation.

The Timesheet screen appears.

In Project Central, you can point to explanatory text that is formatted green on a light gray background to see a pop-up definition.

4 In the Task Name column, select Split Tracks. This is the task you want to delegate to another resource.

5 Click Delegate Tasks.

The Delegate Tasks Step 1 Of 2 screen appears. Your screen should look similar to the following illustration:

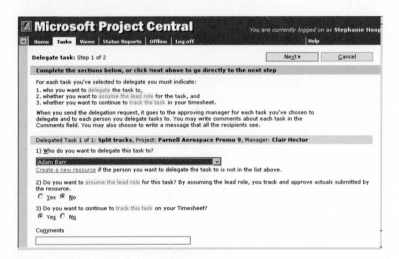

6 In the Who Do You Want To Delegate This Task To? box, click the Down Arrow and then select Ty Loren Carlson.

7 Under Do You Want to Assume The Lead Role For This Task? make sure that No is selected.

8 Under Do You Want To Continue To Track This Task On Your Timesheet? Click No.

9 At the top of the Delegate Tasks screen, click Next.

The Delegate Tasks Step 2 Of 2 screen appears. This screen includes the details of the task delegation for your review.

10 At the top of the Delegate tasks screen, click Send.

Project Central reports that the task delegation has been submitted to the project manager, Clair Hector.

11 Click OK to close the message box.

12 On the Project Central menu bar, click Log Off.

The Project Central login screen appears.

To complete the task delegation, the project manager would next need to approve it in Project Central.

Lesson Wrap-Up

In this lesson, you learned how to work with Project Central both as a resource and as a project manager.

If you are continuing on to other lessons:

1 Close the browser.

2 Switch to Microsoft Project.

3 On the File menu, click Close to close the file. If you are prompted to save changes, click Yes.

If you are not continuing on to other lessons:

1   Close the browser.

2   Switch to Microsoft Project.

3   On the File menu, click Close to close the file. If you are prompted to save changes, click No.

4   On the File menu, click Exit.

Microsoft Project closes.

Lesson Glossary

actuals Project work completed and recorded in a Microsoft Project file. Prior to recording actuals, the project plan contains scheduled or planned information. Comparing planned versus actual project information helps the project manager better control project execution.

bottom-up planning Developing a project plan by starting with the lowest-level tasks before organizing them into broad phases.

resource manager Someone who oversees resource usage in project activities specifically to manage the time and costs of resources. A resource manager might also have project management skills and responsibilities, depending on the organization's structure.

resources People, equipment, and material (and the associated costs of each) needed to complete the work on a project.

stakeholders All people or organizations that might be affected by project activities (those who "have a stake" in its success). These also include those resources working on the project, as well as others (such as customers) external to the project work.

tracking The second major phase of project managment work. Tracking includes all the collecting, entering, and analyzing of actual project performance values such as work on tasks and actual durations.

Quick Quiz

1   What are the two primary means by which Microsoft Project supports online collaboration between members of a project workgroup?

2   What are the two major components of Project Central, and what are they for?

3   You are a resource who needs to enter actuals for your assignments in the Timesheet screen in Project Central. In the Timesheet table, what color are the rows in which you can enter actuals?

4   What is one reason why a resource might want to create a new task in Project Central?

5   When can a resource submit actuals on a task in Project Central that are added to the Microsoft Project file without the project manager's approval?

6   How can a Project Central administrator prevent resources from delegating tasks to each other?

Putting It All Together

If necessary, start Microsoft Project. Open the file that you worked with earlier in this lesson, Parnell Aerospace Promo 9 in the Lesson 9 folder located in the MS Project Core Practice folder on your hard disk. Next, start Internet Explorer or the Browser Module, and connect to the Project Central login screen.

Exercise 1: Log into Project Central as the resource Derik Stenerson. Switch to the Timesheet screen, and record that the work on task "Transfer soundtrack to mag. stock" was completed as scheduled for the time period between 8/13/2001 and 8/17/2001. Next, submit the week's actuals to the project manager and log out of Project Central.

Exercise 2: Log into Project Central as the project manager Clair Hector. Approve the task delegation request that was submitted by Stephanie Hooper earlier in the lesson.

Exercise 3: While still logged on to Project Central as Clair Hector, review the actuals submitted by Derik and then update the Microsoft Project file. To conclude this exercise, log off of Project Central.

LESSON 10

Working with Multiple Projects

After completing this lesson, you will be able to:

✔ *Insert one project file into another to create a consolidated file.*

✔ *Link a task in one project to a task in another project.*

Most project managers must juggle more than one project at a time. These projects might have dependency relationships between them or with other projects beyond the project manager's control.

Microsoft Project has several features to make it easier to work with multiple project files. In this lesson, you consolidate projects and create cross-project links, or **dependencies**.

Practice files for the lesson

To complete the procedures in this lesson, you start with two files. One is named Short Film Project 10, and the other is named Parnell Aerospace Promo 10. Close any open project files (including blank files), and open the Lesson 10 folder in the MS Project Core Practice folder on your hard disk. Open file 10A, and save it without a baseline as Short Film Project 10 in the Lesson 10 folder. Open the file 10B, and save it without a baseline as Parnell Aerospace Promo 10 in the Lesson 10 folder.

Proj2000-6-1
Proj2000-6-2
Proj2000-6-4

Working with Consolidated Projects

Complex projects often involve several people working on tasks at different times, in different locations, and frequently for different supervisors.

A good way to pull together far-flung project information is to use a **consolidated project**. This is a Microsoft Project file that contains other Microsoft Project files, called **inserted projects**. The inserted projects do not reside within the consolidated project, but they are linked to it in such a way that they can be viewed and edited from the consolidated project. If the inserted project is edited outside the consolidated project, the updated information appears in the consolidated project the next time it is opened.

Using consolidated projects allows you to do such things as

Consolidated projects are also known as master projects, and inserted projects are also known as subprojects. In this lesson, we use the terms consolidated and inserted projects.

■ See all tasks from your organization's projects in a single view.

■ "Roll up" project information to higher levels of management. For example, one team's project might be an inserted project for the department's consolidated project, which in turn may be an inserted project for the organization's consolidated project.

■   Divide your project data to match the nature of your project—
for example, by phase, component, or location.

Consolidated projects use the Microsoft Project outlining features. An inserted project appears as a summary task in the consolidated project, except its summary Gantt bar is gray and an inserted project icon appears in
the Indicators column. When you save a consolidated project, any changes
you have made to inserted projects are saved in the source files as well.

In this exercise, you insert a project into a new project.

1   Close all open project files, including any blank files.

2   On the Standard toolbar, click the New button.

The Project Information dialog box appears.

3   In the Start Date box, type **8/6/01** and then click OK.

4   On the File menu, click Save As.

5   Save the file as Consolidated Projects 10 in the Lesson 10 folder.

Next you insert two projects into this new project.

6   On the Insert menu, click Project.

The Insert Project dialog box appears.

7   In the Lesson 10 folder, click Parnell Aerospace Promo 10. Hold down
the CTRL key, click Short Film Project 10, and then click Insert.

Microsoft Project inserts the two projects into the consolidated project
as collapsed summary tasks. Your screen should look similar to the following illustration.

**If you point to the Inserted Project
icon in the Indicators column,
Microsoft Project displays the full
path to the inserted project file.**

Inserted projects initially appear as collapsed summary tasks in
the consolidated project file. Note the Inserted Project icon in the
Indicators column, and the gray task bars.

8   Select the names of Tasks 1 and 2.

9   On the Formatting toolbar, click the Show button, and then click All
Subtasks.

Microsoft Project expands the inserted projects' tasks.

10   On the View menu, click Zoom. In the Zoom dialog box, click Entire
Project, and then click OK.

Microsoft Project adjusts the timescale in the Gantt Chart so that the
complete durations of the two projects are visible. Your screen should
look similar to the following illustration.

If necessary, double-click the right edge of the Duration column heading to widen it enough to see all content in the column.

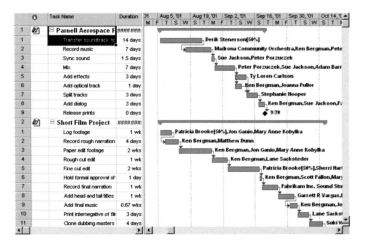

Now any change made directly to the inserted projects will be visible in the consolidated project file. Likewise, changes made to the inserted projects in the consolidated file will be visible in the inserted project file if it is opened individually.

To conclude this exercise, you will add a task to the consolidated project file.

11   In the Entry table, click the name of the second inserted project file, "Short Film Project."

important

This task's ID is 2, but it is not the only Task 2 in the consolidated project file. Microsoft Project preserves the Task IDs from each inserted project file.

12   On the Insert menu, click New Task.

Microsoft Project inserts a new row in the Entry table.

13   In the Task Name column for the new task, type **Plan cast party**

The new task is added to the Parnell Aerospace Promo inserted project.

14   Select the names of Tasks 9 and 10 in the Parnell Aerospace Promo inserted project, and on the Standard toolbar click the Link Tasks button.

Microsoft Project links the two tasks.

15   Close the Consolidated Projects 10 file. When prompted to save the consolidated and inserted projects, save without a baseline.

Here are a few more things to keep in mind when working with consolidated project files:

■   To remove an inserted project from a consolidated project, select the inserted project's summary task. On the Edit menu, click Delete Task.

■   Rather than manually create a consolidated project file and insert projects into it, you can quickly consolidate all open project files. On the Window menu, click New Window. Select the names of the open project files you want to consolidate, and then click OK.

■   If you frequently work on multiple projects that you don't want to consolidate, you can save them as a workspace. The workspace file consists of the names of the open project files, and it allows you to open several files with one action. On the File menu, click Save Workspace.

■   You can add tasks directly to a consolidated project file, independent of any inserted project files. You do this just as you would in a stand-alone project file; just make sure that the point at which you insert the new task is not within an inserted project's task list.

■   To save baseline values of tasks that reside directly within the consolidated project file, select the tasks, on the Tools menu point to Tracking, and then click Save Baseline. Tasks from inserted projects are not affected.

■   By default, Microsoft Project calculates all tasks from inserted projects and any tasks entered directly in the consolidated project as if they were all tasks in a single project file, and identifies a single critical path. However, you can display each inserted project's critical path within the consolidated project. To display this, clear the Inserted Projects Are Calculated Like Summary Tasks box on the Calculation tab of the Options dialog box (available from the Tools menu).

Proj2000-6-3

Creating Dependencies Between Projects

Other than the International Space Station, most projects do not exist in a vacuum. Tasks or phases in one project might depend on tasks in other projects. You can show such dependencies by linking tasks between projects.

Some of the reasons that you might need to create dependencies between projects include the following:

■   The completion of one task in a project might enable the start of a task in another project. For example, another project manager might need to complete an environmental impact statement before you can start to construct a building. Even if these two tasks are managed in separate project files (perhaps because separate departments of a development company are completing them), one project has a logical dependency on the other.

■   A person or a piece of equipment might be assigned to a task in one project, and you need to delay the start of a task in another project until that resource completes the first task. The two tasks might have nothing in common other than that the same resource is required for both.

Task relationships between project files look similar to links between tasks within a project file, except that external predecessor and successor tasks have gray task names and Gantt bars. Such tasks are sometimes referred to as **ghost tasks** because they are not linked to tasks within the project file, only to tasks in other project files.

In this exercise, you link tasks in two project files, and you see the results in the two project files, as well as in a consolidated project file.

1   Open the Lesson 10 folder in the MS Project Core Practice folder on your hard disk, click Parnell Aerospace Promo 10, and then click Open.

2   In the Entry table, click the name of Task 8, "Add dialog."

3   On the Standard toolbar, click the Go To Selected Task button.

To the right of the task's Gantt bar, you can see that one of the re-sources assigned to this task is named Fabrikam Inc. Sound Studio. You want to use this sound studio for work on the short film project after this task is completed. Next you will link Task 8 to a task in the Short Film Project 10 project file.

4   Open the Lesson 10 folder in the MS Project Core Practice folder, se-lect Short Film Project 10, and then click Open.

5   Select the name of Task 7, "Record final narration."

6   On the Standard toolbar, click the Task Information button.

The Task Information dialog box appears. In it, you will enter the file-name and Task ID of the predecessor task in this format:
File Name\Task ID

7   Click the Predecessors tab.

8   In the ID column, click the next empty cell below Task 6, and type **Parnell Aerospace Promo 10\8** (Make sure you are in the ID column when you perform this step.)

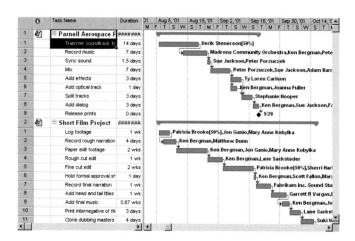

9   Press the Enter key, and then click OK to close the Task Information dialog box.

Microsoft Project inserts the ghost task named "Add dialog" to the project.

10   On the Standard toolbar, click the Go To Selected Task button.

If you point to the ghost task's Gantt bar, Microsoft Project displays a ToolTip that contains details about the ghost task, including the full path to the external project file where the external predecessor task (the ghost task) resides.

The ghost task appears in the project to which it is linked with a gray task name.

The ghost task's Gantt bar is gray.

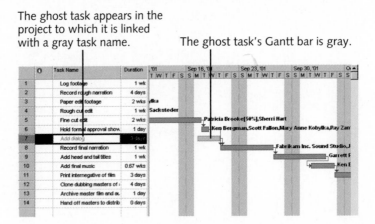

Because the ghost task finishes on 9/20 and the tasks are linked with a finish-to-start relationship, the start date of Task 8, "Record final narration," moves out to 9/20. All subsequent successor tasks are also rescheduled. Next you'll look at the ghost task in the Parnell project.

11 On the Window menu, click Parnell Aerospace Promo 10.

Here you can see that ghost Task 9, "Record final narration," is a successor to Task 8, "Add dialog." Because Task 8 is a successor task with no other links to this project, it has no effect on other tasks here.

The link between these two project files will remain until you break it. Deleting a task in the source file or the ghost task in the destination file deletes the corresponding task or ghost task in the other file.

To conclude this exercise, you will display the link between these two projects in the consolidated project file.

12 Open the Lesson 10 folder in the MS Project Core Practice folder, select Consolidated Projects 10, and then click Open.

You can see the link line between the task "Add dialog" in the first inserted project and the task "Record final narration" in the second inserted project. Your screen should look similar to the following illustration.

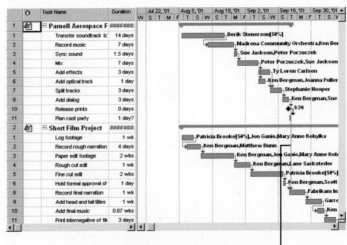

In the consolidated project file, the cross-project link appears as a normal task link.

Because you are looking at a consolidated project file, the cross-project link does not appear as a ghost task.

Here are a few more things to keep in mind when working with cross-project links:

■ When viewing a consolidated project, you can quickly create cross-project links by clicking the Link Tasks button on the Standard toolbar. Dragging the mouse between two task bars will do the same thing.

■ Each time you open a linked project file, Microsoft Project will prompt you to update the cross-project links. You can suppress this prompt if you would rather not be reminded, or you can tell Microsoft Project to automatically accept updated data from the linked project file. On the Tools menu, click Options, and then click the View tab. Under Cross-Project Linking Options For <File Name>, select the options you want.

Lesson Wrap-Up

In this lesson, you learned how to consolidate project files and create task relationships, or links, between projects.

If you are continuing on to other lessons:

● On the File menu, click Close to close the file. If you are prompted to save changes, click Yes, and then save without a baseline. Repeat for the other open files.

If you are not continuing on to other lessons:

1   On the File menu, click Close to close the file. If you are prompted to save changes, click No.
2   On the File menu, click Exit.
3   Repeat for the other open files.
    Microsoft Project closes.

Lesson Glossary

consolidated project A Microsoft Project file that contains one or more inserted project files. The inserted projects are linked to the consolidated project so that any changes to the inserted projects are reflected in the consolidated file, and vice versa. A consolidated project file is also known as a master project file.

dependency A link between a predecessor task and a successor task. A dependency controls the start or finish of one task relative to the start or finish of the other task. The most common dependency is finish-to-start, in which the finish date of the predecessor task determines the start date of the successor task.

ghost task A task that represents a link from one Microsoft Project file to another. Ghost tasks appear as gray bars.

inserted project A Microsoft Project file that is inserted into another Microsoft Project file, called a consolidated file. An inserted project is also known as a subproject.

Quick Quiz

1   What is one way to roll up details from several projects into one summary project?

2   You are coordinating the work of five project teams, each working on a different component of a complex machine. What is one advantage of creating a consolidated project that contains the five component subprojects?

3   What are two reasons why you might want to create a link, or dependency, between tasks in two different projects?

4   What spooky term are external predecessor or successor tasks given?

Putting It All Together

If necessary, start Microsoft Project. Open the file Putting It All Together 10A in the Lesson 10 folder located in the MS Project Core Practice folder on your hard disk, and save it without a baseline as Jane Clayton Interview 10 in the same folder. Then close the Jane Clayton Interview 10 file.

Next, open the file Putting It All Together 10B in the Lesson 10 folder located in the MS Project Core Practice folder on your hard disk, and save it without a baseline as Documentary Project 10 in the same folder.

Exercise 1: The tasks represented in the Jane Clayton Interview 10 project are one major production activity in a larger project, Documentary Project 10. Make the Jane Clayton Interview 10 project a subproject of the Documentary Project 10 file, inserted below the Production task. Make the Production task a summary task.

Exercise 2: Currently the three top-level summary tasks in the Documentary Project 10 file have finish-to-start relationships. Change these relationships so that the post-production task "Log footage" begins as soon as the production task "Interview" is completed.

LESSON 11

Customizing Microsoft Project

After completing this lesson, you will be able to:

✔ *Set default folder options and AutoSave frequency.*

✔ *Copy a customized view from one Microsoft Project file to another via the Organizer.*

✔ *Reset a customized table to the default settings via the Organizer.*

Practice files for the lesson

To complete the procedures in this lesson, you will use multiple files. First, open the Lesson 11 folder in the MS Project Core Practice folder located on your hard disk. Open the file 11A, and save it as Wingtip Toys Commercial 11 in the Lesson 11 folder. Next, open the file 11B, and save it as Short Film Project 11 in the same folder.

Proj2000-1-2

Customizing the Microsoft Project Environment

As with other Microsoft Office family applications, you have several choices about how to work with Microsoft Project. In fact, some of the preferences you set automatically apply in the other Microsoft Office family applications and vice versa. Some of the customization settings you have include:

> One setting that applies across all Office applications is the specific Office Assistant character you choose.

- Specify the folder you wish to open by default in the Open and Save As dialog boxes by selecting the Options command on the File menu. This is a good idea if you tend to keep most or all of your Microsoft Project files in one location.

- Set up Microsoft Project to save the active file or all open files automatically at the time interval you specify.

In this exercise, you will set default folder options, turn on the AutoSave feature, and specify the frequency with which you will be prompted to save your work.

1 On the Window menu, click Wingtip Toys Commercial 11.

The Wingtip Toys Commercial project becomes the active file in Microsoft Project.

2 On the Tools menu, click Options.

The Options dialog box appears.

3   Click the Save tab.

4   Under the File Locations label, select Projects and then click Modify.

   The Modify Location dialog box appears.

5   In the Folder Name box, type the path supplied by your instructor and click OK.

   Next, you will tell Microsoft Project to save files automatically at a preset time interval.

6   Under the Auto Save label, select the Save Every box.

7   Make sure that 10 appears in the Minutes box. Your screen should look similar to the following illustration.

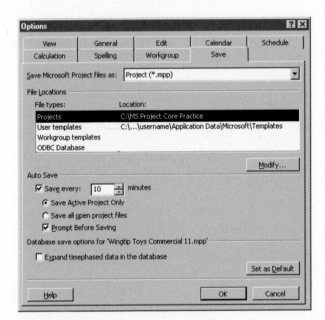

8   Click OK to close the Options dialog box.

   To conclude this exercise, you will see the effects of the file location setting you made.

9   On the File menu, click Save As.

   The Save As dialog box appears. Notice that the suggested location in the dialog box matches the location you specified in the Options dialog box.

10   Click Cancel.

tip

Many personal preference settings reside in the Options dialog box, which opens when you click the Options command on the Tools menu. To view Help about the items on each tab of this dialog box, click the Help button. To view Help about individual items in the dialog box, click the question mark button in the upper right corner of the dialog box, and then click the item you want to know more about.

Proj2000-3-5
Proj2000-5-1

Working with the Organizer

The **Organizer** is the feature you use to share or reset customized elements among Microsoft Project files. The complete list of elements you can copy between files with the Organizer is indicated by the names of the tabs in the Organizer dialog box, which you will see shortly.

One feature of Microsoft Project that you can work with via the Organizer is the **global template**. This is a Microsoft Project template named Global.mpt. The global template provides the default **views, tables,** and other elements in Microsoft Project. The list of elements provided by the global template includes the following:

- Calendars
- Filters
- Forms
- Groups
- Import/export maps
- Menu bars
- Reports
- Tables
- Toolbars
- VBA modules (macros)
- Views

Initially, the specific definitions of all views, tables, and similar elements are contained in the global template. For example, the fact that the default Usage table contains one set of fields and not others is determined by the global template. The very first time you display a view, table, or similar element in a Microsoft Project file, it is copied from the global template to that file. Thereafter, the element resides in the Microsoft Project file. Any customization of that element in the Microsoft Project file (for example, changing the fields displayed on a table) applies to only the one Microsoft Project file, and does not affect the global template.

In this exercise, you will first copy the custom view named Shooting Schedule from one file to another. Then, you will replace a customized Usage table with the Microsoft Project default Usage table by copying it from the Global.mpt file.

1 On the Tools menu, click Organizer.

The Organizer dialog box appears. Your screen should look similar to the following illustration.

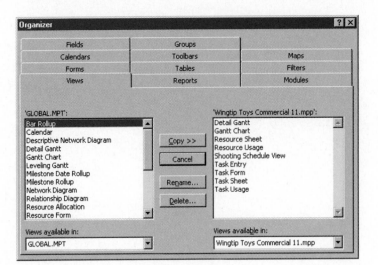

2   Click several of the tabs in the dialog box.

As you can see, every tab of the Organizer dialog box has a similar structure: elements such as views and tables from two different files appear on the left and right sides of the dialog box, respectively.

Notice that the two arrow symbols (>>) in the Copy button switch direction (<<) when you select an element on the right side of the dialog box.

By default, the elements from the Global.mpt file appear on the left side of the dialog box, and the corresponding elements from the active project file appear on the right. Selecting an element on the left side of the dialog box and then clicking the Copy button will copy that element to the file listed on the right. Conversely, selecting an element on the right side of the dialog box and then clicking the Copy button will copy that element to the file listed on the left.

3   Click the Views tab.

4   In the Views Available In list on the left side of the dialog box, click Short Film Project 11.mpp.

The names of the views in the Short Film Project 11 file appear on the left. As you can see, the Short Film Project 11 file does not have the Shooting Schedule View.

5   In the list of views on the right side of the dialog box, click Shooting Schedule View.

This is a custom view you worked with in previous lessons. You would like to copy this view to another project file.

Your screen should look similar to the following illustration.

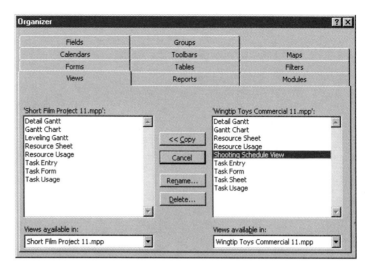

You can also copy in the other direction to overwrite default elements such as views and tables in the Global.mpt file. Be careful though; once you do this, the customized elements are used by all new Microsoft Project files.

6   Click << Copy.

Microsoft Project copies the Shooting Schedule View from the Wingtip Toys Commercial 11 file to the Short Film Project 11 file.

7   Click Close to close the Organizer.

Next, you will replace the customized Usage table in the Wingtip Toys Commercial 11 file with the default "factory settings" Usage table from the Global.mpt file.

8   On the View menu, click Task Usage.

The Task Usage view appears. Your screen should look similar to the following illustration.

	ⓘ	Task Name	Actual Cost	Finish
1	✓	⊟ **Pre-Production**	**$18,145.24**	**9/11/2001**
2	✓	⊟ Review script	$787.50	6/8/2001
		Garrett R. Vargas	$400.00	6/8/2001
		Scott Cooper	$387.50	6/8/2001

The default Usage table contains fields such as Work, Duration, Start, and Finish.

As you can see, this table does not include the default fields you would expect to see in the Task Usage view. Rather than rebuilding this Usage table to display the default fields, you will just copy it from the Global.mpt file. But first, you must switch to another table as you cannot copy or replace the currently displayed table.

9   On the View menu, point to Table: Usage and then click Entry.

10   On the Tools menu, click Organizer.

The Organizer dialog box appears. Note that it is not "sticky;" it does not display the same tab and two filenames that you had last seen in the dialog box, but instead displays the Global.mpt file items on the left, and the active projects on the right.

11 Click the Tables tab.

12 In the Global.mpt table list on the left side of the dialog box, click Usage.

13 Click Copy >>.

14 Microsoft Project alerts you that you are about to replace the Usage table in the Wingtip Toys Commercial 11 file. Click Yes.

15 Click Close to close the Organizer dialog box.

To conclude this exercise, you will switch to the newly copied Usage table.

16 On the View menu, point to Table: Entry and then click Usage.

The Usage table appears.

17 Drag the divider bar to the right to see all of the fields in the Usage table.

This updated version of the table includes the default fields that shipped with Microsoft Project. Your screen should look similar to the following illustration.

This custom view definition includes a custom table and filter, so copying just the view by itself is not very useful. You use the Organizer in a similar way to copy these or other elements between files.

	ⓘ	Task Name	Work	Duration	Start	Finish
1	✓	⊟ **Pre-Production**	**960 hrs**	**72 days**	**6/4/2001**	**9/11/2001**
2	✓	⊟ Review script	40 hrs	1 wk	6/4/2001	6/8/2001
		Garrett R. Vargas	20 hrs		6/4/2001	6/8/2001
		Scott Cooper	20 hrs		6/4/2001	6/8/2001

Using the Organizer in this manner is a handy way to quickly "reset" any view, table, or other item listed as a tab in the Organizer dialog box to the original settings stored in the Global.mpt file.

Lesson Wrap-Up

In this lesson, you learned how to change default save options and work with the Organizer and Global template.

If you are continuing on to other lessons:

● On the File menu, click Close to close the file. If you are prompted to save changes, click Yes. Repeat for the other open file.

If you are not continuing on to other lessons:

1 On the File menu, click Close to close the file. If you are prompted to save changes, click No.

2 Repeat for the other open files.

3 On the File menu, click Exit.

Microsoft Project closes.

Lesson Glossary

global template A Microsoft Project template named Global.mpt that contains the default views, tables, filters, and other items that Microsoft Project uses. You can copy these items from the global template via the Organizer to restore items that had been customized in other Microsoft Project files.

Organizer A dialog box with which you can copy views, tables, filters, and other items between the Global.mpt template and other Microsoft Project files, or between two different Microsoft Project files.

table A spreadsheet-like presentation of project data, organized in vertical columns and horizontal rows. Each column represents one of the many fields in Microsoft Project, and each row represents a single task or resource.

view The primary way you see data in Microsoft Project. The three categories of views are charts, sheets, and forms.

Quick Quiz

1   What is one setting that applies not only in Microsoft Project but all Microsoft Office applications, regardless of the specific application in which you make the setting?

2   The Organizer allows you to do basically one thing. What is it?

3   What is the filename of the Microsoft Project template that supplies the default views, tables, and all other similar elements to all Microsoft Project files?

Putting It All Together

If necessary, start Microsoft Project. Open the file Putting It All Together 11 in the Lesson 11 folder that is located in the MS Project Core Practice folder on your hard disk, and save it as Music Video 11 in the same folder.

Exercise 1: If you completed the steps in this lesson, the AutoSave feature should be turned on. Turn off AutoSave.

Exercise 2: The Resource sheet's Entry table in Music Video 11 has been customized. Restore the Entry table in Music Video 11 to the default settings by copying it from the global template, and then view the restored Entry table.

LESSON 12

Using Microsoft Project with Other Programs

After completing this lesson, you will be able to:

✔ *Take a "snapshot" of a Gantt Chart view.*

✔ *Publish Microsoft Project information in HTML format.*

✔ *Copy and paste data to and from Microsoft Project.*

✔ *Open a file produced in another program in Microsoft Project using import/export maps.*

In this lesson, you focus on various ways of getting data into and out of Microsoft Project. This includes using the Web publishing features of Microsoft Project and other means of importing and exporting data between Microsoft Project and other applications.

Practice files for the lesson

To complete the procedures in this lesson, open the Lesson 12 folder in the MS Project Core Practice folder located on your hard disk. Open the file 12A, and save it as Wingtip Toys Commercial 12 in the same folder.

Proj2000-3-4

Copying Project Information as a GIF Image

When communicating project details to resources, managers, and other **stakeholders**, chances are you will need to copy information out of Microsoft Project and into other programs and formats. Microsoft Project supports the standard copy and paste functionality of most Microsoft Windows programs, and it has an additional feature, called **Copy Picture**, for taking snapshots of a view. You can take these snapshots by choosing the Copy Picture command on the Edit menu or clicking the Copy Picture button on the Standard toolbar.

With Copy Picture, you have different options when taking snapshots of the active view:

■ Copy the entire **view** visible on the screen or selected rows of a **table** in a view.

■ Copy a range of time that you specify or show on the screen.

In some views, such as the Task Form or Relationship Diagram view, this feature is unavailable.

Either way, you can choose to copy onto the Windows Clipboard an image that is optimized for pasting into another program for onscreen viewing (Microsoft PowerPoint, for example) or for printing (Microsoft Word, for example). You can also save the snapshot to a Graphics Interchange Format (GIF) file in a location you specify. Once you save the image to a

GIF file, you can use it in any of the many programs that support the GIF format.

In this exercise, you change what appears in the Gantt Chart view, and then you use Copy Picture to save a snapshot of this view as a GIF file. To begin, you filter the Gantt Chart to show only summary tasks.

1   On the Project menu, point to Filtered For: All Tasks, and then click Summary Tasks.

Microsoft Project filters the Gantt Chart to show only summary tasks. Next you will zoom the **timescale** to see the entire project.

2   On the View menu, click Zoom.

The Zoom dialog box appears.

3   Click Entire Project, and then click OK.

Microsoft Project adjusts the timescale in the Gantt Chart to display the entire project's duration in the window. Your screen should look similar to the following illustration.

4   On the Standard toolbar, click the Copy Picture button.

The Copy Picture dialog box appears.

5   Under Render Image, click To GIF Image File.

Microsoft Project suggests that you save the file in the same location as the practice file and with the same name, except with a .gif extension.

6   Click OK to close the Copy Picture dialog box.

The GIF image is saved.

To conclude this exercise, you will view the GIF image you just saved.

7   On the View menu, point to Toolbars, and then click Web.

The Web toolbar appears.

8   On the Web toolbar, click Go, and then click Open.

The Open Internet Address dialog box appears.

9   Click Browse.

The Browse dialog box appears.

10   In the Files Of Type box, select GIF Files from the drop-down list.

11   Locate the GIF image named Wingtip Toys Commercial 12 in your Lesson 12 folder.

12   Select the GIF image, and then click Open.

13 In the Open Internet Address dialog box, click OK.

Microsoft Project opens the GIF image. If you have Microsoft Internet Explorer as your default program for viewing GIF files, your screen should look similar to the following illustration.

The Gantt Chart view snapshot is saved as a GIF format image, which you can view in a browser or graphics editing program.

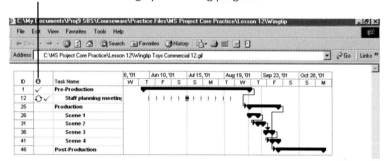

As noted above, what you see is a graphic image of the Gantt Chart view. The GIF image displays the view you displayed in Microsoft Project almost exactly as you had it set up.

14 Close the program you used to view the GIF file, and then return to Microsoft Project.

Creating GIF images of views in Microsoft Project is useful on its own. However, you can also save Microsoft Project data as HTML content for publishing to the Web or to an intranet site. This is the subject of the next section.

Proj2000-3-4

Saving Project Information as a Web Page

Another way to publish Microsoft Project information is to save it as a Web page. Unlike the Copy Picture feature, which produces a GIF image, saving as a Web page is better suited for publishing text. Microsoft Project uses **export maps** that specify the exact data to export and how to structure it. Export maps organize Microsoft Project data into HTML tables; the predefined maps resemble some of the predefined tables and reports in Microsoft Project. You can use export maps as they are or customize them to export only the Microsoft Project data you want.

In this exercise, you save Microsoft Project data as a Web page using an export map, and then you view the results in your browser.

1 On the File menu, click Save As Web Page.

The Save As dialog box appears. Microsoft Project suggests that you save the information as a Web page in the same location from which you opened the practice file. If you see a different location in the Save In box, navigate to the Lesson 12 folder on your hard disk.

2 Click Save.

The Export Mapping dialog box appears.

3 Under the Import/Export Map label, select Export To HTML Using Standard Template, and then click Save.

Microsoft Project saves the data to HTML format. This particular export map produces three tables that contain task, resource, and assignment information from the Wingtip Toys Commercial Project. All three tables will appear on the single Web page that you saved. Next you will view the Web page.

4 On the Web toolbar, click Go, and then click Open.

The Open Internet Address dialog box appears.

5 Click Browse.

The Browse dialog box appears.

6 In the Files Of Type box, select Web Pages from the drop-down list.

7 Locate the Web page named Wingtip Toys Commercial 12 in the Lesson 12 folder on your hard disk.

8 Select the Web page, and then click Open.

9 In the Open Internet Address dialog box, click OK.

Microsoft Project opens the Web page in your browser. If you have Internet Explorer, your screen should look similar to the following illustration.

This is the result of saving Microsoft Project data as a Web page using the Standard HTML template.

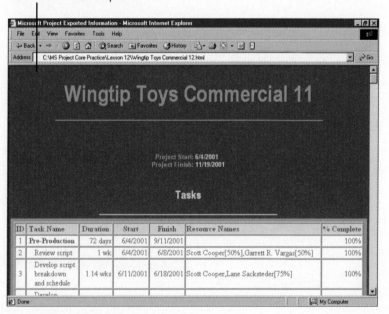

10 Scroll through the Web page to view the Tasks, Resources, and Assignments tables, which contain some of the same information as the Microsoft Project file.

11 Close your browser, and return to Microsoft Project.

Saving information as a Web page allows you to publish large volumes of project information in HTML format.

You can do a few things to fine-tune the Web pages you publish out of Microsoft Project.

The data you can export when saving to a Web page is not tied to the specific view you happen to be in at the time you save.

■ You can edit the export map. In the Export Mapping dialog box, click Edit. The Define Import/Export Map dialog box will appear, providing you a great deal of flexibility in choosing the exact task, resource, and assignment fields you want to export and how you want the exported data organized.

■ If you have previously saved a GIF image with the Copy Picture button, you can include the GIF image in the Web page you create with the Save As Web Page command. In the Define Import/Export Map dialog box, check the Include Image File in HTML Page box, and then choose the filename of the GIF image you want to be included.

■ If you are HTML-savvy, you can edit the resulting Web page after saving it in Microsoft Project. For example, you can add several Microsoft Project–specific tags to a Web page. For a list of those tags, ask the Office Assistant to "Tell me about HTML export templates and tags."

tip
Project managers, resources, and other stakeholders can use Microsoft Project Central to share project information via your organization's intranet. For more information, see Lesson 9, "Managing a Project Team Online."

Proj2000-3-7
Proj2000-3-8

Copying and Pasting with Microsoft Project

You can copy and paste data to and from Microsoft Project using the Copy, Copy Picture, Paste, and Paste Special commands on the Edit menu (or the corresponding buttons on the Standard toolbar). When copying data from Microsoft Project, you can choose one of two options, depending on the results you want.

■ You can copy text (such as task names and dates) from a table, and paste it as text in a destination program.

■ You can copy a graphic image of a view from Microsoft Project and paste it as a graphic image in the destination program. With the Copy Picture command on the Edit menu, you can create a graphic image of a view or a selected portion of a view. As you might recall from the previous exercise, the Copy Picture feature allows you to optimize the image for onscreen viewing (in PowerPoint, for example) or for printing (in Word, for example).

There is an important distinction between using Copy and Copy Picture. Using Copy allows you to edit the data in the destination program. However, using Copy Picture yields an image that you can edit only with a graphics editing program, such as Microsoft Paint.

> **tip**
>
> Many Windows programs, such as Word and Microsoft Excel, have a Paste Special command on their Edit menus. This command gives you more options for pasting text from Microsoft Project into the destination program. For example, the Paste Special command in Word allows you to paste formatted or unformatted text, a picture, or a Microsoft Project Document Object (an **OLE** object). You can also choose to paste just the data or paste it with a link to the source data in Microsoft Project. For more information about using OLE with Microsoft Project, ask the Office Assistant "Tell me about linked and embedded objects."

You also have two options when pasting data into Microsoft Project from other programs.

- You can paste text (such as a list of task or resource names) into a table in Microsoft Project. For example, you can paste a range of cells from Excel or a sequence of paragraphs from Word to Microsoft Project. One example of this is pasting a series of task names that are organized in a vertical column from Excel or Word to the Task Name column in Microsoft Project.

> **tip**
>
> Pasting text as multiple columns requires some planning. First, make sure that the order of the information in the source program matches the order of the columns in the Microsoft Project table. You can either rearrange the data in the source program to match the column order in the Microsoft Project table or vice-versa. Second, make sure that the columns in the source program support the same types of data—text, numbers, dates, and so on—as do the columns in Microsoft Project.

- You can paste a graphic image or an OLE object from another program into a graphical portion of a Gantt Chart view. You can also paste a graphic image or an OLE object to a task, resource, or assignment note; to a form view, such as the Task or Resource Form views; or to the header, footer, or legend of a view or report. For more information about printing views and reports, see Lesson 7.

For the toy commercial project, you would like to add a Gantt Chart image to a document you have prepared for a stakeholder of the project. In this exercise, you copy a snapshot of a Gantt Chart and paste it to WordPad (or to Word, if you prefer). You create the snapshot in the same way regardless of the destination program you have in mind. For example, you could paste the snapshot into a file from a word processor or an e-mail editor.

1   On the Standard toolbar, click the Copy Picture button.

    The Copy Picture dialog box appears.

2   Under the Render Image label, select For Screen, and then click OK.

    Microsoft Project copies a snapshot of the Gantt Chart view to the Windows Clipboard.

    Next you will open a proposal that has been created in a word processor. You can open this in WordPad or in Word if you have it.

3   Do one of the following:

    ●   If you do not have Word installed, click the Windows Start button, point to Programs, point to Accessories, and then click WordPad.

    ●   If you have Word installed, start it.

4   In WordPad or Word, on the File menu, click Open.

5   Locate and open the document named Letter To Client in your Lesson 12 folder.

6   Highlight the paragraph "(insert summary Gantt Chart)."

7   On the Edit menu, click Paste.

8   Microsoft Project pastes the snapshot of the Gantt Chart view from the Windows Clipboard to the document. If you are using WordPad, your screen should look similar to the following illustration.

This image of the Gantt Chart view has been pasted into a WordPad document. In this format it cannot be edited, except as a graphic image.

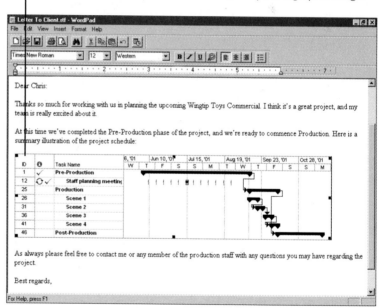

Again note that, rather than pasting this image into a word processor, you could paste it into an e-mail message or another type of document.

9   On the WordPad or Word File menu, click Exit. When prompted to save the document, click No.

Proj2000-1-1
Proj2000-3-3

Opening Other File Formats in Microsoft Project

Information that you need to incorporate into a Microsoft Project document might come from many sources. A task list from a spreadsheet or resource costs from a database are two examples. You might want to use the unique features of Microsoft Project to analyze data from another program. For example, many people keep task lists and simple project schedules in Excel, but Excel has a very hard time with basic scheduling issues like working and nonworking time.

As you might recall from earlier in this lesson, Microsoft Project uses export maps when saving data to HTML and other formats. Microsoft Project uses import maps when opening data from another file format in Microsoft Project. In fact, the same maps are used for both opening and saving data, so they are referred to as **import/export maps**. Import/export maps allow you to specify how you want individual fields in the source program's file to be mapped to individual fields in the destination program. Once you set up an import/export map, it is available to use again.

A colleague has sent you an Excel workbook that contains her recommended tasks, durations, and sequence of activities for a television commercial Industrial Smoke and Mirrors will produce. In this exercise, you open the Excel workbook in Microsoft Project, and then you set up an import/export map to control how the Excel data is imported into Microsoft Project.

tip

If you have Excel installed on your computer, open the workbook named Sample Task List in the Lesson 12 folder. The important things to note about the workbook are the names and the order of the columns, the presence of a header row (the labels at the top of the columns), and that the data is in a worksheet named Tasks. When you are done viewing the workbook, close it without saving changes.

1   In Microsoft Project, on the File menu click Open.
    The Open dialog box appears.
2   Locate the Lesson 12 folder on your hard disk.
3   In the Files Of Type box, select Microsoft Excel Workbooks.

tip

While scrolling through the Files Of Type box, you can see the several file formats Microsoft Project can import. If you work with programs that can save in any of these file formats, you can import their data into Microsoft Project. For more information, ask the Office Assistant "Which file formats does Microsoft Project support?"

4 Open the file Sample Task List.

The Import Mapping dialog box appears.

5 Click the New Map button.

The Define Import/Export Map dialog box appears. In this dialog box, you will identify the source workbook, and you will specify how you want to map the data from the source workbook to Microsoft Project fields.

6 In the Import/Export Map Name box, type **Simple Task List**

7 Under the Data To Import/Export label, select Tasks.

8 Click the Task Mapping tab.

9 In the Source Worksheet Name list, select Tasks.

Microsoft Project analyzes the header row names from the workbook, and it suggests the Microsoft Project field names that are probable matches.

In this dialog box, you specify how Microsoft Project should import data from other file formats, in this case an Excel workbook.

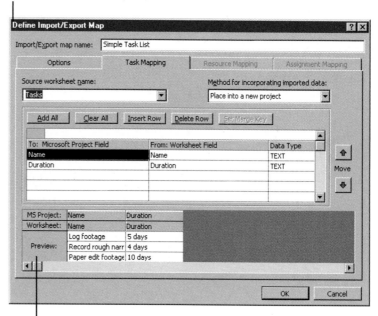

Use the Preview area here to see how the data from another file format will be mapped to Microsoft Project fields, based on the settings you've made above.

10 Click OK to accept the field names it suggests and to close the Define Import/Export Map dialog box.

In the Import Mapping dialog box, note that the new data map appears in the Import/Export Map list.

11 Click Open.

Microsoft Project imports the Excel data into a new Microsoft Project file. Your screen should look similar to the following illustration. (The dates you see on the timescale will differ from those shown because Microsoft Project uses the current date as the project start date in the new file.)

After importing the task names and durations, they appear as an unlinked sequence of tasks, ready for editing.

	O	Task Name	Duration
1		Log footage	5 days
2		Record rough narration	4 days
3		Paper edit footage	10 days
4		Rough cut edit	8 days
5		Fine cut edit	7 days
6		Hold formal approval show	1 day
7		Add dialog	2 days
8		Record final narration	5 days
9		Add head and tail titles	5 days
10		Add final music	3 days
11		Print internegative of film	3 days
12		Clone dubbing masters of :	4 days
13		Archive master film and a	0.5 days
14		Hand off masters to distrib	0 days

12 Close and save the new file as TV Commercial 12 in the Lesson 12 folder. When prompted, save the file without a baseline.

Working with Microsoft Project File Formats

To accommodate new capabilities and features, the Microsoft Project file format has changed significantly with every major release of the product. Microsoft Project 2000 does a good job of opening and saving files in the Microsoft Project 98 format, but it cannot directly open MPP files from versions of Microsoft Project prior to 98. These include Microsoft Project 3.0, Microsoft Project 4.0, and Microsoft Project 95.

On the other hand, Microsoft Project 2000 can open files in the MPX format, which is supported by a variety of project management programs. All previous versions of Microsoft Project could save files in the MPX format, so you can convert old Microsoft Project files to the new format. However, it is a one-way trip. After you convert a project to the Microsoft Project 2000 format, you cannot save it back to the MPX format or to formats of versions prior to Microsoft Project 98.

When saving a Microsoft Project 2000 file in the Microsoft Project 98 format, you will lose data related to features that are new in the later version. These features include those that handle material resources, custom field formulas, and custom box styles in the Network Diagram view. You also lose timescale baseline data. Microsoft Project 2000 displays a warning when saving a project in the older format; from the warning, you can view additional details in Help.

Because of changes in the file format and in Microsoft Project itself, project schedules are calculated differently in Microsoft Project 2000 than in earlier versions. These differences mean that the data that Microsoft Project generates—in some cases, start or finish dates—might change.

Lesson Wrap-Up

In this lesson, you learned how to save Microsoft Project data in formats for use on intranets and the Web and to exchange data between Microsoft Project and other applications.

This lesson concludes the Core Series for Microsoft Project. The Expert Series uses another film production project and addresses more advanced features and activities of Microsoft Project and project management.

If you are continuing on to the Expert series lessons:

● On the File menu, click Close to close the file. If you are prompted to save changes, click Yes.

If you are not continuing on to other lessons:

1   On the File menu, click Close to close the file. If you are prompted to save changes, click No.
2   On the File menu, click Exit.
    Microsoft Project closes.

Lesson Glossary

Copy Picture The feature that allows you to copy images and create snapshots of a view.

export map Specifications for exporting fields from Microsoft Project to other file formats, such as HTML. Microsoft Project includes several export maps, which you can use as they are or modify.

import/export map A set of specifications for importing or exporting specific data to or from Microsoft Project fields. Microsoft Project includes several built-in maps, which you can use as is or modify. Import and export maps are sometimes referred to as data maps.

OLE A protocol that allows you to transfer information, such as a chart or text (as an OLE object), to documents in different programs.

stakeholders All people or organizations that might be affected by project activities (those who "have a stake" in its success). These also include those resources working on the project, as well as others (such as customers) external to the project work.

table A spreadsheet-like presentation of project data, organized in vertical columns and horizontal rows. Each column represents one of the many fields in Microsoft Project, and each row represents a single task or resource.

timescale In views such as the Gantt Chart view and the Resource Usage view, the timescale appears as a band across the top of the grid and denotes units of time. The timescale is divided into a major scale (such as weeks) and a minor scale (such as days). You can customize the timescale in the Timescale dialog box, which you can open from the Format menu.

view The primary way you see data in Microsoft Project. The three categories of views are charts, sheets, and forms.

Quick Quiz

1   You wish to copy a task list out of Microsoft Project and paste it into a text editor. Why is the Copy Picture feature not the best way to do this?

2   What is the Microsoft Project feature you use to control what data is saved to HTML format?

3   You would like to include a picture of a Gantt Chart in an e-mail message. What is one way to do this?

4   What is the Microsoft Project feature you use to control how data from other file formats is imported into Microsoft Project?

Putting It All Together

If necessary, start Microsoft Project. Open the file Putting It All Together 12 in the Lesson 12 folder located in the MS Project Core Practice folder on your hard disk, and save it as Music Video 12 in the same folder.

Exercise 1: Zoom the Gantt Chart to show the entire project. Then copy a snapshot of the Gantt Chart to the Windows Clipboard, and paste it into a new Word or WordPad document.

Exercise 2: Save the project data in Music Video 12 in HTML format, using the Export To HTML Using Standard Template export map.

Quick Reference

Lesson 1: Entering and Organizing Tasks

To start Microsoft Project

1   On the Windows taskbar, click the Start button.
2   On the Start menu, point to Programs, and then click Microsoft Project.
3   On the Microsoft Project Help title bar, click the Minimize button.

To expand a menu and view a dialog box

1   Click the Tools menu.
2   Click the chevron at the bottom of the menu.
3   Point to Customize, and in the submenu that appears, click Toolbars.
4   Click the Options tab. Here you can control the behavior of menus and toolbars in Microsoft Project.
5   Click Close.

To create a new Microsoft Project file

1   On the Standard toolbar, click New.
2   In the Start Date box, type or select the project start date.
3   Click OK to close the Project Information dialog box.

To enter a task list

1   In the Gantt Chart view, click the cell directly below the Task Name column heading.
2   Enter the task name (hint: use a verb phrase), and then press Enter.
3   Continue entering task names.

To enter a task's duration

1   In the Gantt Chart view, click the cell directly below the Duration column heading.
2   Enter the task's duration, and then press Enter.
3   Continue entering task durations.

To enter a milestone

1   In the Task column of the Gantt Chart view, enter the milestone name.
2   In the Duration field, type **0d** and then press Enter.

To create subtasks below a summary task

1   In the Task column of the Gantt Chart view, select the tasks directly below the task you want to make a summary task.

2   On the Formatting toolbar, click the Indent button.

To link tasks

■   To link two adjacent tasks, in the Task column of the Gantt Chart view, select both tasks and then click the Link Tasks button on the Standard toolbar.

■   To link nonadjacent tasks, select the task you want to be the successor task, click the Task Information button on the Standard toolbar, and then click the Predecessors tab. In the Task Name column, select the predecessor task you want.

To adjust task relationships

■   To enter lead or lag time between linked tasks, select the successor task, click the Task Information button on the Standard toolbar, and then click the Predecessors tab. In the Lag field, enter the lag time (positive value) or lead time (negative value) you want.

■   To change the link type between two tasks, select the successor task, click the Task Information button on the Standard toolbar, and then click the Predecessors tab. In the Type field, select the link type you want.

To create task notes or hyperlinks

■   To create a task note, select a task in the Task column of the Gantt Chart view, and then click the Task Notes button on the Standard toolbar. Enter the note text you want, and then click OK.

■   To create a hyperlink, select a task in the Task column of the Gantt Chart view, and then click the Hyperlink button on the Standard toolbar. Enter the hyperlink address and other information that you want, and then click OK.

Lesson 2: Setting Up Resources

To enter basic people resource information

1   On the View Bar, click Resource Sheet.

2   On the Resource Sheet, click the cell directly below the Resource Name column heading.

3   Enter the resource name, type, initials, Max. Units, and other information. Press Tab to move between fields.

To enter basic people resource information

1   On the View Bar, click Resource Sheet.

2   On the Resource Sheet, click the cell directly below the Resource Name column heading.

3   Enter the resource name, type, initials, Max. Units, and other information. Press Tab to move between fields.

To adjust working time

1   On the Tools menu, click Change Working Time.

2   In the For box, select the resource whose working time you want to change.

3   In the Change Working Time dialog box, enter the changes you want, and then click OK.

To set up material resources

1   On the View Bar, click Resource Sheet.

2   On the Resource Sheet, click the next empty cell in the Resource Name column heading.

3   Enter the material resource name, and then press Tab.

4   In the Type field, select Material.

5   In the Material Label field, enter the per-unit label appropriate for this material.

6   Move to the Std. Rate field, and enter the per-unit cost of this material resource.

To enter a resource's pay rates

1   On the Resource Sheet, click the Std. Rate field for a work resource.

2   Enter the resource's standard pay rate in the format payment/pay period, for example 10/h for $10 per hour.

3   If necessary, enter the resource's overtime pay rate in the Ovt. Rate field.

To create resource notes or hyperlinks

1   In the Resource Name column, select the name of Resource for whom you want to enter a note.

2   On the Standard toolbar, click the Resource Notes button.

3   In the Resource Information dialog box, enter the note text you want, and then click OK.

Lesson 3: Assigning Resources to Tasks

To assign a single resource to a task

1   On the View Bar, click Gantt Chart.

2   On the Standard toolbar, click Assign Resources.

3   In the Task Name column in the Gantt Chart view, select the task to which you want to assign a resource.

4   In the Name column in the Assign Resources dialog box, select a resource, and then click Assign.

To view scheduling formula values

1   Select a task with resources assigned to it.

2   On the View menu, click More Views.

3   In the Views box, click Task Entry, and then click Apply.

4   In the Task Form at the bottom of the Microsoft Project window, identify the three variables of the scheduling formula:

- The task's duration in the Duration field
- The resource's units in the Units column
- The resulting work value for the task assignment in the Work column

To assign multiple resources to a task

1   On the View Bar, click Gantt Chart.

2   On the Standard toolbar, click Assign Resources.

3   In the Task Name column in the Gantt Chart view, select the task to which you want to assign a resource.

4   In the Name column in the Assign Resources dialog box, select a resource, and then click Assign.

5   Repeat for additional resources.

To disable effort-driven scheduling

1   In the Gantt Chart view, click the name of the task for which you want to disable effort-driven scheduling.

2   Do one of the following:

- In the Task Form, clear the Effort-Driven check box, and then click OK.

    -OR-

- On the Standard toolbar, click the Task Information button. Click the Advanced tab, and then clear the Effort-Driven check box.

To assign a material resource to a Task

1   On the View Bar, click Gantt Chart.

2   On the Standard toolbar, click Assign Resources.

3 In the Task Name column in the Gantt Chart view, select the task to which you want to assign a material resource.

4 In the Name column in the Assign Resources dialog box, select a material resource.

5 In the Units column, enter a fixed-unit quantity of the material resource, and then click Assign.

Lesson 4: Fine-Tuning Your Project Plan

To apply a task calendar to a task

1 In the Gantt Chart view, select a task.

2 On the Standard toolbar, click the Task Information button.

3 Click the Advanced tab.

4 In the Calendar box, select the task calendar you want to apply.

5 If you want the task calendar to override resource calendar settings, check the Scheduling Ignores Resource Calendars box.

To change a task type

1 In the Gantt Chart view, select a task.

2 On the Standard toolbar, click the Task Information button.

3 Click the Advanced tab.

4 In the Task Type box, select the task type you want.

To interrupt work on a task

1 On the Standard toolbar, click the Split Task button.

2 Move the mouse pointer over the task's Gantt bar where you want to start the split, and then drag to the right.

To create a recurring task

1 In the Gantt Chart view, select the task above, into which you want to insert a recurring task.

2 On the Insert menu, click Recurring Task.

3 In the Recurring Task Information dialog box, select the options you want.

To apply a constraint to a task

1 In the Gantt Chart view, select a task.

2 On the Standard toolbar, click the Task Information button.

3 Click the Advanced tab.

4 In the Constraint Type box, select the type of constraint you want to apply.

5 If you choose a semi-flexible or an inflexible constraint type, type or select a date in the Constraint Date box.

To view the critical path

1   On the View menu, select More Views.

2   In the More Views dialog box, select Detail Gantt, and then click Apply.

To view resource allocations over time

●   On the View bar, click Resource Usage.

Resource
Usage

Lesson 5: Filtering, Sorting, and Grouping Project Information

To sort data in a view

1   Switch to the view and table you want to sort.

2   On the Project menu, click Sort, and then select the field by which you want to sort the view. To specify a custom sort, select Sort By, and then, in the Sort dialog box, choose the options you want.

To group data in a view

1   Switch to the view and table you want to group.

2   On the Project menu, click Group By: No Group, and then select the criteria by which you want to group the view. To specify different grouping options, select Customize Group By, and then choose the options you want in the Customize Group By dialog box.

To filter data in a view

1   Switch to the view you want to filter.

2   On the Project menu, point to Filtered For, and select More Filters.

3   In the More Filters dialog box, choose the filter you want and then click Apply.

Lesson 6: Formatting Your Project Plan

To format bar styles on the Gantt Chart

1   On the Format menu, click Bar Styles.

2   In the Bar Styles dialog box, select the options you want.

To draw text boxes or other objects on a Gantt Chart

1   On the View menu, click Toolbars, and then select Drawing.

2   On the Drawing toolbar, click the object or shape you want to draw, and then draw it on the chart portion of a Gantt Chart view.

3   To set options for the drawn object (for example, to link it to one end of a Gantt bar), double-click the object's border, and choose the options you want in the Format Drawing dialog box.

Resource
Sheet

To display a text field

1   On the View bar, click Resource Sheet.

2   Click the column heading to the right of where you want to insert a text field.

3   On the Insert menu, click Column.

4   In the Field Name list in the Column Definition dialog box, click one of the text fields named Text1 through Text30.

5   In the Title box, type the name you want to appear in the column heading for this field.

6   Enter whatever other options you want, and then click OK.

To create a custom table

1   On the View menu, point to Table: Entry and then click More Tables.

2   In the More Tables dialog box, do one of the following:

   ● To create a new table, click New.

   ● To redefine a table, select the table name, and then click Edit.

   ● To create a table based on another table, select the table name, and then click Copy.

3   In the Table Definition dialog box, choose the options you want.

To create a custom view

1   On the View menu, click More Views.

2   In the More Views dialog box, do one of the following:

   ● To create a view, click New. Select Single View or Combination View in the Define New View dialog box, and then click OK.

   ● To redefine a view, select the view name, and then click Edit.

   ● To create a view based on another view, select the view name, and then click Copy.

3   In the View Definition dialog box, choose the options you want.

Lesson 7: Printing Project Information

To create a custom report

1   On the View menu, click Reports.

2   Click Custom, and then click the Select button.

3   In the Reports box, select an existing report on which to base the new report, and then click the Copy button.

4   In the <name> Report dialog box, select the options you want.

To group data in a view

1   Switch to the view and table you want to group.

2   On the Project menu, click Group By: No Group, and then select the criteria by which you want to group the view. To specify different grouping options, select Customize Group By, and then choose the options you want in the Customize Group by dialog box.

Lesson 8: Tracking Progress Against the Project Plan

To save a baseline

1   On the Tools menu, point to Tracking and click Save Baseline.

2   In the Save Baseline dialog box, select Save Baseline and then click OK.

To display the Task Sheet view and Work table

1   On the View menu, click More Views.

2   In the Views box, select Task Sheet and click Apply.

3   On the View menu, point to Table: Entry and click Work.

To display the Resource Sheet view and Work table

Resource Sheet

1   On the View bar, click Resource Sheet.

2   On the View menu, point to Table: Entry and click Work.

To display the Task Usage view and baseline work details

Task Usage

1   On the View bar, click Task Usage.

2   On the Format menu, point to Details and click Baseline Work.

To record that work has been completed as scheduled

Gantt Chart

1   On the View bar, click Gantt Chart.

2   On the Tools menu, point to Tracking and click Update Project.

3   Make sure the Update Work As Complete Through option is selected. In the adjacent Date list, type or select the date you want, and click OK.

To record that work has been completed as scheduled

1   On the View menu, point to Toolbars and click Tracking.

2   In the Task Name column, select the task you want.

3   On the Tracking toolbar, click the 100% Complete button.

To record the percentage of a task that has been completed

1   In the Task Name column, select the task you want.

2   On the Standard toolbar, click the Task Information button.

3   Click the General tab.

4   In the Percent Complete box, type or select the value you want, and click OK.

To track work by time period

1   On the View bar, click Task Usage.

2   On the Format menu, point to Details and click Actual Work.

3   In the timescale grid, select the Act. Work field for the task or assignment and date you want.

4   Enter the actual work values you want.

To view cost variance for tasks

1   On the View menu, click More Views.

2   In the Views list, select Task Sheet and click Apply.

3   On the View menu, point to Table: Work, and click Cost.

4   Look over the task variance.

5   On the View bar, click Resource Sheet.

6   On the View menu, point to Table: Work and then click Cost.

To sort resources by cost variance

1   On the View bar, click Resource Sheet.

2   On the View menu, point to Table: Work and then click Cost.

3   On the Project menu, point to Sort and click Sort By.

4   In the Sort By box, select Cost Variance, and click Descending.

5   Make sure the Permanently Renumber Resources box is cleared, and then click Sort.

To reschedule uncompleted work

1   On the Tools menu, point to Tracking and then click Update Project.

2   Click Reschedule Uncompleted Work To Start After, and in the Date box select the date you want.

3   Click OK to close the Update Project dialog box.

Lesson 9: Managing a Project Team Online

To enable Project Central communication in Microsoft Project

1   On the Tools menu, click Options.

2   Click the General tab.

3   In the User Name box, type the name by which you wish to log on to Project Central.

4   Click the Workgroup tab.

5   In the Default Workgroup Messages For box, Select Web for Project Central–based communication.

6   In the Microsoft Project Central Server box, type the URL of your Project Central server, and then click OK.

To send a TeamAssign message

1   On the Tools menu, point to Workgroup and then click TeamAssign.
2   In the Workgroup Mail dialog box, make sure that All Tasks is selected, and then click OK.
3   If the Planning Wizard appears with a message about Windows user accounts, click OK.
4   Click Send.

To log into Project Central and view messages

1   Start Internet Explorer or the Browser Module.
2   In the Address box, type the Uniform Resource Locator (URL) address of your Project Central Server login screen.
3   In the User Name box, select the name under which you wish to log in and then click Enter.
4   If a message box about your password being blank appears, click No.

To view a TeamAssign message in Project Central

1   On the Home menu, click Messages.
2   In the Subject column, click TeamAssign to display the message.
3   Click Close.
4   To delete the message, click Delete Message.

To record and submit actuals

1   On the Tasks menu click Timesheet.
2   Under Show, make sure that Scheduled Work and Summary Tasks are checked.
3   In the Show Timescale Period From and To boxes, select the date range you want to see and then click Apply.
4   Select the Actual Work cell for the task and date you want, and enter the actual value you want.
5   At the top of the Timesheet screen, click Send Update.

To create a task and send an update

1   On the Tasks menu, click New Task.
2   In the Project box, select the project for which you want to create a new task.
3   Enter the other options you want for the new task.
4   At the top of the New Task screen, click Create Task.
5   At the top of the Timesheet page, click Send Update.

To accept resource submissions and update Microsoft Project from Project Central

1   Log in to Project Central as a project manager.
2   On the Home menu, click Messages.

3   Select the resource submission message you want.

4   Click Update.

5   After Project Central updates Microsoft Project, click Yes to delete the message.

To delegate a task and send an update

1   Log in to Project Central as a resource.

2   On the Tasks menu, click Delegation.

3   In the Task Name column of the Timesheet, select the task you wish to delegate to another resource.

4   Click Delegate Tasks.

5   In the Delegate Tasks screens, choose the options you want.

6   At the top of the Delegate tasks screen, click Send.

Lesson 10: Working with Multiple Projects

To create a consolidated project file

1   On the Standard toolbar, click the New button.

2   Enter a project start date, and then save the new project file.

3   On the Insert menu, click Project.

4   In the Insert Project dialog box, locate and select the Microsoft Project file you want to insert into the consolidated project file. To select multiple files, hold down the CTRL key while you click the names of the files.

5   Click Insert.

To create links between projects

1   Switch to the project file that contains the task you want to make the successor task.

2   In the Entry table, click the name of the task you want to make the successor task.

3   On the Standard toolbar, click the Task Information button and then click the Predecessors tab.

4   In the ID column, click the next empty cell below any other predecessor tasks, and enter the name of the predecessor task from the other project file in this format: File Name\Task ID.

5   Press the Enter key, and click OK to close the Task Information dialog box.

Lesson 11: Customizing Microsoft Project

To set Save settings in the Options dialog box (Tools menu)

1   On the Tools menu, click Options.

2   Click the Save tab.

3   Under the File Locations label, select Projects and then click Modify.

4   Type or select the default file location you want, and then click OK.

5   Under the Auto Save label, select the Save Every box.

6   Click OK to close the Options dialog box.

To copy a view with the Organizer

1   On the Tools menu, click Organizer.

2   In the list of views on the right side of the dialog box, select the view you want to copy.

3   In the Views Available In list on the left side of the dialog box, select the name of the open but not active file to which you want to copy the view.

4   Click <<Copy, and then click Close.

To copy a table from the global template to a Microsoft Project file

1   In the active Microsoft Project file, switch to a table other than the one you wish to replace.

2   On the Tools menu, click Organizer.

3   Click the Tables tab.

4   In the Global.mpt table list on the left side of the dialog box, click the table you wish to copy to the active Microsoft Project file on the right.

5   Click Copy >>, and then click Close.

Lesson 12: Using Microsoft Project with Other Programs

To save a snapshot summary tasks as a GIF image

1   On the Project menu, point to Filtered For: All Tasks, and then click Summary Tasks.

2   On the View menu, click Zoom.

3   Click Entire Project, and then click OK.

4   On the Standard toolbar, click the Copy Picture button.

5   Under Render Image, click To GIF Image File, and then click OK.

To save Microsoft Project data as a Web page using an export map

1   On the File menu, click Save As Web Page.

2   Click Save.

3   Under the Import/Export Map label, select Export To HTML Using Standard Template, and then click Save.

To copy a snapshot of a Gantt Chart and paste it to WordPad

1   On the Standard toolbar, click the Copy Picture button.

2   Under the Render Image label, select For Screen, and then click OK.

3   Start WordPad and create a new document.

4   On the Edit menu, click Paste.

To open the Excel workbook in Microsoft Project and set up an import/export map

1   On the File menu click Open.
2   In the Files Of Type box, select Microsoft Excel Workbooks.
3   Select the Excel workbook.
4   In the Import Mapping dialog box, click the New Map button.
5   In the Import/Export Map Name box, type a name for this map.
6   Under the Data To Import/Export label, select Tasks.
7   Click the Task Mapping tab.
8   In the Source Worksheet Name list, select the name of the worksheet you want.
9   Click OK, and then click Open.

Index

A

B

C

About the Authors

Carl S. Chatfield, PMP

Carl is a documentation manager in the Microsoft Project User Assistance team at Microsoft. He has worked on Microsoft Project since 1998 and prior to that had worked on the Excel and Office teams at Microsoft since 1991.

Carl is a graduate of the master's program in Technical Communication at the University of Washington and has been certified as a Project Management Professional (PMP) by the Project Management Institute. He lives in Redmond, Washington.

Timothy D. Johnson, MCP

Tim is a support professional in the Microsoft Project Support group at Microsoft. He has supported customers in the use of Microsoft Project since version 3.0 and is a Microsoft Certified Professional (MCP) Product Specialist. He lives in Issaquah, Washington.

Rebecca H. Chatfield, Ph.D.

Rebecca is a database designer. She has worked as a database design consultant since 1990 and has research interests in the sociology of technology, organizations, and participatory design. Rebecca received her Ph.D. from the University of Washington in 1999. She lives in Redmond, Washington.

MICROSOFT LICENSE AGREEMENT
Book Companion CD

IMPORTANT—READ CAREFULLY: This Microsoft End-User License Agreement ("EULA") is a legal agreement between you (either an individual or an entity) and Microsoft Corporation for the Microsoft product identified above, which includes computer software and may include associated media, printed materials, and "online" or electronic documentation ("SOFTWARE PRODUCT"). Any component included within the SOFTWARE PRODUCT that is accompanied by a separate End-User License Agreement shall be governed by such agreement and not the terms set forth below. By installing, copying, or otherwise using the SOFTWARE PRODUCT, you agree to be bound by the terms of this EULA. If you do not agree to the terms of this EULA, you are not authorized to install, copy, or otherwise use the SOFTWARE PRODUCT; you may, however, return the SOFTWARE PRODUCT, along with all printed materials and other items that form a part of the Microsoft product that includes the SOFTWARE PRODUCT, to the place you obtained them for a full refund.

SOFTWARE PRODUCT LICENSE

The SOFTWARE PRODUCT is protected by United States copyright laws and international copyright treaties, as well as other intellectual property laws and treaties. The SOFTWARE PRODUCT is licensed, not sold.

1. GRANT OF LICENSE. This EULA grants you the following rights:

- **a. Software Product.** You may install and use one copy of the SOFTWARE PRODUCT on a single computer. The primary user of the computer on which the SOFTWARE PRODUCT is installed may make a second copy for his or her exclusive use on a portable computer.

- **b. Storage/Network Use.** You may also store or install a copy of the SOFTWARE PRODUCT on a storage device, such as a network server, used only to install or run the SOFTWARE PRODUCT on your other computers over an internal network; however, you must acquire and dedicate a license for each separate computer on which the SOFTWARE PRODUCT is installed or run from the storage device. A license for the SOFTWARE PRODUCT may not be shared or used concurrently on different computers.

- **c. License Pak.** If you have acquired this EULA in a Microsoft License Pak, you may make the number of additional copies of the computer software portion of the SOFTWARE PRODUCT authorized on the printed copy of this EULA, and you may use each copy in the manner specified above. You are also entitled to make a corresponding number of secondary copies for portable computer use as specified above.

- **d. Sample Code.** Solely with respect to portions, if any, of the SOFTWARE PRODUCT that are identified within the SOFTWARE PRODUCT as sample code (the "SAMPLE CODE"):

  - **i. Use and Modification.** Microsoft grants you the right to use and modify the source code version of the SAMPLE CODE, *provided* you comply with subsection (d)(iii) below. You may not distribute the SAMPLE CODE, or any modified version of the SAMPLE CODE, in source code form.

  - **ii. Redistributable Files.** Provided you comply with subsection (d)(iii) below, Microsoft grants you a nonexclusive, royalty-free right to reproduce and distribute the object code version of the SAMPLE CODE and of any modified SAMPLE CODE, other than SAMPLE CODE, or any modified version thereof, designated as not redistributable in the Readme file that forms a part of the SOFTWARE PRODUCT (the "Non-Redistributable Sample Code"). All SAMPLE CODE other than the Non-Redistributable Sample Code is collectively referred to as the "REDISTRIBUTABLES."

  - **iii. Redistribution Requirements.** If you redistribute the REDISTRIBUTABLES, you agree to: (i) distribute the REDISTRIBUTABLES in object code form only in conjunction with and as a part of your software application product; (ii) not use Microsoft's name, logo, or trademarks to market your software application product; (iii) include a valid copyright notice on your software application product; (iv) indemnify, hold harmless, and defend Microsoft from and against any claims or lawsuits, including attorney's fees, that arise or result from the use or distribution of your software application product; and (v) not permit further distribution of the REDISTRIBUTABLES by your end user. Contact Microsoft for the applicable royalties due and other licensing terms for all other uses and/or distribution of the REDISTRIBUTABLES.

2. DESCRIPTION OF OTHER RIGHTS AND LIMITATIONS.

- **Limitations on Reverse Engineering, Decompilation, and Disassembly.** You may not reverse engineer, decompile, or disassemble the SOFTWARE PRODUCT, except and only to the extent that such activity is expressly permitted by applicable law notwithstanding this limitation.

- **Separation of Components.** The SOFTWARE PRODUCT is licensed as a single product. Its component parts may not be separated for use on more than one computer.

- **Rental.** You may not rent, lease, or lend the SOFTWARE PRODUCT.

- **Support Services.** Microsoft may, but is not obligated to, provide you with support services related to the SOFTWARE PRODUCT ("Support Services"). Use of Support Services is governed by the Microsoft policies and programs described in the user manual, in "online" documentation, and/or in other Microsoft-provided materials. Any supplemental software code provided to you as part of the Support Services shall be considered part of the SOFTWARE PRODUCT and subject to the terms and conditions of this EULA. With respect to technical information you provide to Microsoft as part of the Support Services, Microsoft may use such information for its business purposes, including for product support and development. Microsoft will not utilize such technical information in a form that personally identifies you.

- **Software Transfer.** You may permanently transfer all of your rights under this EULA, provided you retain no copies, you transfer all of the SOFTWARE PRODUCT (including all component parts, the media and printed materials, any upgrades, this EULA, and, if applicable, the Certificate of Authenticity), **and** the recipient agrees to the terms of this EULA.

- **Termination.** Without prejudice to any other rights, Microsoft may terminate this EULA if you fail to comply with the terms and conditions of this EULA. In such event, you must destroy all copies of the SOFTWARE PRODUCT and all of its component parts.

3. **COPYRIGHT.** All title and copyrights in and to the SOFTWARE PRODUCT (including but not limited to any images, photographs, animations, video, audio, music, text, SAMPLE CODE, REDISTRIBUTABLES, and "applets" incorporated into the SOFTWARE PRODUCT) and any copies of the SOFTWARE PRODUCT are owned by Microsoft or its suppliers. The SOFTWARE PRODUCT is protected by copyright laws and international treaty provisions. Therefore, you must treat the SOFTWARE PRODUCT like any other copyrighted material **except** that you may install the SOFTWARE PRODUCT on a single computer provided you keep the original solely for backup or archival purposes. You may not copy the printed materials accompanying the SOFTWARE PRODUCT.

4. **U.S. GOVERNMENT RESTRICTED RIGHTS.** The SOFTWARE PRODUCT and documentation are provided with RESTRICTED RIGHTS. Use, duplication, or disclosure by the Government is subject to restrictions as set forth in subparagraph (c)(1)(ii) of the Rights in Technical Data and Computer Software clause at DFARS 252.227-7013 or subparagraphs (c)(1) and (2) of the Commercial Computer Software—Restricted Rights at 48 CFR 52.227-19, as applicable. Manufacturer is Microsoft Corporation/One Microsoft Way/Redmond, WA 98052-6399.

5. **EXPORT RESTRICTIONS.** You agree that you will not export or re-export the SOFTWARE PRODUCT, any part thereof, or any process or service that is the direct product of the SOFTWARE PRODUCT (the foregoing collectively referred to as the "Restricted Components"), to any country, person, entity, or end user subject to U.S. export restrictions. You specifically agree not to export or re-export any of the Restricted Components (i) to any country to which the U.S. has embargoed or restricted the export of goods or services, which currently include, but are not necessarily limited to, Cuba, Iran, Iraq, Libya, North Korea, Sudan, and Syria, or to any national of any such country, wherever located, who intends to transmit or transport the Restricted Components back to such country; (ii) to any end user who you know or have reason to know will utilize the Restricted Components in the design, development, or production of nuclear, chemical, or biological weapons; or (iii) to any end user who has been prohibited from participating in U.S. export transactions by any federal agency of the U.S. government. You warrant and represent that neither the BXA nor any other U.S. federal agency has suspended, revoked, or denied your export privileges.

DISCLAIMER OF WARRANTY

NO WARRANTIES OR CONDITIONS. MICROSOFT EXPRESSLY DISCLAIMS ANY WARRANTY OR CONDITION FOR THE SOFT-WARE PRODUCT. THE SOFTWARE PRODUCT AND ANY RELATED DOCUMENTATION ARE PROVIDED "AS IS" WITHOUT WARRANTY OR CONDITION OF ANY KIND, EITHER EXPRESS OR IMPLIED, INCLUDING, WITHOUT LIMITATION, THE IMPLIED WARRANTIES OF MERCHANTABILITY, FITNESS FOR A PARTICULAR PURPOSE, OR NONINFRINGEMENT. THE ENTIRE RISK ARISING OUT OF USE OR PERFORMANCE OF THE SOFTWARE PRODUCT REMAINS WITH YOU.

LIMITATION OF LIABILITY. TO THE MAXIMUM EXTENT PERMITTED BY APPLICABLE LAW, IN NO EVENT SHALL MICROSOFT OR ITS SUPPLIERS BE LIABLE FOR ANY SPECIAL, INCIDENTAL, INDIRECT, OR CONSEQUENTIAL DAMAGES WHATSOEVER (INCLUDING, WITHOUT LIMITATION, DAMAGES FOR LOSS OF BUSINESS PROFITS, BUSINESS INTERRUPTION, LOSS OF BUSINESS INFORMATION, OR ANY OTHER PECUNIARY LOSS) ARISING OUT OF THE USE OF OR INABILITY TO USE THE SOFTWARE PRODUCT OR THE PROVISION OF OR FAILURE TO PROVIDE SUPPORT SERVICES, EVEN IF MICROSOFT HAS BEEN ADVISED OF THE POSSIBILITY OF SUCH DAMAGES. IN ANY CASE, MICROSOFT'S ENTIRE LIABILITY UNDER ANY PROVISION OF THIS EULA SHALL BE LIMITED TO THE GREATER OF THE AMOUNT ACTUALLY PAID BY YOU FOR THE SOFTWARE PRODUCT OR US$5.00; PROVIDED, HOWEVER, IF YOU HAVE ENTERED INTO A MICROSOFT SUPPORT SERVICES AGREEMENT, MICROSOFT'S ENTIRE LIABILITY REGARDING SUPPORT SERVICES SHALL BE GOVERNED BY THE TERMS OF THAT AGREE-MENT. BECAUSE SOME STATES AND JURISDICTIONS DO NOT ALLOW THE EXCLUSION OR LIMITATION OF LIABILITY, THE ABOVE LIMITATION MAY NOT APPLY TO YOU.

MISCELLANEOUS

This EULA is governed by the laws of the State of Washington USA, except and only to the extent that applicable law mandates governing law of a different jurisdiction.

Should you have any questions concerning this EULA, or if you desire to contact Microsoft for any reason, please contact the Microsoft subsidiary serving your country, or write: Microsoft Sales Information Center/One Microsoft Way/Redmond, WA 98052-6399.

PN 097-0002296